Barley, Bombs and Bagels

MYRTLE RUSSELL

Chaville Press
London

2016

Published by **Chaville Press**
148 Friern Park
London
N12 9LU

Copyright © **Myrtle Russell 2016**
First published 2016
ISBN 978-0-9930063-1-9

Cover designed by DesignbyCaroline.co.uk
Text arrangement by Sheila Gewolb
Typeset by Cristina Guidone-Charles
Printed and bound in Great Britain by Jellyfish Print Solutions

All rights reserved. Without limiting the rights under copyright reserved above, no part of this publication may be reproduced, stored or introduced into a retrieval system, or transmitted, in any form or by any means (electronic, mechanical, photocopying, recording or otherwise), without the prior written permission of both the copyright owner and the publisher of this book.

Contents

Foreword		11
Introduction		15
Chapter 1	Countdown to War	17
	In the Beginning	
	Early Warnings	
	Preparing for the Inevitable	
	Introducing our Family Heroes	
Chapter 2	Britain at War	23
	The Balloon Goes Up	
	'Goodbye' to the Old, 'Hello' to the New	
	The Changing Face of Britain	
	Surviving on Shortages	
	The Phoney War	
	Norwegian Connections in the House	
	A Lost Country in Sixty-two Days	
	Uproar from Both Sides	
	A New Broom to Sweep Clean	
	The Miracle of Deliverance	
	Here to Fight Another Day	
Chapter 3	War in Europe	39
	Frenchmen on Opposite Sides	
	Meres-el-Kabir	
	On Our Own	
	Saved by the Few	
Chapter 4	War Comes to London	43
	My Testimony to Horror and Fortitude	
	The Effects that Changed London	
	Tragedies	
	The London Spirit	
	Uncle Monty	
	"Oh to be an Evacuee!"	
Chapter 5	America Enters the War	55
	A Meeting of Minds	
	Land-grabbers on the March	
	A Vicious Enemy	
	Brutality and the Big Mistakes	
Chapter 6	My Personal War	59
	Early Reminiscences	
	A Power-change at Home	
	A March and a Road Block	
	A Quandary and a Decision	

Launched 1914: Fully-grown 1939
On My Way
A Change of Scene
The Land Girls' Lot
It Wasn't All Work
Brief Encounters
A Letter from Somerset

Chapter 7   Changing Fortunes of War..77
The Tide Changes
Strangers in a Friendly Land
Letting One's Hair Down
The Weekend Battery-charger
Robbie and Me
A Change of Scene and a Shock to the System
'On Your Bike Girl'!
Market Gardening
The Last Throw of the Dice
Let the Children Learn

Chapter 8   After the War was Over..91
Meeting Fate at the Balfour
Raymond Re-introduced
"If Only ..."
Dead or Alive?
The Past and the Present – What Now?
Aftermath
The Blessed and the Damned

Chapter 9   A Story about the War..101
The Bridge
Off on My Travels
Hayes
A Bit More About Me
Adam – A Difficult Decision
Adam – A Dual Responsibility
The Tragedy of Slapton Sands
Let the Children Go
The British Schindler
Paying Tribute to Heroes
In Remembrance
From the Tricorn to the Slouch
From Flanders Fields
Canada in Yorkshire
The Righteous Smiths

Overlord Embroidery
A Missed Appointment
A Double First
Under Occupation
I Was There
The Republic of Ireland – A Story of Two Halves

Chapter 10   A Broader Perspective 131
A Directional Decision
Prologue to Overlord
Where, Why and When?
And the Winner is – Normandy
The Silly and the Sensible
Operation 'Now you see it – now you don't'
Time and Tide Wait for No Man
Time Off for the Boys
Erwin
Dawning of a New Day
Dunkirk in Reverse
The Famous Fighting Five
Business is Brisk in the Channel
Hobart's 'Funnies'
One Tank Going Cheap
Coming-home Warriors and the Backroom Specials
Overview
Mission Achieved
Make-believe v. Reality
A Lady of Merit
Operation Market Garden – Not a WLA Story
No Good News Coming out of Holland
Extra Bits and Pieces

Chapter 11   The Balkans 153
All Change in Central Europe
Wartime Machinations in Greece
British Interference
Greece – a Battle and a Defeat
Crete – a Battle and a Defeat
Cretan Repercussions
Resistance

Chapter 12   A Middle Eastern Tale 163
The Melting Pot of Europe
Battleground Syria – 1940 not 2016
Churchill's Headache

	My Connections	
Chapter 13	Mediterranean Action..168	
	France and Spain	
	Spain under Franco	
	From Sidney to Roger	
	Meanderings and a Haircut	
	A Man to Remember with Love	
	Iraqi Troubles 20th Century – What's New in the 21st Century?	
	It Ain't Finished Yet	
	Not Quite a Gamble or a Boat Ride	
	The Agony of Malta	
	From London E1 to the Med and Back	
	Germany's Business and a Follow-up	
	A Russian Demand – the Iranian Dilemma	
	Operation Torch	
	Algerian Patriots	
	Me in Fancy Dress	
	Me and the Foreign Office	
	The Apes and the Tunnels	
	The Colours of Italy – Red, White and Green	
	Travelling On, the War Continued	
	The Sands of the Sahara	
Chapter 14	My German Travels.. 191	
	I Never Wanted to Go, but I Did	
	Rupert's History	
	Touring in Berlin and an S&S Lunch	
	Old Stones and the New	
	I Didn't Feel Much like Waltzing	
Chapter 15	Onwards to Holland,..196	
	A Square or Two of Edam	
	A Dutch Heroine	
Chapter 16	Trouble in the Baltic...199	
	By Royal Assent	
	An Attempt to Finish the Finns!	
	A Toxic Mix	
	Who was Fighting Who?	
	Finland's Raw Deal	
Chapter 17	More Trouble in the Baltic..205	
	The Devil's Advocates	
	Stage One: The Soviets	

Stage Two: The German Turn
The Jewish Population under Siege
The Reasons and the Results
Prologue to Latvia
The Set-up to Murder
The Killing Squads in Action
The Rigan Ghetto
A Plan for Mass Murder
The Jeckeln System
Their Last Vision – the Trees of Rumbula
The Gypsy Holocaust
The Aftermath
Here We Go Again – and It's Really Not Funny

Chapter 18   Poland and Russia 221
Dairy People Times Two
A Polish Carve-up
The Ghetto and a Little Light Music
Krakow – A Place not for Pleasure
The Russian Nightmare
Four Men in Long Coats and Three Around a Table
A Role Model to Follow
The Legacy of Hitler and Stalin
From the Sublime to the Ridiculous

Chapter 19   Malaya, Singapore and India 230
Geography of Malaya
A Strike from the East
Japan on the March
The Tragedy of Singapore
Revenge
Warriors' Day
The Brave Sons of India
One Country, Four Divisions
What Happened to the Mules and What Happened to Me
Jack Jacobs
A Personality to Admire

Chapter 20   Ceylon and Burma 243
They Did More Than Grow Tea
Ceylon Goes to War
Political Disharmony
My Dear Little Sri Lankan Student
On the Road to Mandalay – In Memory of Rudyard Kipling

                    Churchill v Curtin
                    Churchill Faces His Nemesis
                    The Burmese Retreat
                    A Song on the Brain – Not Cake in the Tum
                    The Battle of Kohima
                    Defeat on an Empty Stomach
                    We Are Mindful Every Year in November

Chapter 21   War in the Pacific 254
                    The Dutch East Indies
                    Introduction to the War in the Pacific
                    The Who and the Where
                    Defeat and Victory
                    My Education of the Affair
                    The End of the Story and It's Quiz Time
                    Japan's Come-uppance

Chapter 22   Southern Africa 261
                    Southern Rhodesia then, Zimbabwe now
                    Herzog v Smuts
                    A Fan Club Membership of Two
                    They Did Good

Chapter 23   Australia – Part One 264
                    Initiation to Oz
                    Australia Attacked
                    My Backpack at the Ready
                    Canberra
                    Historian on Board
                    Diary of the Army
                    Hope I Have My Pencil Sharpener
                    Political Manoeuvres
                    The USA Down-under
                    War in the Skies
                    Non-stop Activities of the Royal Australian Airforce
                    "Goodbye Mr S"
                    My Australian Adventure
                    Letter from Australia
                    A Letter from Down-Under. 10th Feb 1985

Chapter 24   Australia – Part Two 280
                    The Oz Civilian Story
                    New Stuff for the Statute Book
                    Post-war Australia
                    Massacre on Bangka Island

Soap
New Guinea – Its Rise and Fall
The War on Australia's Doorstep
New Tyres and Loads of Petrol Going Cheap

Chapter 25 New Zealand..289
I Concur with the General
The Second Half of the ANZACs Did as Good as the First
Lupines and Sheep and a Helicopter Ride

Chapter 26 Japan Attacks the USA..292
A Churchillian Prophesy
Time-scale to Disaster
Time-scale Part Two
Armageddon
Britain at War with Japan
A Miscalculation – An Unforgiving Population
The Doolittle Raid
An Atrocity and a Surrender
An all-American Programme with an Exception

Chapter 27 Canada..301
Canada – It Didn't Have to be, but it Did
A Fight to the Death in the Atlantic
A Meeting of the Giants
An Ever-busy Navy
The Army Takes its Turn
The Tragedy of Hong Kong
Their Names Liveth for Evermore
The Blunder of Dieppe
Canada in France, Holland and Italy
The Boys in Blue Take a Lion's Share
Have They Medals? They Should Have
Tulips, all Colours Especially Orange

Chapter 28 The Price We Paid...313
Chapter 29 Conclusion..315
One Final Word

Picture & map references

Raymond, aged 20. Newly-conscripted, 1939..................21

Myrtle, aged 14, and brother Leslie, aged 11.
1939 - one month before the declaration of War...............22

Tag issued to children being evacuated..........................25

Ration Book cover...27

Norway 1940..31

Raymond proudly displaying his medals, 1945................36

Raymond, 1942. If this picture was in colour, the
beret (with badge insignia) would show as red...............38

Air Cadet Monty, aged 18. 1941..................................52

Myrtle, aged 7, with parents Hetty and Myer,
and brother Leslie at a family wedding, 1932................62

The Battle of Cable Street..64

Myrtle, aged 18. 1943..76

Not quite five generations, but four is a worthy picture –
Myrtle with her mother, Hetty, daughter Sheila
and granddaughter, Rochelle......................................81

Myrtle, aged 21, eight weeks before her wedding
to Raymond in 1946. With her parents and brother,
and an aunt...93

Myrtle and Raymond's wedding day..............................93

Myrtle aged 63 – always with
her head in a history book!......................................102

Myrtle, aged 24. Cardiff 1948.
With Raymond and baby Sheila.................................104

Myrtle, aged 50, with Alf Russell. He died four months
later, aged 55, after fighting a losing battle with lung cancer.....106

Myrtle, aged 54. At daughter Marian's wedding with
son, Adam, and daughters Sheila, Diane and Simone............109

Kindertransport Memorial at Liverpool Street Station.
With great-grandsons Matthew (13) and Jonathan (10)..........115

Tipperary, Ireland...130

South Holland and Belgium 1944...............................152

The Balkans – South-east Europe...............................162

The Middle East 1940 – showing the
vulnerability of the Suez Canal and beyond..................165

Tapestry of Marc Chagall's Reuben window.................170

One of Myrtle's hand-knitted teddies depicting Wales....181

War cemetery in France.
They lay as they died – side by side..........................190

Myrtle aged 59, 1984. In her clinical teacher uniform.......198

The Baltic States..204

German newspaper 1943 – in the Museum of Krakow......224

Malaya and Borneo 1941..231

Map showing the Japanese advance in Burma, 1944......253

Great-uncle Aaron (sitting 4th from left) and great-aunt
Gertie (standing 2nd from left). Early 20th century..........285

Myrtle aged 62, 1987. Fox Glacier, New Zealand..........291

Canadian War Memorial..311

Foreword

Dear Reader

Before you embark on your journey through this book, you need to have a sense of the mammoth achievement writing it has been for my mother, Myrtle Russell.

I would like to pay tribute to this elderly lady, who, in her 92nd year, has managed not only to paint a picture of life in London during World War Two, but has painstakingly researched the backdrop to this black period in our history to help make sense of how and why war happens.

To complete the book, mum sat at her computer for up to 16 hours a day for nearly a year. Her determination to get it finished demonstrates the tenacity and grit which has dominated a life full of tragedy, not only has she been widowed twice and left to bring up five young children alone; she also lost her only son as a young married man in his 30s.

This book is written in her own inimitable style, full of colloquialisms and forthright opinion, to describe her anathema of war and its awful consequences. To quote a friend who has helped with proof-reading:

"In our crazy world of Brexit and Donald Trump, Myrtle's story is hugely significant in reminding us that we are all human, we are all equal, and throughout history countries have needed the support of other nations. The world is getting smaller by the day and the only way we can live harmoniously is with unity."

I commend this book to you – enjoy!

Sheila Jeanne Gewolb (née Woolfe)

December 2016

Acknowledgements

To my eldest daughter, Sheila, who adding to her many commitments has given so much of her time and energy in the editing of this book. It was a marathon undertaking bearing in mind my educational shortcomings as to "Where do the commas and the verbs go"?

I acknowledge the encouragement and interest of my Uncle Monty. It was his feed-back in the early stages of this effort that installed the confidence on which I based the will to continue.

To Keith Martin, my friend, "Thank you". It was his Christmas Day message at 9am telling me that my work deserved to be published that led to the eventual outcome.

My deep appreciation and love to all three.

I would also like to thank Caroline Sloneem who designed the imaginative front cover, and Cristina Guidone-Charles for her typesetting skills and enthusiastic support. You have both helped to bring my words to life and make the book more enjoyable.

Introduction

I did not deliberately sit down and set out to write a book. I left school at the age of 14 and had neither the ability nor the inclination, nor did I consider that I had any great experience that would give me the know-how to put pen to paper.

In 1994 one of my daughters offered my services to go into the primary school of one of her children, Kira, to enhance the school's activities to celebrate the 50th anniversary of the Normandy landings. They wanted me to tell 8–10 year old youngsters my experience of living in London through the war. Which I did, very basically, and without notes. It went well. Six years ago I was invited to talk to sixth formers on the same subject in the school which another grandchild, Josh, attended. This time not basically, in fact very detailed. Once again without notes.

Last year I was asked by a voluntary organization to talk to a group of 10–11 year old pupils, and this time I needed to offer a middle-of-the-road account: I did hand write a couple of pages of pointers. I consider that those three talks were successful.

On returning home from that last event I decided to use my computer, my use of which is but basic, and to type up those notes. I did not stop for the next three months. Once started I was galvanized. My life during the six war-time years uprooted my every day normal routine into flash-back mode. I just could not believe it and neither could I fathom how I was able to transfer it through the medium of the written word. I did so on sixty five pages of A4 paper and I gave it to a publisher friend for feed-back. If good enough I intended to have just sixteen copies printed, one for each of my adult grandchildren. The report I had back wowed me – "You should publish!"

Accepting that if this was his opinion, I reviewed my work and decided that this early effort presented but the bare bones of what I was capable of. This year I devoted another six months glued to my PC, enlarging and fleshing out those earlier skeletal beginnings.

In this book, I have mentioned the names of many people who were part of my story. Except for close family members, and people who have been honoured for their war sacrifice which is publically recorded, I have not used any real names, and any similarity is purely coincidental.

I have, in places presented hand-drawn maps to guide my readers through the maze to explain where I was and what had happened in the time when battles were fought. If I cannot claim academic status as a historian, I am no cartographer either.

My appendages are not strictly maps in the full sense of the word. I have only shown the named places that are appropriate and relevant to my stories. I do not have the knowledge to add all the geographical minutiae that a true representation of any place would show.

I am of the opinion that some explanation is necessary to understand the presentation of this book. Basically it is a work of two halves. The first part is the story of my life, seen from the viewpoint of actually living through the war years, aged 14–20. The second part is a perspective of that time of hostilities through the thoughts and emotions of a woman of mature years. I was in a position to do this by the means of extensive travelling, mostly in my post-retirement days.

Apart from visiting sites in the United Kingdom, which were of particular prominence in the execution of the war, I traversed the world, except for the few regions which had not been engulfed or connected to that conflagration. I toured, or had connections with, the lands of the Mediterranean and all countries European; the Baltic and the Balkans. I was hosted by the Slavs in Poland and Russia. The East added to my experiences in its regions, Near, Middle and Far. I trod the sands of North Africa, and had connections with the South of that country as well as that land once fondly remembered as Southern Rhodesia.

I spent three months in Australia, back-packing 15,000 miles when I was sixty, learning of the implications of the war on that continent and its near neighbour New Guinea. I repeated that enterprise in New Zealand; with less mileage and so taking less time. I was in a position to remember the epic of the war in the Pacific and the countries of the Indian Ocean, India, the one-time Ceylon and Burma. Towns in Malaysia, previously Malaya, and the once-called Siam have witnessed my presence. I was able to recall an earlier connection to Borneo. I witnessed the effects of the war in the United States of America and in Canada and I heard of an incident which occurred off the coast of Alaska.

For the moment my luggage is moth-balled. I am home, and many years after my adventures, I wrote this book.

Chapter 1

Countdown to War

In the Beginning

I lived through the Second World War. I am a very old lady now and whilst I can still remember how it was at that time, I am recording the history of the war and my experiences during it. To begin with I think that it is important to understand the trajectory which led to the Second World War within a time span of little more than twenty years since the end of the First World War, and although I am not old enough to be able to relate that intelligence from a direct first hand point of view, I can record my impressions from my knowledge of history.

The First World War ended on the 11th November 1918. The British and her Allies defeated the Germans and an armistice was signed. A year later The Treaty of Versailles was drawn up and validated. The terms written into the Treaty rendered Germany utterly vanquished. The conditions and stipulations were extremely harsh. Germany lost territory including their previously held province, Alsace-Lorraine. Huge reparations had to be paid. Strict rules were set up which would prevent Germany from rearming military personnel and military equipment. Inflation was sky high. A barrow-load of the currency, the German Mark, was the price of a packet of butter. That is if one could find butter to buy. In addition, Kaiser Wilhelm was deposed, and went to live in Holland, never to return. Germany was ruined and humiliated. In June 1919 another covenant was proposed. 'The League of Nations' was devised and brought to fruition. The aim of the League was to safeguard European countries should trouble arise in the future.

In the inter-war years, under the Terms of the League of Nations, Treaties and Pacts were devised. They were called Non-Aggression Pacts which incorporated France and Poland and Britain as Allies in any future wars. Hitler, the German leader, flaunted the terms of the Treaty of Versailles. He began, unlawfully, to build a stock of war materials and the training of young men for military purposes. In 1937 and 1938 he annexed Austria and Czechoslovakia. The latter was peacefully and politically changed in 1993. The new state incorporated certain neighbouring states and is now called the Czech Republic.

In September 1938, the British Prime Minister, Neville Chamberlain went to Germany, under the auspices of the of the League of Nations to remind Hitler of the terms of the Treaty and to get assurances from him that he had no further intention of expanding Germany. Chamberlain arrived back, and from the top of the aircraft steps when he landed at Heston aerodrome in Middlesex, he waved the piece of paper bearing Hitler's signature and promise. Chamberlain pronounced, "We will have peace in our time". It was a statement that people remembered and still do. It was a misnomer. It was not worth the paper it was written on. Hitler was a liar and a fraud.

I watched that scene, from Heston, in a newsreel report, showing in a local cinema. In 1938 only the 'rich' had television. As a matter of fact I had already watched TV in 1936, on 2nd November when the BBC put out its inaugural programme, in the house of a friend's friend. My direct acquaintances did not have that endowment. We sat in a darkened room on dining room chairs set out in rows facing a TV of exceedingly small proportions. In 'old' measurements, seven inches, square! I still remember the programme. A young lady gave a rendering of a popular song. Perhaps it was one that the crooner, Bing Crosby, had made famous. I can't recall the name of it. Bing was my number one favourite. The Frank Sinatra of an earlier era. Sometimes the present day BBC show clips from pre-war presentations and I have that initiation into the TV so clear in my mind. Gosh I was 11 years old. Heck, over 80 years ago!

* * *

Early Warnings

Hitler had been a corporal in the German Army. He was angry and bitter about the defeat of Germany and the terms of the Treaty of Versailles. He joined a band of 'like-minded' men and he rose in the ranks. He became the German Chancellor (leader) in 1933. He was a demagogue and he ruled Germany by dictatorship and brutality. He was obsessed with the idea that Germans should be of pure stock, Aryan, that is blue eyed and blonde. He began to plan the strategy of 'The Final Solution'. His aim was the extermination of Romas (Gypsies), the disabled and infirm, homosexuals and Jews.

In April 1933, a group of Nazi students undertook 'The Burning of the Books'. Books written by classic liberals, socialists, communists and Jews among others who were viewed as being subversive or as representing opposing ideologies to the Nazi state.

It is said that "those who burn books, burn bodies". It foretold the future.

'The Night of the Long Knives' was the name given to an event played out in Nazi Germany for three days in the summer of 1934, one year into Hitler's chancellorship. A series of extra-judicial executions were carried out in his name; certain proof of a genocidal mind and tendencies. Eminent politicians, who he regarded as a threat to his rise to power, were targeted. Old scores were settled and the victims subjected to attack and elimination. Courts and other legitimate assemblies were swept aside. The purge strengthened and consolidated his power; he became supreme head over a subjugated population. This foray of barbarous animalistic exhibition should, I think, have been a dire warning to other European states of what lay in store for the future. Initially, eighty five people were killed in that 'putsch', (German for 'thrust' or 'blow'), but it is estimated that the number was probably much higher, possibly several hundreds. More than a thousand were arrested, and were some of the first prisoners in the concentration camps.

On the night of 9th November 1938, an event called 'Kristallnacht' took place in Germany. Translated as 'Crystal Night', this event was known as 'The Night of Broken Glass'. Synagogues, Jewish shops, schools and homes were vandalized. A hundred Jewish people were beaten and killed. As an aftermath to that terrible night thirty thousand were rounded up and sent to Concentration Camps. From 1935 to 1945 six million people of the Jewish Faith were murdered.

* * *

Preparing for the Inevitable

In spite of Chamberlain's flag waving, the British Government were worried. They did not feel that they could trust the word of this unreliable, crazy, land-hungry man. They began preparations to contain him.

Portable air raid shelters were delivered to every household. They were of two types. One was the Anderson Shelter, which was suitable if you had a garden and which you dug into the earth until it was half submerged. We had that type. I remember my Dad sweating away one Sunday morning with a garden spade. Later, during the raids when there was not enough warning to get to the public shelter, we used that Anderson. We sat in it with just a torch for light. It was cold, dank and smelly and we stayed in it, sometimes for hours, until the 'All Clear' siren went.

Incidentally, my Dad refused to go to a shelter, be it ours or later on, the public one. He stayed at home in his bed. He used to say: "Gotta get up for work in the morning."

The other type of shelter was the Morrison Shelter. That was the one allotted to you if you had no garden. You fixed it to the underside of your kitchen table. And there a family sat when the siren went. John Anderson and Herbert Morrison were members of the Government. Large buildings reinforced their basements for public use.

Gas masks were issued to every person. The adult model was the size of a toaster and it came in a cardboard box with a shoulder strap. Children had 'Mickey Mouse' designs on their replicas, and little tent-like envelopes with gas mask protection were issued for babies. A plan was arranged for the evacuation of school children from cities and towns to areas where it was considered to be safer than in more populated parts.

Air Raid Wardens were recruited and trained. When they were eventually needed they did a magnificent job. They were issued with whistles to attract the attention of colleagues and rattles to warn the public in the event of a gas attack. The wardens were elderly men, too old for the Armed Forces, and young lads, not yet old enough to fight. These youngsters were issued with cycles and they acted as messengers between Air Raid Wardens and ARP (Air Raid Precautions) sectors. Fit young men were recruited for the AFS, The Auxiliary Fire Service, and they dealt with the fires caused by the raids.

* * *

Introducing our Family Heroes

A young man in his early twenties, married to my cousin and father of a small daughter, organized himself to do his duty. His name was Israel Deitch. We all called him 'Izzy'. He thought that he would stay in London with his little family rather than be called for the Armed Services abroad. He volunteered for the AFS and was killed on duty during a raid. Close by St. Pauls Cathedral in London, there is a memorial to those who gave their lives serving in the Fire Service during the war, and his name is there inscribed.

A Minister for War was appointed. His name was Hoare Belisha. As a matter of interest he was the person earlier on who had devised the zebra crossing idea.

The yellow globe atop the crossing pole was, (and probably still is by some people), known as a 'Belisha Beacon' in his honour. His next claim to fame, which he left as his legacy, was for a plan, considered and enacted pre-war, to conscript all young males who were aged 21 in, and after, July 1939, to be liable for military service. A young man called Raymond, who was 21 in that month, was 'called up' and directed into The Royal Artillery. Privates in that regiment are called 'Gunners'. And so out of 'civvies' and into uniform – Raymond was now a 'Gunner'.

In 1938, and in the run-up to the war, I was 13 years old, and mature enough to understand what was happening around me. I realized what was likely to take place. I was very worried, very nervous, and very afraid. The Spanish Civil War had been fought since 1936, and there had been air raids. I remembered it, and thought of it with dread.

On 1st September 1939, in spite of all his promises and assurances to the British Prime Minister Neville Chamberlain, and with disregard to the covenant of the League of Nations and The Treaty of Versailles, Hitler marched into Poland. Early in the morning, two days later on, September 3rd, Chamberlain delivered an ultimatum. He allowed Hitler until 11am to abandon the incursion. He warned him that if he did not comply, and a withdrawal from Poland was not evident by that time, we would be at war with Germany. No reply was forthcoming, and Hitler's aggressive manifestation proceeded. It was the starting pistol that plunged the entire world into an abyss of death and destruction – misery, heartache, suffering and atrocities. The tragedy of the Second World War.

Raymond, aged 20.
Newly-conscripted, 1939

At 11.15am on that fateful morning, Chamberlain spoke to the nation on the wireless, now called a radio. I listened to that speech. It was preceded by the sound of Big Ben, the famous chimes from the clock perched high over our seat of government in Westminster. It sounded ominous. We all knew what was to follow. It was the death knell to everything that had gone before. To many it was indeed a tolling for the dead. It did not auger well for the future. I feel the shiver of dread as I remember it now.

Myrtle, aged 14, and brother Leslie, aged 11. 1939 - one month before the declaration of War

Chapter 2
Britain at War

The Balloon Goes Up

Where was I? What was I doing when I listened to the declaration of war? To set the scene, it is necessary to tell you that one of the very first requirements on that day was to ensure that all your windows were 'blacked out'. Failure to do so would render you liable to imprisonment. It was vital that German bombers had no guidance as to the whereabouts of their chosen targets. You either painted your windows or you hung heavy black lined curtains, and you criss-crossed the windows with narrow strips of gummed brown paper preventing the glass from shattering if a loud retort should resound from a nearby explosion. So where was I?

With my Mum and Dad and my brother Les, we were at my Aunt Millie's who lived quite close to our house. The Phillips family, (for that was their name), had a wine and spirits shop. Leading from the shop to the 1st floor was a very long staircase with a window. I was perched on top of a ladder fixing the black-out curtain. (Sorry if that was a bit long winded but it evokes a memory I will never forget.)

No sooner had we heard Prime Minister Chamberlain's announcement when the air raid sirens went – a terrible wailing sound. We all grabbed our gas masks and rushed down to the cellar which the authorities had delegated as a public shelter for any person wishing to use it, such as my uncle's customers or people in the street seeking refuge. A large red letter 'S' was displayed outside as were on all public shelters. Aunt Millie's cellar was almost purpose-built for emergency use. It stored their bottled stock. We were in shock and maybe we needed a reviving tot, but declined to sample its contents. The inclination was not to manifest fear at that awful time. So we sat there, wearing the gas masks although no gas alert was given and very soon the 'All Clear' sounded. We all had a nice cup of tea thankful that it had just been a false alarm.

We very quickly became accustomed to the new routine of war-time living. I became an avid newspaper reader and searched out all the news I could concerning the finer points of the situation. I elucidated the knowledge that our wartime partners would be France and Poland and we were to be known as the Allies.

To add to the news that worried us all was that on the 23rd August, nine days prior to Hitler's invasion of Poland, a pact was signed between Russia and Germany. Basically it was a non-aggression arrangement. Call it whatever, it was anything but non-aggression. When Hitler marched into Poland the Russian army did too. It was an attempt to annex that country between them. The agreement was signed by Molotov for the Soviets and Ribbentrop for Germany – foreign ministers for their respective masters, Stalin and Hitler. Both armies advanced and it was not too long before their troops met, shook hands and carved up Poland between them. In 1941, the chickens came home to roost when Russia was invaded by their previous erstwhile collaborators. They were not so friendly then.

At a later date in October and November 1940, that 1939 pact was negated. Hitler had a much better idea; he wanted Poland for himself and maybe a bit more besides. Fast forward one year to 1941. His day dream came to fruition and he invaded Russia and it was then when that country joined us as a member of the Allied coalition. By our declaration of war against Germany we undertook to honour the conditions of the Non-Aggression Pact forged in the years after the First World War.

Germany was partnered with Italy, governed by the Fascist dictator, Mussolini. They became allies in war until 1943. Mussolini, a weak and cowardly character, changed his allegiance when the war was being fought in Italy, and the successful Allies were overrunning that country. Benito, for that was his name, thought it wise to hedge his bets as to who would win the war. In 1941 when Japan, let loose on its path of aggression, ruled by its Emperor Hirohito, cuddled up to the other two beauties Germany and Italy, they became known as the Axis.

* * *

'Goodbye' to the Old, 'Hello' to the New

We were at war and everything changed. All the street lights went out. People went out in the dark and never forgot to take a torch. Everyone carried their gas mask. Places of entertainment were closed so that people were not gathered in large crowds. Later on, when an invasion was likely, named signposts within the UK were either removed or the names obliterated. The Child Evacuation Plan was geared into action.

As part of the Government preparation policy for war, a plan had been devised whereby all school children and mothers with pre-school children would be evacuated to less densely populated places where it was considered to be less likely to attract aerial bombardment. Some parents, in a position to do so, sent their offspring, under private arrangements, to seek sanctuary in Commonwealth countries, out of the war zone entirely.

As early as the summer of 1939, when officials realized that war was becoming more and more a possibility, local councils made arrangements for the requisition of trains and buses, and comprehensive lists were drawn up of foster homes. The scheme was known as Operation Pied Piper. When it eventually went into an actuality, three and a half million children were evacuated in the first four days of the war. It was the biggest and most concentrated population movement in British history.

And so it came to pass. The first few days after the declaration, train stations were packed with thousands of children all labelled and with their little attaché cases and clutching their dollies or teddies, being herded by their teachers and railway staff. There were all the weepy mums saying good bye, and crying offspring too. On arrival at the destinations, the children disembarked to the phrase echoing around stations by prospective foster parents – "I'll have that one!" I was 14 and had already left school so I stayed at home. My brother Leslie, then aged 11, left and was sent to Preston Park, Hove, in Sussex.

Tag issued to children being evacuated

The Changing Face of Britain

I went to work with my Dad. I started at a factory owned by Simpsons. Some might know that Simpsons is a firm of bespoke tailors and outfitters. They still operate from their retail premises in Piccadilly, London. In wartime, their obligation and our labour aided the war effort, and were manufacturing all types of military uniforms. Our particular team turned out khaki clobber for Tommies (British soldiers). The material, hard wearing for those foot-sloggers, was tough and heavy to handle. It was 'good-bye' to soft fairy-like mitts. I sat at that sewing machine, on the same bench as my Dad, in a continuous row of fellow machinists for four years, until I was 18. We 'clocked-on' at the factory entrance every morning at 8am and 'clocked out' when we left at 6pm. We did a five and a half day week. My Dad had been a trouser maker for civilians pre-war. Now we were 'doing our bit'.

Single men and women aged between 18 and 41 were mobilized for the Armed Forces or for work of national importance in factories producing war utilities – ammunitions, tanks, bombers and fighters, guns and the like. Some people were considered exempt from conscription in what was known as Reserved Occupations. They continued to do their vital jobs at home. The category included farmers, train drivers, the police, government officials and miners, to name but a few. Young men living in or near a coal mining area were called up to work in the pits. They were called 'Bevin Boys' named for the minister Ernest Bevin who devised the scheme. A cousin in Cardiff, an aspiring pharmaceuticals student left his studies and went down the mines. He was the most unsuitable and unlikely miner ever, but he did the job without complaint. His mother, aunt Sonnie (Sonya) scrubbed away at the black coal dust-ingrained gear, also without complaint. Pit-head bath or shower facilities had not yet become an innovation.

Woman at home did full-time work. Nobody grumbled or skived off. They became bus drivers and toiled in factories. They joined the Police and directed traffic and they worked on the railways. They volunteered for the NAAFI (Navy, Army and Air Force Institutions) which was an organization originally conceived by the Government in 1921 to provide recreation establishments for service personnel. They sold goods which might be required by such persons, and they offered refreshments. They were sited world-wide, wherever the armed forces operated. They could even be found on ships of the Fleet. Women became ambulance drivers. They swept the streets and emptied the dustbins (the equivalent of today's 'wheelie bins').

I very recently encountered a lady 'postie' who delivered at my flat in lieu of our regular postman, who was taking a break. He is not the type of fellow to take a 'sickie', so I dare say he was on holiday. He's a lovely man and I know his wife. I am doing this 'commercial' in the hope that I can off-load a copy of my book when it's ready! He might like to read what I think about him. Anyway, I unexpectedly came face-to-face with his replacement. It was a shock – it immediately rendered a flashback to the forties when lady mail deliverers were the norm. I could not believe it. We had a friendly chat and I told her of her predecessors. If I were younger I think I would apply for a like-wise job. I bet one could work off plenty of those fat producing calories! The working women and volunteers of the Second World War were the life-blood of our nation here at home.

Ration books and Identity Cards were distributed to everyone. By some fluke of memory, I can recall my identity number: AVUX2743. (Not bad for an old girl!) Food was rationed and was issued on a weekly basis. Meat, butter, cheese, sugar and milk were allotted in meagre quantities. For example your cheese ration for one week, was that which you would use for one small snack sandwich today. Potatoes and bread were unrationed, but the flour used for bread making was a very poor quality. It was probably a mixture of different types of grain. The bread was dark and tasteless. If you were hungry you ate it.

The war-time Ministry of Food was headed by Lord Woolton. It was his responsibility to make sure that Britons were fed. I wonder if the toast he had for breakfast was as I have mentioned 'dark and tasteless'? I would wager that Harrods, London, had their own bakery, and I bet that their bread was pure white and delicious!

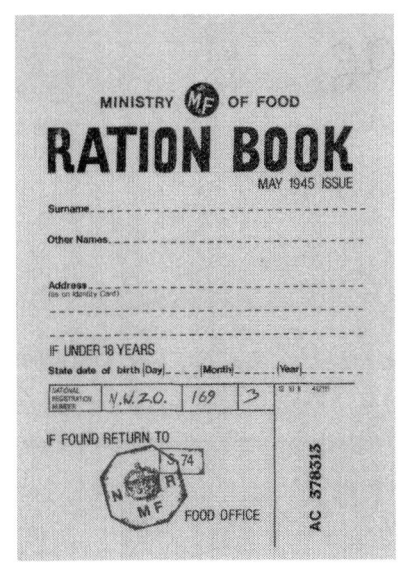

Ration Book cover

Surviving on Shortages

Eggs were not on ration but they were scarce and hard to come by. Grocers did have them occasionally. Unless you were a regular customer there was no availability to you. The grocer's 'relos' and friends were the recipients and eggs were a commodity for the Black Market – 'under the counter' profiteering. The scarcity of eggs lasted till well after the war. I remember paying one shilling (5p) for one when the official price was less than one old penny. I bought it for the tea for my young child. That was in 1948, three years after the end of the war. I remember where that transaction took place. The lapse of time renders it unnecessary to name the person and the shop!

My Dad decided that we should try a bit of self-sufficiency. He bought a couple of hens, and housed them in a wire mesh sort of enclosure in our back garden and we waited for some nice warm eggs. Unfortunately the venture lasted all of three days. Rats had infiltrated where we never had them before. So my Mum got the poor old hens slaughtered and whilst we were deprived of eggs for breakfast we did have some good old chicken soup for our Friday night meal!

If you were in luck you would get some dried egg powder at your local shop. It didn't taste much like egg but in scrambled form it looked a bit like it and it eked out the rations. Housewives spent hours queuing outside a shop if rumour had it that there was something special on offer like fish or rabbit or dried egg.

Later on sweets were rationed. Chocolate had completely vanished. People got slim and some say healthier. It was years before sweets were on general sale. I clearly remember going into a shop in Penarth, near Cardiff, to buy 'off the ration' sweets for my children. I had two by then. Sweet rationing only ended in February 1953.

Clothes were later rationed. We were all allocated a points system. One was entitled to so many 'points' and different items of clothing had a point value. For example, a dress might be 10 points; a pair of trousers might be 6 points. A gentleman's suit might be valued at 24 points. One was very restricted and perhaps saved them up to buy a special garment for a special occasion. A prospective bride, if she was very lucky, knew someone who knew someone who had access to an old used parachute, (which was made of silk), and could be recycled into a wedding dress. The family would pool their coupons so that the bride could buy some new underwear or honeymoon clothes.

People learnt to repair, alter and rejuvenate their apparel. They did so through necessity. Other items required by a war-time population, but were unavailable, inspired us to compromise or adjust accordingly. I would like to give one example of the restrictions laid down by government ministries. Narrow elastic was not to be found in any shop. Shipping from abroad brought in war supplies or was used to transport our armed forces to various areas where we were engaged. Elastic, a rubber by-product, was manufactured from raw material grown in Burma. There was no likelihood that we were going to use vessel space to import that commodity. The Ministry faced and surmounted that problem with alacrity. It had to be proved that that narrow gauge article was vital for the repair of ladies underwear.

I have a hang-up left over from the war. Even today, when I no longer need to, I sew up the ladders in my tights and I darn the holes in my socks. I have another post-war foible. I am unable to part with anything, be it to the charity shop or discarded in the rag bag. In the unusual event that I am compelled to do so I bid it "Good Bye" with reluctance.

Have some pity for my family when in due course it will be their chore to clear my flat.

* * *

The Phoney War

Here in Britain, the change from peace to war carried on apace. Gardens, both private and public, lost their flower beds and were replaced with vegetables. Railings were removed, and the metal was recycled into armed motor vehicles and such like. All the lovely food stuffs that we take for granted today vanished from the shops. Citrus fruit and bananas disappeared. After the war, when supplies started to return to normal, I watched a six year-old child attempt to eat a banana. She did not know that it was necessary to peel it! People you knew were no longer to be seen. Everywhere they were leaving to fight for King and Country. In tune with everyone else, I was glued to the wireless, listening to the news. I can still hear the familiar voice of Alvar Liddell who read the news every night at 9pm. Even today, after 70 years, I am a news addict.

Poland was very quickly taken by the Germans following their 'Blitzkrieg' invasion. Subsequent to that event there was a sustained period of military inactivity.

It was a case of being 'All quiet on the Western Front'. In fact Chamberlain speaking to fellow conservatives at a party meeting said that Hitler "had missed the bus". Had he? A couple of days later, on the 9th April 1940, Germany officially invaded a neutral and unsuspecting Norway. The intervening seven months were to be known as the 'Phoney War'.

* * *

Norwegian Connections in the House

A debacle in the House of Commons of the British Parliament during the two days, 7th-8th May 1940, was the direct result of a French and British attempt to defend the Norwegian ports of Narvik and Trondheim in April of that year.

Norway at the outbreak of World War 2 was neutral; a quiet peaceful country attempting to keep out of the limelight, away from the turmoil that was bursting forth around it. It was unfortunate for its own good that it was reckoned to be a vital and valuable prize for any would-be conqueror, and both the United Kingdom and Germany were well aware of this fact. Narvik and Trondheim, nestling on the western coast of that land, and a gateway to the Atlantic Ocean, were the number one targets within the sights of both the belligerent nations.

Germany needed these exits for the exportation of iron ore from Sweden and the British needed to ensure that they were kept free from the possibility of being the departure points of the enemy's battleships and U-Boats ready to interfere with our shipping in the Atlantic. Also to prevent the use of airstrips in that locality for the Luftwaffe to undertake air activities on a wide scale over that ocean. These twin ports were particularly essential when it is considered that in the winter months much of the Baltic Sea eastward of Norway is frozen over. A successful invasion of that Baltic country by either side had the potential to strike a severe blow against the other.

* * *

A Lost Country in Sixty-two Days

The assault and defence of Norway first saw the light of day on the 3rd April 1940. Without warning Germany covertly ordered supply vessels out to sea in advance of a main naval force. Alerted by this underhand move the Allies dispatched sixteen submarines and twelve destroyers to the area within the next two days.

The weather was bad, thick fog and heavy snow gave the Germans an advantage. On the 8th April contact was made between the two navies and both sides suffered heavy losses during ongoing sea battles.

The Norwegian government issued mobilization details, but their coastal ships failed to defend the western ports. Hitler sent his land forces to invade on the 9th April and the United Kingdom and France sent an expeditionary force to do likewise in its defence. Battles took place in central and eastern Norway. A defence was mounted of those two ports, Narvik and Trondheim, to keep them free from German hoards, which in the end they were unable so to do. Further south the port of Bergen suffered the same fate, and Oslo, the country's capital was captured soon afterwards. The King, Haakon Vll and the Royal Family together with parliament fled to the United Kingdom.

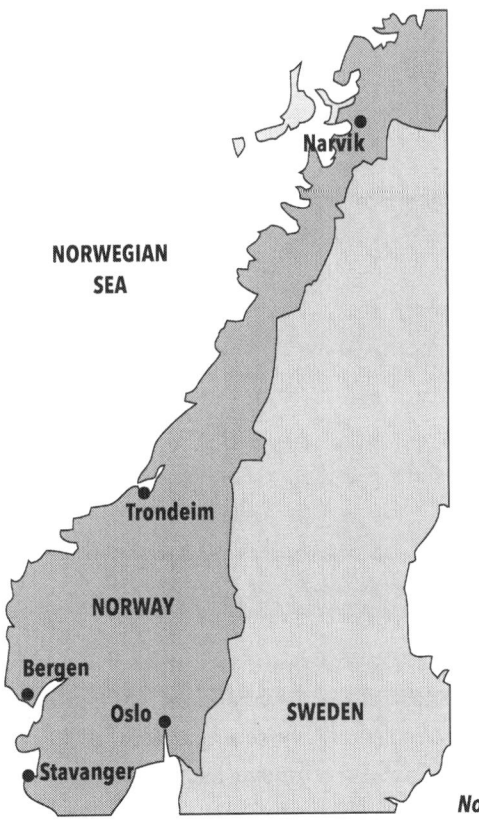

The subsequent German invasion of Holland, Belgium and France in the early days of May 1940 gave the Allies no choice but to withdraw their aid to Norway. The French and the Flemish were now having to fight for the defence of their own land across the English Channel and we were having to utilize our anti-aircraft guns at the time of German bomber raids over British cities. Norway was finally taken in a matter of sixty-two days.

Norway 1940

Uproar from Both Sides

This brings me back to square one. A Conservative majority government met in the British parliament to debate the Norwegian affair which led to Hitler's victory in that country. It came to be known in history as the Norwegian Debate. The decision to defend the Norwegian ports had been taken, and was planned for early in April.

The military preparation for the expedition was poor and under-estimated in man power and viable armour. Guns, transport and tanks were in short supply and the troops lacked training in those Norwegian arctic conditions. The snow lay thick on the ground and snow shoes or skis were items not thought of by those engaged in the planning arrangements. It was a diabolical miscalculation from the start with disastrous effect. Relationships between the Army Chiefs and the Naval Commanders were divisive and a stalemate situation between them was hardly a surprise. As a result of mismanagement two-and-a-half thousand men of the Royal Navy were lost at sea and fifty of the RAF did not return home. One thousand nine hundred soldiers were killed or wounded; all to no avail.

Dissatisfaction came to a head regarding Chamberlain's leadership and his ineffectual handling of the war. The debate in the House on those days in May 1940 gave rise to heated arguments and hostility. There erupted a massive outcry against the PM and he was frequently interrupted and mocked by members on both sides as he spoke. Quoted by one were the words spoken by Oliver Cromwell to the Long Parliament in 1653: "You have sat too long here for any good you have been doing. Depart I say, and let us have done with you. In the name of God, go!"

The Prime Minister sought the help from some of his friends but they remained silent. Mr Lloyd George appealed to him to relinquish his office. He was said to be unfit to discharge his duties in the conduct of the war. Lloyd George was a personality of long-standing in the Commons. His political career began in 1890 when he was first elected as a Liberal member for the Carnarvon Boroughs which he held until his death in 1945. The political career of this staunch Welsh nationalist rose rocket-like. In 1916 he became Prime Minister in a World War 1 Government, after serving as Minister of Munitions in 1915 and Secretary of State the following year. It was he in 1916 who first advocated the Convoy System and persuaded the Royal Navy to utilize it. He was the head of the British delegation at the 1919 Peace Conference which saw the birth of the Treaty of Versailles.

In 1921 he became instrumental in the establishment of the Irish Free State, now the Republic of Ireland. Later his posts were President of the Board of Trade, and Chancellor of the Exchequer. He certainly was a voice to be reckoned with. In 1938 he distanced himself from Chamberlain's appeasement attitude and he disfavoured the PM's policies. His powerful speech in the Commons during the May debate did much to undermine Chamberlain's case.

Neville Chamberlain became Prime Minister in 1937. When war broke out he had been in office for two-and-a-half years during which time Great Britain had suffered a series of diplomatic defeats and humiliations. The event of the Munich return with Hitler's promise of non-aggression was not easily forgotten. Under his leadership a complete breakdown of our foreign policy was undeniably obvious and after the disaster in Norway the House of Commons could place no confidence in his ability to lead us to victory. It was eventually decided that the formation of a National Government was the answer. Today a National Government would be known as a Coalition, and the Labour and the Liberal Parties were asked to take up the responsibility to create it together with the Conservatives. On the 10th May, when the Germans invaded the mainland continental countries, Chamberlain finally bowed to pressure and resigned, especially when the Opposition leaders stated that they would not serve under him.

* * *

A New Broom to Sweep Clean

A decision was now imminent: "Who would succeed him"? Three days after the start of the Norway Debate Chamberlain went to Buckingham Palace to offer his resignation to the King, George Vl. Chamberlain looked for Lord Halifax to succeed as PM and the King, in conversation, thought so too. But Lord Halifax refused, offering as the reason for his refusal that his seat in the House of Lords was not compatible with that of the role of Prime Minister in the lower House. Well there was some suggestion that Halifax had had some dealings with Adolph Hitler in the past. He was in favour of contacting the Axis via Italy and suing for talks after our Dunkirk retreat from France, (as described in the next section). For my money it was a bloomin' good job that he turned down the role of premiership. When the war went badly for us in the coming months, who is to say that feelers for a negotiated peace would not have been on the table?

Winston Churchill, then First Lord of the Admiralty, was the only other contender. Some were haunted by his 'Gallipoli' past but he had had a good parliamentary record since, and the Labour and Liberal leaders were prepared to take up service under his watch. And so it was that Winnie became top dog. On the evening BBC news on that 10th May 1940 an announcement was forthcoming to that effect. Churchill retired to bed at 3am the next morning having organized the make-up of a new War Cabinet which included the heads of the Services Ministries – all in six hours! Labour's Clement Atlee was now Deputy Prime Minister, and Sir Archibald Sinclair, representing the Liberal Party, joined the coalition as Secretary of State for Air. The vote in the House gave 381 for and zero against the newly-formed coalition. The 'Ayes' had it. Our newly-elected Prime Minister spoke to the members. He said: "I have nothing to offer but blood, toil, tears and sweat". Well that's what was on offer, and we the public accepted. An eventual victory would be ours; we got there in the end.

* * *

The Miracle of Deliverance

In the very early days of the war, Britain sent the army to France. It was called the BEF – British Expeditionary Force. Raymond was one of those soldiers. Hitler had invaded France and Belgium; German code name 'Fall Gelb', (Case Yellow), and there the Germans engaged the British Forces. Our Army retreated and was gradually driven back towards the sea. That withdrawal developed, until what remained of the BEF, those troops who had survived the German guns and the bombs, found themselves on the beaches of Dunkirk.

The call went out for a rescue. More than seven hundred boat owners and their small craft answered that they were ready for whatever they were asked to do. There were boats of every description – pleasure yachts, privately owned motor launches, fishing boats, and many others, including paddle steamers that once ferried holiday makers for a 'day out' in Southend or Margate.

Indeed as a child, the four of us, (my immediate family and me), used to enjoy a day out in Margate. We would board the paddle steamer at Tower Bridge, on the river Thames. I recall its name – the 'Golden Eagle'. I remember the thrill as the Bridge opened and raised its sides as we left the Port of London and sailed between those two elevated roads.

Today that only happens for the Queen, although Winston Churchill was accorded that honour at his State Funeral, at the time of his death on the 24th January 1965 aged 90.

But I digress, and ashamed that I should do so, to find myself rambling on about inconsequential trivialities. The evacuation by sea, designated Operation Dynamo resulted in The Dunkirk Evacuation. That is what it was called, and that is how it is remembered. The Armada of that rescuing flotilla comprised any small boat that could sail. Some were not designed for sea waters. Most of them were river craft but they took their places ready to cross the English Channel. In those small vessels they saved the residue of the British Army; many of them made repeated journeys in spite of the disadvantage of not being able to understand naval signals at night, a necessary requirement requiring a response from those erstwhile sailors in their unlighted craft. They were at risk of being the victims of 'friendly fire'. Soldiers waiting patiently in long lines on the beach for hours until it was their turn to leave were strafed by German dive bombers.

The carnage and the noise were terrible. Many were killed. They died as they waited to be rescued. The small boats carried their human cargo to the waiting big ships, too large to sail into the shallow water, whereas the little ships could get closer to the shore, and those exhausted men came home. Their equipment had been lost or abandoned. They left behind an enormous amount of pertinent war hardware; nearly 3,000 guns, more than 650,000 tons of ammunition and 85,000 army vehicles. Some came back having lost their boots. In addition seventy of the rescuing boats did not return and the Royal Navy suffered the loss of thirty warships.

A retreat it was but a victory too. To have rescued so many from those beaches, away from that 'hell on earth' situation. In total 300,000, including French troops, some Poles and some of the Belgium Army were rescued during those seven days in 1940, from the 26th May to the 3rd June. But many more were not, and they lie in France.

The history of that situation is an integral part of our British heritage. It will be remembered and immortalized as long as Britain exists. Mr Churchill called it a 'Miracle of Deliverance'. To parliamentary members he said: "We must be very careful not to assign to this deliverance the attributes of a victory. Wars are not won by evacuations". Those who came home lived to fight another day. But that is the official history and there is a more personal history to record.

Raymond, who was serving with the BEF, was one of those enervated young men waiting his turn to be rescued. He was fortunate to have come so far, unharmed, and to have arrived at that place. His luck held. He was rescued by an Irish mail boat. That heaven-sent little boat saved his life. That small vessel was one of the last to leave the French beach. It was one of the 'Little Ships', as they came to be known.

After the war, when decorations were issued to those who had served, Raymond was awarded the Dunkirk medal. Now in 2016, Raymond is no longer with us. His daughter, Sheila, proudly wears that medal every year when she marches along-side veterans and progeny of those warriors long since gone, on Remembrance Sunday in November which takes place at the Cenotaph in Whitehall, London. Raymond's Dunkirk medal, a small symbol of that time, is recognized and admired by many. With my youngest daughter, Simone wearing her dad's medals, and myself, (sporting my replica Land Army badge that I received from a 'grateful country' in 1995, 50 years after the end of the war), we three take an immense pride in attending this event. It is an emotional experience. We march to the stirring music of the military bands. We veterans, who sadly grow less in number each year, follow contingents of today's armed forces. We gather and 'fall in' to parade, in spite of the now ageing old-timers, to pay our respects to, and to remember those who were not as fortunate as we who survived.

Of the estimated Jewish population, (400,000 in 1940), 70,000 Jewish men and women served in the British Armed Forces. These figures do not include Commonwealth personnel or any of the 30,000 who voluntary enlisted in the British Forces in Palestine.

Raymond proudly displaying his medals, 1945

Here to Fight Another Day

At this point I think it is appropriate to continue the story about Raymond. He is, after all, the hero of the piece.

After his return home from Dunkirk, he was taken to Salisbury Plain, and was encamped there under canvas. The British Army was in disarray. The men came off the beaches individually, disorganized and disarranged, separated from their regiment or unit. Gradually the British public were fed the story of the evacuation, and if a family had a son or husband or brother fighting in France, anxiety was natural. Raymond's folk in Cardiff were no exception. They were soon informed that Raymond was safe, and where he was. His father left Cardiff to seek out his son.

Salisbury Plain covers a large area, and row after row of look-alike tents where no formal address existed, presented an almost impossible task to trace one person. But Dad, Mr Shocolinsky, was undaunted. He marched up and down between the rows of tents yelling "Shocko where are you?" – Shocko being the abbreviation of the family name. Such perseverance deserves its reward, and father and son were reunited. Raymond said that being bivouacked there, without organized routine or action, boredom beset these usually active soldiers. With nothing to do and not knowing what would happen next, the men became restless. Until a day dawned which changed everything in general, and Raymond's army career in particular. A group of army officers informed the men that a new regiment was about to be formed and asked for volunteers to join up and to be part of it. And many of them did, including Raymond.

The new authority was to be known as the 1st Airborne Division. Its role in the British Armed Forces was the training of personnel in the art of parachuting from aeroplanes, and to fly and land in engineless gliders. They were to be identified by exchanging their khaki forage caps, hitherto worn by all non-commissioned officers and privates in the British Army, for a new army innovation: berets. And for this elite corps of men, the new style of head wear would be red! When he recounted this experience to me, Raymond added a rider. He told me that when he arrived home on his next leave wearing his red beret, his mother opened the front door and said "You are not coming in here wearing that hat!"

At the same time as being asked to volunteer, the men were asked to submit sketches for a new cap badge. Raymond was blessed with an artistic talent and he could sketch and draw. He was not an artist in oils or water colour. He was, in fact, colour blind. So he drew and sketched in black and white and the design he submitted was accepted.

That insignia is still worn today by men of that regiment. It is Raymond's bequest.

Raymond, 1942.
If this picture was in colour,
the beret (with badge insignia)
would show as red

Chapter 3
War in Europe

Frenchmen on Opposite Sides

The British Evacuation from France did not end the fighting. The French and Germans were engaged in a series of skirmishes which resulted in a weakening of the defenders and defeat was evident. The victorious Germans entered Paris unopposed, marching in victory through the Arc-de-Triomphe and copy-catting the march of the French military when they celebrated their victory after the Great War. A camera team was in attendance and at the cinema I watched Adolph in that city gloating over his view of the Eiffel Tower from a bridge over the River Seine. I have no idea of the nationality of that set-up but the authenticity of it was true. I squirmed in my cinema seat. The photographs that appeared in the newspapers showed a happy Fuhrer, gazing and laughing, and so satisfied with his conquest. That picture is engraved into my brain, corroding into feelings of utter repugnance.

The Frenchman, Charles de Gaulle was a soldier of merit within the annals of military history. He was a very tall man in stature and phlegmatic in character and usually presented a demeanour of impassive imperturbability. He exiled himself in England when France was lost and transferred his fervour and allegiance to Winston Churchill and the Allies. He became leader of the so called Free French. Broadcasting in his language from the BBC on its worldwide news transmissions, he exhorted those Frenchmen and women, living overseas in the French held territories and in Great Britain, to join him and his Free French comrades. In total they eventually formed a fighting force to be reckoned with in the Allied cause. He was a resistant statesman. At the time of the French collapse he was the Under Secretary of State for National Defence. Subsequently he rose to the rank of General.

Following the Fall of France, (as it is remembered), the French Marshal Petain sued for an armistice with Germany. He was an elderly gentleman, a surviving soldier from the Great War. The armistice was signed in July 1940, giving Petain jurisdiction to set up a nominal government and to rule for his German masters. Hitler decreed that the signing of this Armistice document should take place in the same railway carriage in the Forest of Compiegne as a humiliating reversal of the treaty signed on 11th November 1918 by a defeated Germany.

France was subjugated and became a German puppet state. The town of Vichy was to be Petain's seat of government and he was allowed full rights of power under Hitler's 3rd Reich. In addition most of the French Colonies came into his province and remit.

* * *

Meres-el-Kabir

It came to pass that our Prime Minister still had reason to worry about an, as yet, unresolved problem relating to the fiasco across the English Channel. When at the time of Petain's take over, the French Fleet was still intact and lying in harbour in a place called Meres-el-Kabir in French Algeria. It was a very dangerous and disconcerting train of thought. Churchill pleaded with the then French Admiral Darlan to allow those ships to set sail for England or Canada but the plea was ignored.

A combined sea-and-air British bombardment was an unavoidable complication. The French Navy anchored on that Algerian coast on the 3rd July 1940 was obliterated. The consequences were harsh; one thousand French servicemen died along with the destruction of their ships. Mr Churchill was seriously worried that these vessels would have ultimately surrendered to the Germans. Their guns trained on the ships of our Navy giving them superiority over ours.

The French Admiral promised that that would not happen. Mr Churchill, at that time, still fretting over our retreat from Dunkirk and of the French surrender, surmised that it was too precarious to take that risk of having that fleet intact and unharmed.

His decision to carry out the attack at Meres-el-Kabir remains a controversial subject for debate, even to the present time. It is agreed that times were desperate and we could not afford to risk the chance of facing that fleet in mortal combat. The French, on the other hand, argue that we should have trusted Darlan and taken him at his word. They declare that we acted without honour. They considered that it was a betrayal and this attitude festered for generations. Perhaps it still does.

* * *

On Our Own

After the Evacuation of Dunkirk, Hitler invaded Denmark, Holland, Norway, Greece, Luxembourg and the Channel Islands. The only European countries unaffected were Switzerland and Sweden, which remained neutral, as did Portugal.

Spain was in the grip of the Fascist Regime under General Franco – though not an active ally of Germany, he was a sympathiser and friend of Hitler.

Britain stood alone against the might of Germany and its superior war machine.

Life in the occupied countries under Hitler was very difficult and dangerous for the indigenous population. Living under Nazi rule was tenuous and uncertain, depending how you reacted to it, and who you were. As well as other people, hundreds of thousands of Jews were herded into cattle trucks and taken by train to concentration camps, where they were beaten, starved, and suffered every form of cruelty, treated in the most inhuman manner and murdered. That was the Holocaust – the name by which that terrible time is written into history. Those poor unfortunate humans, who for no other reason than their status in life, or their religious belief, were the victims of that scale of barbaric sadism.

Every year, on the 27th January, which is the date on which Auschwitz, the most notorious of the concentration camps was liberated three months before the end of the war, civilized democratic countries, worldwide, remember and pay homage to the survivors, and to those who died, and to their families. That day is designated as 'Holocaust Memorial Day', and services and solemn programmes are arranged by civic dignitaries, government officials, religious leaders and many others. It is important that we remember, that we teach our children, and we do not forget. We should strive to make the world a good and safe place for us, and for those who come after us, to live in without fear, and in peace, and in a society championing as a priority, a tolerance for the culture and religion of others as well as our own.

* * *

Saved by the Few

The war has so far been recorded until the 10th July 1940. On that day, the tide of hostilities gave us a new aspect to consider. Squadrons of German bombers and fighters appeared over the southern counties of England. They attacked the RAF bases in that area, bombing and machine gunning aircraft on the ground, and aircraft in their hangars. RAF crew quarters were destroyed and personnel killed. Where possible, and when they had the opportunity, our airmen took to the skies in their fighters and they fought the enemy in 'dog fights' in the air.

Hundreds of raids were mounted, always in daylight. The strategy of the Germans was to obliterate the RAF as a fighting force. This episode in the war became known as The Battle of Britain. Its duration was four months, and the last raid was on the 31st October 1940.

The famous Spitfire fighter plane had its baptism of fire. It was the first time they were used in action. Thanks should go to Mr Reginald Joseph Mitchell, the Spitfire's designer, and to the brave young men who fought in those planes, in their late teens and early twenties, many of whom died in them. They and the ones who survived are all heroes. Our Prime Minister, Winston Churchill, delivered a speech to the nation. He said "Never in the field of human conflict has so much been owed by so many to so few". I listened to it on the wireless.

In my heart I blessed them all, the dead and those still alive. When the speech was over I stood up and shouted – "Three cheers for good old Winnie". Not very respectful, I confess, but his name was Winston after all!

Chapter 4
War Comes to London

My Testimony to Horror and Fortitude

It happened that a new phase of the war came to pass. It began in earnest on the 7th September 1941. Previous to that date, London had been subjected to spasmodic daylight air raids, but on that day, late in the afternoon, the savage onslaught meted out by the German Luftwaffe, (German Airforce) was initiated.

That was the first day of the London Blitz. The word 'blitz' was abbreviated from the German word 'blitzkrieg', translated into English as 'lightning war'. That's what the Germans called their rapid advance into the European countries which they attacked and invaded. They did it in a very short time. The defences of these states were no match for the might of Germany.

So what took place, and where was I on that day? My mother had a Saturday job. She worked in a shop that dealt in leather goods. Handbags, luggage, and other items of that nature. The shop was situated in a very busy market called Crisp Street, in the East London district of Poplar. Poplar is an area adjacent to the London Docks.

It was nearly shop closing time on that Saturday. I would think it was approximately 4pm. I was in the shop waiting for my Mum to finish work so that we could go home together to get the tea ready for the family, when the air raid sirens sounded. It was as if the end of the world was nigh. The noise of the crash of falling bombs, and the roar of the anti-aircraft guns was deafening. Very quickly the sky turned red reflecting the fires that were devouring the dockland warehouses. Three hundred and fifty bombers with six hundred fighter escorts discharged their high explosive cargo killing more than four hundred and fifty and seriously injuring 1,300 Londoners.

The market ceased trading. The shops all closed and my Mum and I journeyed home on whatever bus we could that was still in service. We did not voice our fears but we both knew that the fires would guide the German bombers back again that night. And our assumption became an actuality. That is exactly what happened, and it wasn't until the early hours of the next morning that the 'All Clear' gave us relief from the night we spent in our Anderson shelter. I carry that memory with me, even now.

Life after that first day of the Blitz presented us with a new regime of living, for fifty seven consecutive nights, from 7th September to November 3rd 1941. At dusk the sirens wailed out their warning – "Take Cover, run for your life". It was Hitler's hope that by neutralizing the capital and breaking the spirit of its citizens into defeat, Churchill would sue for peace. How wrong he was. Londoners rose to the challenge.

In the first thirty days, 30,000 bombs descended from the sky; almost 6,000 of our fellow citizens were killed; and 12,000 badly injured. But we coped and accepted the terror. Somehow we were proud to be taking our share in this war. We learnt to adjust to a new routine. Every evening after getting home from work and having eaten our evening meal, with our bedding at the ready and our sandwiches packed, we set off to our nearest public shelter, conveniently five minutes' walk from home. Incidentally it was the basement of the factory where my Dad and I worked, although the shelter was available to all, whether you were employed there or not. There we slept and ate our sandwiches and drank tea from our Thermos flask, and stayed until daylight broke and the 'All Clear' blew.

Humping our bedding and empty food boxes and drained flasks, we wended our way homeward. "Will it still be there?" we wondered. Thousands of people would find an empty space or debris where home once was, and maybe the rescue teams were already removing bricks and stone if it was thought that the family were still inside and had not gone to another place to find a safe haven where they could sit out the raid. One incident remains in my memory. We left the shelter one morning and the pet shop near our home was on fire. We could hear the howls of the trapped animals being burnt alive. One could hear the noise of claxons of ambulances, and fire engines, and rescue appliances, rushing through the streets. The fires needed to be quelled, heavy lifting gear was required, and injured folk waited for the transport to hospital. Everywhere the rubble remained of destroyed houses piled high as if in protest against the fate which caused it thus. Its once inhabitants, now homeless.

***

The Effects that Changed London

Apart from the casualty lists, the destruction of property was universal, both of private dwellings and important London buildings. Many government buildings in Whitehall repeatedly took hits. The Houses of Parliament were damaged by incendiary bombs which set the debating chamber alight.

The Germans almost succeeded where Guy Fawkes had failed. Churchill set up his headquarters in specially prepared basement accommodation called The War Rooms, where he worked by day and cat-napped at night. Those rooms have survived to this day. They are open for public viewing. I have taken the opportunity of doing so. I was transfixed as I stood there remembering the war and what that great man did for us British. In my opinion he was the greatest Briton ever.

Sixteen churches, built by Sir Christopher Wren in the 17th century, were destroyed or damaged. St. Pauls Cathedral was hit but luckily saved by the courage and resourcefulness of the ARP the AFS (Auxiliary Fire Services) and the rescue workers. Buckingham Palace suffered damage from the salvos of falling bombs. King George VI and his Queen, Elizabeth, visited the East End of London in its travail, and was able to empathize with staunch East-enders. They too had had their home damaged. Unlike many of the other royals of foreign states, our King and Queen stayed at home to be with their people. I am sure that they were advised to leave for their own safety and live out the war years in a Commonwealth country, but no, they chose to stay. Even if their bread was not 'dark and tasteless', they remained at home.

In the middle of September, a new aspect of the Blitz occurred. The bombers changed their tactical approach. They showered London with delayed-action bombs on railway lines, important road junctions, factory approaches and main routes in and out of London, as well as other essentially vitally important sites. With primitive equipment not yet developed, (which we might use with today's know-how), squads of soldiers were called into action to dig up these deadly appurtenances and to defuse them. They became known as Bomb Disposal Squads and Unexploded Bomb Detachments, and sad to relate, they had their share of fatalities.

The German High Command had other surprises for us Londoners. On the 15th of October during the night of a full moon, 480 German raiders let lose 386 tons of high explosive bombs and 70,000 tons of incendiary devices, rendering the city to be the victim of a blazing inferno. The AFS fought a gallant battle that night and the lesson was learnt. The government asked for civilian volunteers to offer their services as fire watchers. It was as Churchill said, "not down to the cellar, up on the roof". So it came to pass that Londoners reinforced their resolve and were privileged to feel that they were part in fighting this war. My Dad was issued with a steel helmet, and became a name on a rota. But he still had to get up in the morning for work, after a few hours' sleep.

On another night during the blitz, the Germans deliberately attacked our capital when the River Thames was at its lowest tide. The incendiaries rained down, and in a repeat performance, once again London was engulfed in flames. The high explosives, which preceded the fire bombs, had resulted in an enormous amount of damage, and put out of action the water hydrants. Together with the unavailability of Thames water, it was indeed a miracle that the brave and courageous men of the Auxiliary Fire Service prevented a re-run of that event in 1666 when London burned.

Recalling that incident has revived another item of information concerning our river which I think is interesting and I hope that my readers might think so too.

Tidal waves of the Thames can sometimes reach to a level of 8 feet. Being that I received my education before the era of metrification, I am still in the land of imperial measures, but having sought help from my 10 year-old great grandson, I am able to tell you that 8 feet equates to a measure of two-and-a-half metres, so high tide is no understatement. Well if some interference of that amount of water was to happen, a great lot of bother for us Londoners and our city is obvious.

There was a gentleman by the name of Guy Maunsell. He was a renowned civil engineer with a highly respected reputation. In the run up to the declaration of war, he had the foresight to imagine the problems that tidal meddling would incur. And it is easy to guess that the intervention could come from the German Luftwaffe. Strategic bombardment of the river would result in an enormous rise of an already high tide and London would drown. Mr Maunsell, with his team of co-workers, devised a London 'Tidal Bible', and together a solution was sought and agreed on.

This plan came to light and was acted upon. There existed some very vulnerable positions along the river bank, which were the most likely points where the water would overflow including The Houses of Parliament, and places, which if not protected would flood the low lying tunnels of the London Underground Railway, submerging, and causing devastating loss of life.

Every tube station was fitted with steel floodgates at each end of the platforms, where the trains entered and left. Hydrophones were installed beneath the water so that sound waves of the flowing water could be measured. Special defences were erected to deal with the problems of the risk of flooding at the seat of government in Westminster. When the sirens sounded at high tide, the system would leap into action and London would not suffer.

One station on the system's Northern Line, was indeed flooded in one particular incident. But the ingenuity of these blessed men was remarkable, and they saved the heart of our homeland.

* * *

Tragedies

Thousands of Londoners sought night-time shelter in the stations of the underground tube system. They took possession early every evening, before the 'Banshee Howlings', as Mr Churchill described the warning air raid sirens, calling them to 'Take Cover!' The people bunked down in families on station platforms.

I recall two terrible incidents that took place at that time. In addition to the high explosive bombs and the incendiary bombs and the delayed action bombs, land mines were unleashed from the German aircraft. One catastrophic night, a land mine dropped from the sky and into the ventilator shaft of one of the tube stations. Hundreds were killed. Remembering Londoners, such as I, will never forget that tragedy.

Bethnal Green tube station is on the Central Line on that transport system, and like so many others, was utilized for night-time sheltering. In that heavily-populated area in London's East End, thousands took refuge. That evening on the 3rd March 1943, much later than the end of the official Blitz, and when aerial bombardment on London only sometimes occurred, the sirens warned the public that a raid was imminent. Crowds of the local inhabitants rushed to the station to take cover. A heavy but orderly flow of them descended the blacked-out unlighted stairs leading to the platforms. On the third step from the bottom, a middle-aged woman and a child fell. A mass of 300 persons were descending behind them and it became a struggling, heaving tangled mass of humanity. 173 people, mostly women and children, were crushed and asphyxiated. The Government blacked-out the news for 36 hours and a report from them gave the reason of the disaster as an accident, caused by a crowd driven by panic from the noise given off by the discharge of anti-aircraft guns sited in the nearby Victoria Park. My family and I, as a child, would spend our Saturday summer afternoons in this park, and my Dad would row us for a trip around its boating lake.

The official Coroner's inquest report stated there was nothing to suggest that those doomed ill-fated people were in panic; that it was an orderly flow and that there was no stampede or surging. Some fifty years after this calamity, a commemorative plaque was erected at that site. I was there at its unveiling.

Most of those there at that solemn event were perhaps not even born in 1943, or at least were too young to remember first-hand, what had happened there. I wept as I witnessed the ceremony and I bow my head in sorrow as I write of it.

In reality, the tube stations were the safest places in which to shelter, but many Londoners did not shelter at all. They stayed at home, and slept in their beds, or went to places where one could go for safety in cellars or basements. Reinforced areas such as these were not able to withstand a direct hit. There was only a slim chance of survival against blast or shattered glass or falling debris or embedded splinters. Hospitals and medical staff were overworked and over-stretched by the work load, and additional ward capacity for the thousands of mutilated men, women and children.

On the 3rd November 1941 the sirens were silent. It was the first night that we went to bed at home for two months. I remember it well. The silence was eerie and odd. Frankly we wondered what was wrong. We soon discovered why. The Germans, now realizing that we were not going to be demoralized or cowed into defeat, changed their objectives.

Their bombardment became widespread around the British Isles, and every town and city of importance suffered. As it had been in London, these communities took the full brunt of the Nazi onslaught. Damage and loss of life was excessive. In highly industrial areas, factory workers ceased their labours to take shelter, and war production paused. Ports and harbours were bombed and shipping was affected. I did hear of one specific incident which took place in Sheffield on December 12th 1940 when a hotel suffered a direct hit from a single bomb. Seven storeys were reduced to 15 feet of debris. The hotel boasted ten reinforced cellar rooms; only one was left intact, trapping its occupants. I also remember when the Prime Minister visited Birmingham after another attack to witness for himself the inflicted town, and to commiserate with its people. He stood by a long newly-dug mass grave for the dead of that atrocity.

* * *

The London Spirit

I hope that I have been able to present a fair, and comprehensive account of that time. Most of which I have recorded has been a sorry tale of death and destruction, melancholic and depressing. I think that it is right and proper to redress a balance, and I feel that I might have an opportunity to do so by adding a postscript.

Life in the shelters was no picnic, but we coped and made the best of it. I tried hard not to be disgruntled with the inconveniences. I tried to think of those unfortunate people where battles were being played out, and how they were suffering from shortages, hunger and deprivation, without recourse, and had reason to be afraid. I thought of the news of the day, and wondered how people, living in the occupied countries were faring under Nazi oppression. Life was not perfect, but so far my family and I were safe and together, and I tried to overcome my discomfort and dissatisfaction.

Community spirit during the blitz was remarkable. This sentiment was widespread in that war-time period for the entire six years, no matter where you were, or the company you were with. In the shelter where we gathered night after night, we melded into a comfortable companionship. We played board games with the children, and with each other while the young ones slept. Someone bought in a wind-up gramophone and others supplied records, and we sang, very loudly, to drown out the inferno of the noise going on outside. We told stories and jokes and made general conversation – "What did you do today? Did you get some apples from the corner shop?"

We felt fierce pride and patriotism at that time, and I still do in retrospect, when I think of the manner in which we of our capital city conducted ourselves whilst weathering the storm. I well remember those nights we spent in the basement of Simpson's factory where we sheltered, and feel it is incumbent on me to tell of it. We mourned together in sympathy, when a wife received the news that her husband had been 'killed in action', or we offered solicitous support if she was told that her man was reported 'missing', as the delivered telegram said.

We got out our knitting and produced socks for soldiers, although sometimes a pair did not quite match in length or the heel appeared to be not quite in its traditional position, and we made tiny garments for an expected baby, and cooed over it in admiration when it arrived. Those who wanted to machinate the needles and could not, we taught in our organized craft sessions. My Mum taught me to knit when I was four years old, so in my early teens I boasted of my expertise.

We became child-minders if a mum was working late in her wartime job, and we undertook the shopping if shop hours prevented people on shift hours from going to the shops themselves. If someone's sandwiches were forgotten, or her wartime food allowance was exhausted, we shared ours. Our various religious beliefs were acknowledged and respected, and we celebrated each other's festivals. We offered assistance and advice to a child needing help with school homework, and often pacified a difficult obstreperous youngster. I read our local library dry of its books. I devoured the classics, alternating with light fiction, enjoying a wide breadth of material. I even learnt to spell; compensating for the deficiency that resulted from my brief three years of education at senior school level, although I have to admit that in very old age I have lost some of that skill, and I have by my side my trusted and resourceful Oxford English Dictionary! We chatted about our lives and showed each other photographs of pre-war holidays and of precious wedding day memorabilia. One might wonder why these time-passing pursuits were female orientated. Easy! Men not eligible for the armed forces worked locally, and slept at home. To repeat what my Dad used to say: "Gotta get up for work in the morning". And so becoming tired, we eventually snuggled down into our makeshift beds and prayed for a safe night and the blessings for a secure day tomorrow.

When you left the shelter in the morning, you breathed a sigh of relief to see that your house was still on its foundations, and you offered up a silent "Thank you" because you were on your feet. Once home you washed, ate your breakfast and you went to work.

It was a time of history, and a time of unspeakable horror of life for those living through it. It was said of the London Blitz: "Londoners could take it", and in spite of what we endured we did. My immediate family and I survived to tell the tale. But the memory of it, which happened so many years ago, is etched into my sub-conscious and I will never, ever forget it.

* * *

Uncle Monty

Other places, apart from London were attacked from the air: coastal towns, large cities and areas of industrial importance. The head of the Luftwaffe, Field Marshall Hermann Göring, had boasted to the German population that Berlin would never be bombed. And it was – he miscalculated. He underrated the British. As a reprisal, or call it revenge, a long, long night of terror and disaster rained down from the skies onto the town of Coventry.

Large numbers of German bomber squadrons flew in, dropped their deadly cargos and caused mass murder and wholesale destruction of property including the centuries' old Cathedral. The aftermath of that night left that once thriving beautiful city and its citizens devastated. That incident is, and will be remembered, as one of the landmark events of the Second World War.

And here I can relate to my uncle who was the navigator of a Halifax bomber in the RAF. He was born in 1923, and aged 18 in the second year of the war, he was conscripted into the Air Force. He started his training and became an Air cadet. Air cadets were easily recognisable. As part of their blue RAF uniform they wore the usual blue forage cap with a white 'flash'. Air cadets were in training for Bomber Command.

Many cadets were sent to Canada for their RAF tuition and education in the discipline. An equivalent scheme was offered by training facilities in Southern Rhodesia. Uncle Monty, as is his name, underwent his training here at home. Once fully trained, he wore his officers' uniform, now displaying the single-wing insignia of 'Air Crew'. My Mum's baby brother was now a fully 'paid-up' member ready to do his duty. Bomber aircraft pilots wore a double winged insignia. Other crew – gunners, bomb-aimers and navigators wore the single-winged insignia I have already described. It is interesting to note that they plotted the route with pencil, compass and note paper. No modern electrical and digital equipment in those days.

Our uncle had his fairy godmother watching over him. The average number of sorties that one could expect to do, the data logged officially, was eight. That was the survival rate. Uncle Monty did thirty two.

Bless him, he is still with us. This year, 2016, he will be 93 years old. He is fourteen months older than me and we grew up together. We shared summer holidays at my grandma's house and we have never been other than very good friends. Sometimes he stayed with us and my Dad, being his brother-in-law, was not in a position to scold him if he misbehaved. I was the elder sibling at home so I always had to take the blame for any mischief afoot. Well, sorry, I have wandered well off the beaten track! Monty is a now a guide at the RAF Museum in Hendon London, and I hope he tells the story of his war time experiences to the folk who visit, particularly to the children. He wears his Distinguished Flying Cross (DFC) every year at the annual Remembrance Parade, newly polished and shining. He wears it with pride and it is noticed and admired. There was only a limited number of these medals awarded.

Not many young men survived to tell their story. The DFC was awarded to officers of the RAF. The Distinguished Flying Medal (DFM) was the recognition of bravery for non-commissioned officers. Never mind the medal, it is unbelievable that he could have flown in those 'crates' over Germany on so many occasions and come home safely. He must have been the mascot of the squadron. Good on you Mont!

So who is the hero and who is the villain? We cursed them when the German bombs were falling on us from the skies and they cursed us when British bombs fell from theirs. "But we were at war" some will say, especially if a loved one had been affected or they had lost their home; a lifetime of treasured items, gone. "They did it to us" some said. It is only with hindsight can we think about it with clarity. During the war when we heard on the wireless that: "There has been a heavy raid over Dusseldorf last night", we said "Bloomin' good job, they do it to us".

Morality and ethics, on the agenda of those in charge, and in the planning of the raids, was not very high on the list. I suppose they also thought: "Well we are at war".

My Uncle Monty never speaks of it and I don't think many men in his situation do either. Is it guilt? I know that he annually meets up with his former crew mates and like me he has recorded his war time memoirs, but of the raids that he was witness to, he remains silent.

Air Cadet Monty, aged 18. 1941

"Oh to be an Evacuee!"

My brother Leslie was very lucky. He was billeted in a house reflecting the affluence of the family. They had offered to take in two boys and so it was that he was together with his school friend. Even after all these years, I recall his name – it was Malvin Rosen. The family, Saunders, gave the two lads a very good home. They were well cared for and the Saunders respected their Jewish faith. Les learnt much from his foster family. When he eventually returned home he taught me a posh game of cards, Cribbage. I remember how to play it and if I could discover another Cribbage player I would enjoy a game!

At the time, we did not know how fortunate Leslie was. After the war, it was revealed that some children, mostly those who were sent to farms, were badly treated, almost slave-like, and did long hours working on the land and in their foster homes. Later on in my story, I will have an opportunity to relate my own bad experiences when allocated to a private billet.

My brother was fostered in Hove for two years. My mother, who I have to admit was rather partial to her youngest child, withdrew him from the government scheme. The three of us, Mum, Leslie and me, travelled to Somerset to a small market town, Chard, near Taunton. My parents had decided that we had endured the London Blitz to the limit, and in any case my mother wanted to be reunited with her boy.

Against official advice, many children had returned home to areas still under German aerial bombardment. It was blatant stupidity on the part of parents who ignored the government directive. More than 80,000 Londoners were killed in the London Blitz. One in ten was a child, killed or seriously injured. And this is the London count, notwithstanding the casualty lists of other regions of the United Kingdom under attack. In London 100,000 homes were destroyed and 1 million were damaged. It was foolhardy, bordering on criminality, to bring the children home.

And so leaving Dad behind to 'house sit', and continuing to earn his 'daily crust', we three 'set up shop' in Chard. I was 16. I dare say I settled into our new life. We lived with an elderly man and Mae, his middle-aged spinster daughter, who kept house for him. She was a kindly introverted soul. I think that she tried to hide a deformity. We became 'paying guests', and I found work there.

I got a job in a glove factory. I walked miles to get there. I didn't mind the exercise but I hated the job. I worked for only one morning. I ate my sandwiches at lunch time and walked back to our digs. I never returned. I denied myself the opportunity of learning the art of glove making. I became a shop worker in the Chard branch of The International Stores, (nothing to do with foreigners). It was one of a chain of grocery and provision outlets. The forerunner of our supermarkets, but where one was served by counter staff. I was quite happy to be employed in that situation. It was sociable as well as wage-earning and very pleasant to chat to customers with their West Country twang: "Ah ee lass".

I was not too keen on the manager, Mr Martin. He was as thin as a rake, presented a brusque manner and bustled about like a bee with a sore bottom. I suspect that he took me on owing to shortage of labour, but did not approve of my East London accent although I was polite to the clientele, as is my natural persona. I had the impression that he was rather wary of us from 'the Smoke'. I worked there until mother decided that she had had enough of country life and she probably missed my Dad, so we left that rural scene and returned to London.

It was time for me to go too. Mr Martin caught me with a tomato in my mouth. Not good for shareholders – shop staff eating stock lowered the profit margin. Mr Martin did not sack me. He told me off in his crisp clipped vernacular. And I missed my Dad too.

The only reason why I was sorry to leave Chard was because every Saturday a bus load of REMEs, (Royal Electrical Mechanical Engineers), would roll in with their instruments and loads of blokes, and we females would have a Saturday night 'hop' to go to. I did enjoy them. We did the Hokey Kokey and the Lambeth Walk and all other novelty gambols current to that era. Even today if I hear the dreamy slushy song Blueberry Hill that was Number 1 in the 'Top Ten' at that time, (or would have been if such a transmission programme had existed), I feel romantically slushy too. I feel the inclination come over me. I think I should go back to wallow in this nostalgia!

When I returned home I resumed my station at the Singer sewing machine that I had vacated when we left for Chard. I went to work once again with my Dad at Simpsons as I did at the outbreak of war.

Chapter 5
America Enters the War

A Meeting of Minds

Mr Churchill and President Roosevelt of the United States were friends. Churchill's mother was American, and he was lauded in that country. He was relying on the president's help, in some small measure, even though America was a declared neutral. They often met to discuss the war situation. Churchill sometimes went to the States projecting charm, as only Churchill could, and guile, to coax his pal for support and aid. On occasion they were known to meet mid-Atlantic on board a British war ship.

In August 1941, they met in Newfoundland, Canada, the outcome of which was a broad statement of British war aims, and the United States position should it be drawn into the conflict. They both approved of the setting up of an organization similar to the League of Nations. It was to be known as the Atlantic Charter.

The USA had no enthusiasm to be dragged into a European conflict, a mirror image of President Woodrow Wilson's reluctance to become involved in the European upheaval 1914–1918. Roosevelt arranged a scheme called 'Lease Lend', by which they sent us food and basic commodities. It was not gifted. We were billed and paid with interest. The account was settled just a few years ago, decades after the end of the war. In addition, we received some of their clapped-out old ships. They were called Liberty Ships. The purpose of the gesture was to help compensate for the heavy shipping losses, owing to the action of the German U-Boats. I am of the opinion that the name of that project was truly appropriate. It was indeed a liberty to offer us those derelict old vessels.

The battle of the U-Boats in the Atlantic Ocean continued until the brilliant cryptologist Alan Turing developed a machine to break the German Enigma code at Bletchley Park, near Milton Keynes, in Buckinghamshire. It is officially considered that the war was shortened by two years by the outcome of the wonderful work carried out by Turing and his gifted team. I am not offering an apology for this aside. I have been seeking a 'slot' to introduce Mr Turing, and in focusing on the U-Boat campaign, I have found my opportunity.

I have visited Bletchley Park and was overawed by the wonder of it. I was able to watch the Enigma code-breaking machine in action. It is hard to imagine the genius that lay behind its inventiveness. I feel such a small cog in the wheel when I think of my own, small contribution to the war effort, and in all honesty, everything else in general.

* * *

Land-grabbers on the March

In 1941, two seismic events changed the course of the war. On the 22nd June of that year, Hitler invaded Russia. The count at the end of the war was 21,000,000 Soviets killed: military personnel and civilians.

Six months later, on 7th December of that momentous year, on the opposite side of the world Japan, without warning or preamble, bombed and obliterated the United States naval base at Pearl Harbour on the Pacific Ocean off Hawaii. That brought America into the war. Germany declared war on the USA on the 11th December, and President Roosevelt declared war on Germany and Japan a few hours later. In his declaration broadcast, Roosevelt said the day of the attack would be remembered as "a day of infamy".

If one chose to be facetious, one could easily imagine a couple of inane schoolboys indulging in a slanging match in a school playground, challenging each other in silly exchanges, declaring war on each other in that time frame. But it was not an event to invoke humour. It was not funny – it was no ha-ha matter.

I saw images of the Pearl Harbour disaster, and all other world changing events of a critical nature, screened retrospectively in cinemas. There was no 'on the spot' coverage as it applies today. We had no television set at home, which was of no great concern. Transmission was suspended for the duration.

* * *

A Vicious Enemy

Japan was now our common enemy. The Japanese had engaged our forces in Asia, and captured Singapore. It was a bitter and very serious blow. We lost a vitally strategic region, and tens of thousands of fighting men. The Japanese rounded up thousands of British ex-patriots, who lived there. Both the Military and civilians; men, women, and children, were taken prisoner and force-marched hundreds of miles to camps.

History would later reveal the utter brutality with which these unfortunates were dealt with. They were beaten, starved, and under enforced labour, worked until they dropped dead from exhaustion. They lived in unspeakably diabolical conditions. Those few who did eventually come home, when the war with Japan was over, did so as living skeletons and with lifelong psychiatric problems.

* * *

Brutality and the Big Mistakes

I witnessed the effects of the Japanese brutality first-hand. A young man, married to a cousin, returned home from a Japanese prisoner of war camp in what was then Siam. He returned home after the end of war with Japan in August 1945.

He suffered the conditions that I have already defined. He lived close to my home and I saw him frequently. He was painfully thin, and barely recognizable from the fit, strapping person who had left home a few years previously. His condition manifested itself both physically and mentally. He had terrible nightmares and an interrupted sleep pattern. He suffered severe and chronic gastric problems in addition to frequent illnesses, owing to loss of immunity and weakness. He was a totally different person from the man who went to war. The post-war quality of his life was so very poor, and he is no longer with us.

After their capture of Singapore, the Japanese invaded the islands in the Pacific Ocean. They were a fierce and ferocious enemy. At one moment in time, they were almost at the point of invading the northern coast of Australia. The Americans engaged them in long drawn-out battles for supremacy to drive them out of the islands, at the cost of many American lives during the vicious and prolonged actions.

Hitler was now fighting on an eastern front in Russia. The Germans made good progress in their initial onslaught, but gradually the Russians held them in spite of the very heavy losses in men and machines. When the Russian winter set in, Hitler faced the same fate that Napoleon had suffered 125 years earlier. The German Army was ill-equipped for the treacherous ice and snow, and freezing temperatures. Hitler's ill-gotten plans had gone awry. He had not thought it necessary to provide for bad weather conditions, assuming that his Army would be firmly entrenched in warm comfort, in places vacated by a beaten foe, by the time winter arrived. He was wrong. And his army suffered frostbite and wet body-clinging clothes encrusted with ice.

His armed vehicles and tanks would not move because the fuel was frozen. Perhaps the Gods had chosen right over wrong.

By now it was recognized that he had made two mistakes:

1. That he had entangled himself with the mighty 'Russian Bear'.

2. That he had missed the opportunity of invading Britain after the collapse at Dunkirk. He should have followed those 'Little Ships' across the Channel, when our Army and defences were at rock bottom.

This story of the Second World War has now reached the year 1941. As events progressed during this year, so they did in 1942. The pattern of war is similar in some respects, however, two new campaigns were initiated. One was an important progression in the war-time frame, and the other involved me.

Chapter 6
My Personal War

Early Reminiscences

At the outbreak of war, a dispensation was issued by the Chief Rabbi allowing those serving away from home, to eat non-kosher food if kosher was not available. Further on in my story, when I was living away from home, I ate what was provided, but I did not eat pork or bacon or ham or rabbit. Perfectly good and wholesome food I know it to be, but Jewish canon law forbids it. I never ate it at home, and I was reluctant to break the habit when I later lived away. When forbidden meat was served, I ate only vegetables. Alternative vegetarian meals were a luxury of the future.

I was reared in a traditional Jewish home. We kept all the rules and Torah commandments that is, as far as the economic ethos would allow. In the late 1920s and the 1930s, unemployment was rampant. Men would gather at street corners and the first question on the lips was: "Are you working?" Many children in my class at school were absent. They had no shoes. We, at home, were lucky. My Dad was never out of work, but his terms of employment insisted on a five-and-a-half day week. He went to work on Saturday, the Sabbath. My uncle Henry, a father of two, had no job and was unemployed for as long as I can remember. Religion had no part in that fact. A job was just not available. The rest of the family, that is the working ones, chipped in as much as they could afford every week to support Uncle Henry's brood. Pittance dole money could be drawn, but benefits were only available if you consulted a fortune teller who maybe could tell you the future. When I was a widowed mother in 1957, I lived on a minuscule widow's pension, and there were times when my young ones ate but I did not; no mileage from the system at that time!

I had a friend when I went to school. Her name was Shirley Black. Her Dad was ultra-religious, and perhaps because he had skills, he probably could have found a work placement. But he would not work on Saturday, and his family lived in a near starvation level. I think a Jewish charity helped out, but there was not enough to eat in that household. I remember those years so vividly. But as I said earlier, we did all that was required of us at home. My Mum lit the candles on Fridays at dusk, and we never went to a public event on that evening.

On the Sabbath, forbidden to labour, we read our books or met up with friends and relatives. We did not write, or cut using scissors, or knit, or any task that was considered as work. We ate kosher food and we celebrated the Festivals to the T. I was well able to pass on our way of life to my own children and my brother did the same when he had a family.

When I was a youngster, perhaps from the age of seven, I attended a weekly class to master the art of reading Hebrew. It was held on school premises, after hours. The classes, held in all areas in London, were sponsored by the then London County Council, the forerunner of the present Greater London Council. I did not learn. The teacher, a Mr. Frankel, had favourites, one in particular, a fair-haired, blue eyed little girl. Perhaps I was jealous, or not too bright. I did not like our teacher and I eventually left with no knowledge of the written Hebrew word. My brother was taught in classes organized by the Synagogue. He was of Bar Mitzvah age (13) in 1941 when the war was raging and events of that nature were not feasible. He did rectify that discrepancy when he was very much older, in fact in his eighties.

I too made up for lost opportunity. On one of my excursions undertaken many years later, I went to a Saturday morning service in Adelaide, Australia. As is the custom in orthodox synagogues, the genders sit separately and I was escorted to the ladies gallery. The officiating Rabbi looked up and noticed a stranger. He beckoned to a little boy, who having instruction, approached me with a prayer book which I was not able to read. I felt pretty well ashamed of myself. On my arrival back in London, I took a course of six weekly hour-long lessons in an adult educational programme in our local place of worship. I am not fluent, but I did make up the shortfall, and I can easily follow a service when need be.

* * *

A Power-change at Home

In 1932 I was seven years old and even at that tender age to walk to our local library with my Dad was the highlight of my week. My reading material was of the school story variety and the adventures of their inmates, mostly stories for boys of the dare-devil type. Even well before my 8th year I was an avid reader. I also displayed an unusual interest in listening to the news on our wireless. We had just been converted from gas power that we used to light our home and from the coal burning fire in our living room for warmth, (the rest of the house was unheated and we 'froze' in winter), to electricity.

My Dad was now in a position to discard the antiquated forms of enlightenment that we had to discover what was happening in the outside world, namely his 'crystal set', and the wind-up gramophone that we used for our entertainment. Wow! Dad brought home a wireless and we now had the thrill of plugging it in to the newly installed socket on the wall, twiddling the knobs and lo and behold we could sing and dance to the piped music. It was then that I discovered the connection that would give us the opportunity to learn what was happening in the wide world outside. Wow again! I began to interest myself in the daily news broadcasts and I heard and remembered the news I was listening to concerning the Manchurian invasion in 1931–32 and the goings-on which were taking place in the Far East. I was already reading the newspapers. My Dad was a Labour supporter and he brought home the Daily Herald, a paper of that time.

When I was 11 years old I transferred from primary to secondary education. The school was co-educational which was unusual in those days. It was middle-of-the-road in educational ratings. Those were in the days of the selective '11 plus' exam which segregated children into three categories. Low marks regulated one to a 'Secondary School' which taught a basic curriculum; high marks destined one for Grammar School; and then there were 'in-betweeners' like me, who achieved neither the best nor the worst, although at the time I was given to understand that I missed out the higher rating by just a few marks. Nevertheless the school I was allocated offered a very high educational standard. We were taught a foreign language which the secondary schools did not and we were taught secretarial skills, shorthand and bookkeeping which neither of the other two categories did. We were destined for a better class of employment than the lower rated pupils. Our teachers were dedicated. We had music appreciation which serves me to this day. I can name every instrument when I go to a concert – classical is my preference. We had cookery and housekeeping and laundry, (which I hated), slots. I am still averse to ready-made supermarket foods and in those days, in the 1930s, washing machines and dishwashers were unheard of. We had parental guidance and I learnt how to bath a baby! My brother Les went to a renowned grammar school. He matriculated at 18, (the forerunner of 'A' Levels), was later articled and qualified as a chartered accountant when he finished his National Service in the RAF.

I am writing about this episode in my life as there is a connection to the Second World War. The school I went to, St. George's in the East Central School, as was its title, was less than a five minutes' walk from Cable Street, London E.1. In the borough of what is today Stepney. A mixed Christian and Jewish population, we lived cheek-by-jowl. We gelled together with no thought of not respecting our different religious practices and we celebrated each other's festivals. As children we played together in the streets and our mums gossiped together no matter to whom. No one knew of anti-Semitism; we had never heard the word and if we did we did not know its meaning. That's how it was for everyone, young and old, the men and the women of London's working class people of the East End.

Myrtle, aged 7, with parents Hetty and Myer, and brother Leslie at a family wedding, 1932

* * *

A March and a Road Block

The end of the 1914–1918 Great War ushered in a war-torn Europe. Economic depression and mass unemployment was rife throughout. As a child I remember seeing one-legged men and other disabled ex-servicemen selling matches on the streets. Politicians here spread the slogan: "A land fit for heroes". Never!

On the Continent, in Germany and France, democracy was turned on its head. Political factions sprang into prominence. Fascists, those of the population embittered with the defeat of their land and the hardships which were the aftermath of the war in Germany, and Communism spread to France taking a lead from the Czarist collapse in Russia and the rise of the doctrine of the ideology of Karl Marx. Britain was not unaffected in the political turmoil.

In 1933 Hitler came to power. His doctrine was to blame Jews for all the problems that had beset the nations. Some of its tentacles spread to Britain. In East London the Jewish population, the majority of whom lived in poverty, a hand-to-mouth existence, were targeted. Sir Oswald Mosley, head of the British Union of Fascists (BUF) held a mass rally in 1934 here in London. The turnout was enormous. They called themselves 'Blackshirts', taking the name from Hitler's Nazi party followers 'Brownshirts', and they mirrored the Nazi policy of its abhorrence of Jews and others not considered part of their own ideology. Their uniforms reflected their title.

On Sunday the 4th October 1936 Mosley prepared to march with 3,000 of his cohorts through the East End of London. They attempted to do so through Cable Street, a heavily populated location where Jewish people lived. In the area over 20,000 anti-Fascists gathered in protest; a solidarity of Labour Party supporters, Irish dockworkers, Communists and members of trade unions. Their shouted slogan was "They Shall Not Pass". The clash was fermented by 6,000 of the Metropolitan police, some on horse-back, there to ensure that Mosley's turn-out was not disrupted. Despite the strong likelihood of a violent outcome the Government and police refused to ban the march.

The anti-Fascist hoards built roadblocks. The police attempted to clear the road to facilitate a viable passage through but the demonstrators fought back. They used sticks and rock, chair-legs and other improvised weapons. Rubbish, rotten fruit and vegetables and eggs were hurled by the women from windows of houses along the way. A series of running battles ensued, police versus the protesters. One hundred and fifty people were arrested, and an estimated 175 policemen were injured. But Mosley's Fascists did not get through: they disbanded and left the scene, moving the meeting to Hyde Park, London.

Many of the arrested demonstrators accused the police of harsh handling. Most were charged with minor offences of police obstruction and fined £5, (about a week's wages for a factory worker), but several were found guilty of affray and sentenced to what was then, hard labour. The Battle of Cable Street as history has remembered it was a major factor leading to the 1936 Public Order Act which required police consent for political marches and forbade the wearing of political uniforms. This has been widely accepted as a significant factor in the BUF's political decline prior to World War 2.

The Battle of Cable Street

I vividly remember that day. I was 11 years old and living in close proximity to the area I was enthralled by the crowds milling around locally in such large numbers. Of course I was not allowed to join the protesters, (I think I probably complained at the embargo), but my Dad was there and arriving home, (without being arrested), was able to tell an excited little 'un all about it.

The school I attended and the library I walked to with my Dad are within the confines of that locality, and sometimes I wish I could have witnessed it first-hand. In the 1990s a large mural depicting the event was painted on the side of St. George's Town Hall, (next to the library), in Cable Street, later to become the Town Hall of Stepney Borough Council. I sometimes visit my old happy hunting-ground, and now in the year 2016, eighty years after it happened in 1936, I think of it and remember it still.

* * *

A Quandary and a Decision

In 1942, I was 17 years old. In another year I would be due for conscription. Well in advance I considered my options. I thought carefully about the various women's services. The ATS – Auxiliary Territorial Army; the WAAF – The Woman's Auxiliary Air Force. I weighed up the pluses and minuses of the WRNS – The Woman's Royal Naval Reserve. All of those titles are self-explanatory. I could have learnt to drive a bus, or taken a job as a road sweeper, or become a canteen assistant or a nurse.

(Many years later I did just that!) However, I did not fancy that back then; fainting at the sight of blood would not do anyone any good. I wasn't so squeamish when I got older. All these opportunities were open to females. Or for that matter, I could have stayed with my Dad in the factory, still working the sewing machine turning out gear for squaddies.

Two of my cousins who lived close by, eventually went to work in a munitions factory, also close by, which enabled them to go home after their shift to their mum and dad, where a good hot meal awaited them, and a good hot bath. Wartime regulations allowed only five inches of hot water, but by a small twist of the tap, you could add a bit more for luck!

I thought: "I can do better than that – I will do something that will suit my nature". To work away from home would be interesting. It was time I left the nest. I did not relish the thought of coming under the command of an officer or a sergeant, and I was not too taken with the idea of working with my cousins. I felt I had little in common with either one. I loved my Dad dearly, but I had worked with him for four years, so I felt it would make a change to leave the factory for 'pastures new', (quite ironic when you realise that I ended up working on the land). I found myself in a quandary wondering which I should plump for.

I decided to volunteer for the WLA – the Women's Land Army. Without telling Dad, I disappeared from the factory one day after lunch, and presented myself to the WLA recruitment officer in their premises in Oxford Street, London, and signed up. If you volunteer at least you know what you are going to do, and more or less where you are going to be. To wait for 'call up' you go where you are sent, and who knows, I could have been directed to the factory where I was already working, or to the munitions-making establishment where my cousins worked. The Women's Land Army gave you the freedom of individuality, and that was the main reason for my decision. The Armed Forces bestow upon you a service number, and that is your identity.

When I got home after my 'skived off' afternoon my dad demanded to know where I had been, without so much as a 'by your leave', and he was furious when I told him what I had done. He was very angry and said I should cancel my recruitment and go to work with my cousins round the corner. I defied him which I had never done before. Even at 17 years old you did what your parents said. But I had made up my mind and I was determined to do it.

Launched 1914: Fully-grown 1939

I had considered the Women's Land Army with care. I had obviously heard of it, and for some unknown reason I was drawn to it. Maybe it was the hand of fate, if you believe in that philosophy. I wrote to them and requested some literature. They obliged by return of post. They needed me.

I received a run-down of its history, which I digested with relish, and it gave rise to my own thoughts on the subject. It was a British organization, created during the First World War in 1915, under the auspices of the then Board of Agriculture. By the end of that war there were more than 250,000 women working on farms – 23,000 of that number were recruits of the WLA.

By rule of thumb, as in any war, Britain used all the means it could to be self-sufficient, and to be able to feed the nation. No food was imported from overseas. Shipping losses were heavy; in tonnage, and especially in lives. The shipping we relied on was to bring in war supplies from America and for the transportation of military personnel to the various arenas of combat. A cousin in the Air Force, Ruby was his name, was lost at sea during one of these transportations. He is remembered when we visit the memorial at Runnymede by the River Thames near Windsor. His name and hundreds of like souls are etched into the stone.

In preparing for a state of hostility, pre-1939, the government quickly realized the prospect of a dearth of agricultural workers, and agonized over a solution if food output was to be increased. The history of The Great War exploded into resurrection. Men, hitherto engaged in agriculture, were 'called-up' for military service and replacements were necessary to fill the void. The modern Women's Land Army came to fruition in June 1939. Less than a year later, the head count had already reached 80,000. The nation had to be, and was going to be, fed!

In the Second World War, that branch of service was the responsibility of the Ministry of Agriculture. Their remit was to ensure that the production of food should be raised to the highest possible level. The Land Army women became farm labourers. They did the heavy manual work in the fields; they learnt to drive tractors and use farm machinery. They tended livestock and milked the cows, by hand. No modern appliances 1939 to 1945!

They were company for the farmers wives left at home, when their menfolk left to fight.

They became part of the social scene, in the sometimes small communities in which they lived; perhaps in an isolated rural hamlet or village. Many a local lad learnt the wiles of female 'townie' lasses.

Many traditional farmers still at home under the Reserved Occupation edict were critical of the Land Army scheme but were won over by government argument, and I daresay, some ministerial bullying! They soon realized the value of these ladies, and appreciated the work they did. "However would we manage without them, when Government quotas for increased output, are forever being levied at us?" was the farmer's interjection!

* * *

On My Way

Following regulations, no matter what kind of national work you did, a medical examination was compulsory. I was a young healthy teenager so that was not a problem. My Mum's weekly Friday night chicken soup helped – 'Jewish penicillin!' A dental examination, however, proved a very sore point.

School children were subjected to regular dental checks by an Education Department dentist, who visited schools. If treatment was needed you would be sent to a dental surgery. I required treatment on every occasion. Mostly for extractions. By the time I left school aged 14, it is a wonder that I had any teeth left at all. And the first thing I did the week after I left school, when I started my first job, was to buy myself a tooth brush. Good and loving parents I had; I was reared in a caring and safe environment. But dental hygiene was not on the agenda.

I toddled off to the dental school at Guy's Hospital, London, and there I spent the best part of the next two weeks being treated to a complete dental 'make-over'. And to reinforce the benefit, all the newly-filled cavities were carried out using gold inlays, (pre NHS days but I received this treatment free, gratis and for nothing!). Wow! Did that mean that I would have to sleep with my head in a security safe? Those gold inlays lasted for years and years. I would not be surprised if I still had some.

Commenting on this recollection, I would like to say that I learnt a very useful lesson. From the age of six months old, I would take my children with me for my dental visits. They would sit on my knee whilst the examination was being carried out.

They learnt to accept the fact that the dentist was a friend, and that it was in order to be a bit apprehensive but not to be afraid. Now as adults they all sport perfect teeth, and even me, being quite an elderly lady, still have plenty of those molars and incisors to brush every day.

The uniform of the WLA was delivered to my address. The parcel contained a reefer coat and heavy-weight breeches, both items light brown in colour. An emerald green woollen sweater, long fawn colour socks, brown lace-up shoes, cream colour shirt, a light brown colour slouch hat, and the WLA badge, which was worn on a green tie. I nervously tried it on. It fitted perfectly but it felt very strange to be wearing such unusual apparel, particularly the breeches, because up to then women did not wear trousers.

Trousers were introduced in the Land Army of World War I. Obviously it was a better mode of clothing for that type of employment, than the ankle length skirts as was the custom for women at that time. Trousers were strongly frowned upon. The young women were afraid of being accused of 'cross-dressing'. The government 'feminised' the uniform, stressing the importance the role the women would play in the British war effort. It was true enough, but even in those far-off days it was the buttering-up of government spin that won the day.

I quite liked the breeches; well they were different, except for when travelling on the London underground railway system. Using the escalators one day, I was approached by a gentleman, (well I was not adverse to that). He advised me, in hushed tone of voice: "Your skirt is tucked up at the back, and I can see the shape of your bottom". Heigh ho! I wonder if it was his birthday!

I was sent a travel warrant, and instructed to travel on March 1st from Kings Cross Railway Station, London, to Grantham, where I would be met. No one wasted time during the war: due for national war work at the age of 18, I was on my way – 18 years plus 2 weeks.

* * *

A Change of Scene

Before I left home that morning, rigged out in the spanking new gear, I went into the garden and gathering up half a handful of soil, rubbed some of it on my coat. I did not savour the thought that I looked a novice, and new to the job.

The journey to Grantham, (in later years famous as the childhood address of the British Prime Minister, Margaret Thatcher), proved to be the forerunner of my first Land Army adventure.

Travelling during the war was a hectic affair. Trains were always over-crowded, mostly with Service personnel. Unless you were early at the terminus you never had a seat. There were no pre-booking facilities. Train corridors were jam-packed with passengers, together with their cases or as with Service people, their kitbags.

Although I boarded the train early, I had no seat. I joined the merry throng in the corridor. I say 'merry'. Times were hard, and we lived with danger, but people were not grumpy or complaining. The spirit of 'bonhomie' abounded. People were matey, they helped each other. We knew that we lived for the day, and we took 'the bull by the horns', and made the most of it. That is how it was everywhere, and that is how it was on that train.

A soldier, sitting on his kit bag close by, started to chat. It transpired that he lived quite near to my home address. He told me that his name was Herbert Lewis; that his family were in 'shoes' and that he too was travelling to Grantham, back on duty after being home on leave. He didn't give his age, but I guessed him to be in his late twenties, and quite a bit my senior.

His eventual destination was the same village that I would be escorted to by the young Land Girl who met me. How about that for 'starters'! The name of the village was Allington, a few miles from Grantham. I was taken to a Land Army hostel where thirty nine other young women lived. They were a mixed group; they came from all places in the U.K. Their ages ranged from 18 to 29. There were a few other Londoners, and two other Jewish girls. One hailed from London and the other from Chapel Town, the Jewish area of Leeds.

The majority of Land Girls already lived in rural areas. More than a third came from the industrial north and from London. I was one of them. Myrtle, the uniform machinist left London, and Myrtle the Land Girl, had arrived as a hostel inmate, in a small village out in the sticks.

The hostel was run and supervised by a warden, Miss Perkins, her assistant, and a cook. There were rules, and these three people made sure that they were strictly adhered to. I remember on one such occasion, I was spoken to by the boss who warned me that a gentleman I had been dating, an Army officer no less, was married.

Thinking about it now I wonder how the heck she knew he was married! When a young lady 'went out', (as dating is called now), there was a certain snob value when you caught the eye of a serving officer, a much higher-ranked individual than a private, and with inflated pay, you tended to regard yourself as 'superior'. Miss Perkins had no cause to worry. The officer was just a friendly companion who escorted me to the theatre in Grantham occasionally. I was not a husband-snatcher.

The girls were hired out to local farms when they were required. That is, for agricultural work. It was interesting in as much you went to lots of different venues, and one never got bored and we were much in demand.

* * *

The Land Girls' Lot

A lorry from the farm you were allocated to would arrive at 8am. One would climb aboard at its rear, one foot on the back wheel, hoisting the other leg over the tail gate, and sometimes just flopping into its interior. At times, when the season demanded, we would be called for at 6am, and at harvest time we would work until it got dark at 10pm. During the war years we had what was called 'Double Summer Time' whereby we altered our clocks as we do today, but by putting them two hours ahead instead of one. It gave us extra daylight hours in the evening. It meant that it got light later in the morning but we Land Girls were used to all sorts of inconveniences. We worked in dungarees and black boots. When it was wet we had wellies. We wore head scarves, turban fashioned, in the depths of winter. When the mornings were cold, the front bit of hair protruding from the scarf would become encrusted with ice, and froze.

Lincolnshire is good agricultural land. We grew corn crops; wheat and barley. We planted potatoes, and picked them at a time when they were still being unearthed by manual means. We grew sugar beet, which was sent to the factories to be converted into the sweet stuff. We minced the swede crop for animal feed. We worked in the hot sun at harvest time, in the old fashioned way, following the tractor, standing the sheaves of corn into stooks to dry in the sun, and then heaving them, using pitchforks, to build a corn or hay rick. The available machines were of pre-war stock, and it was man, or in this case Land Army power, who did most of the heavy work. Factory production in Britain was outputting war appurtenances and not farming appliances.

Modern agricultural machinery, as we know it today, was not fashionable or affordable, or perhaps not yet on the drawing board. When the time came for the rick to be dismantled, so that the corn could be threshed, we did that too. Many times it was my position, high up on the top of the structure, pitchfork in hand, 'forking' the heavy sheaves into the threshing machine below me.

We tended livestock. I well remember one incident which was not funny at the time, but one I like to think of. On arrival one morning, the farmer choose me to look after a herd of sheep; a couple of hundred of them. He left me the sheep dog, and with my packed lunch and plenty of hedges to sit under for shade, I thought I was in for a picnic and an 'easy-peasey' day. Nothing of the kind! The sheep ran amok. They went through gaps in the hedges, of which there were aplenty, into the adjacent corn growing fields. I yelled at the dog: "Go get them"; he cocked his head, looked at me and took no notice. "Wish you luck" he was thinking! All of that long hot day I could be seen sprinting around the field, chasing those four legged woollies with that cussed dog watching!

I had never worked so hard in my life. And I was worried. Whatever would the farmer say when he saw the trampled-down wheat. I need not of have been so anxious. It was said that the London girls adapted to country life quickly, and worked well on the land. At that moment he was probably thinking: "bloomin' women – useless". We worked darn hard. But we had our reward. The area was teeming with the male sex. Lincolnshire, having such a flat terrain, was ideal for RAF bases and airmen there to man them.

* * *

It Wasn't All Work

After work, we would return to the hostel worn out with fatigue, starving hungry, filthy and dishevelled. In no time, we washed and changed into our formal uniform, ate whatever had been prepared for us, and arranged our hair in the Forties' hair style: a 'Lana Turner' bang in the front and a curled roll around the back. We would make up our faces with a pat of face powder on a powder puff and a smidgen of lipstick, which we frugally used. All that stuff was now unobtainable in the shops.

Like a bunch of happy-go-lucky school girls we would saunter down to the village to the 'YM' – Young Men's Christian Association (YMCA). By the time we arrived it was heaving with lovely young men. We knew many of them and our company was always appreciated. We would have 'char and a wad' – tea and a bun, and would settle for a good evening out.

The YM is an organization built on the principal of giving succour to individuals; a bed and food to those who need it. An elderly philanthropist living in Allington, had opened the downstairs floor of his house as such a venue for the likes of us and other Servicemen and women, living away from home, and needing a space to socialize. The doors were open to all regardless of age or creed, belying its name. This benefactor was religious and teetotal. He enforced strict rules. No alcohol and no 'hanky-panky'. We all spent many happy hours in that YM. We did enjoy the refreshments and the company and the good feeling of a deserved evening out after a hard day's work, well done. Contrary to the ethics of the original principal, the premises had no boarding facilities.

Someone would start to play the piano and we would sing and lark about, and we would all have a very happy and fulfilling end to a great day. Usually one of the fellows would walk you back to the hostel and you could rely on the fact that he would want to see you again. There was no dearth of male company. Sometimes I would have a multiple group of young men waiting for me outside the hostel who I had promised to go out with, and I would say to one of them: "Okay, I'll go out with you this evening".

We were restricted. We had to be in by 10pm. There was just time to call into the only pub in the village or to go back to be with everybody else in the YM. If you had a special reason, you could ask permission for a late pass. That was the occasion when I was admonished for going out with a married man. He had tickets for a rare concert in Grantham, and I knew that I would be late, and asked for sanction which was granted, together with the "mind what you're doing" warning.

Looking back, when situations of that kind were unheard of, we never ever thought of such unusual relationships. It was, after all, only 1943. I think that the warden and her assistant were same sex partners. We thought it normal that in a hostel set up with limited space, that they should share a room. I shared mine with 39 people in a dormitory with tiered bunks. I was lucky. Mine was an upper one and I had a bit of air space.

I think I have come to the point when I must refer again to Herbert, the young man I met on the train. He was housed in barracks in an army base situated across a field behind our hostel. The base was the home to Italian prisoners of war, and Herbert was a guard.

The Italians also worked the land, and my love of the opera was conceived and born at that time when they sang as they worked.

Herbert and I started a relationship. We saw each other most evenings when he was off duty. He was keen. My priority was to enjoy my free time with causal friends who had similar views, and who had no wish to be so intensely involved. I was perfectly happy to be in the company of the less serious. Living away from home for the first time, in a completely new and different environment gave me a relish for freedom and the opportunity to develop my personality. I was not yet prepared to enter into a serious commitment.

I was basking in my newly found autonomy. And I was still only 18.

* * *

Brief Encounters

When he returned back from leave, Herbert's mother sent the message that she would like to meet me. She also sent some typically Jewish food. I remember the gefilte fish in a jar and the home-baked cake. I really relished the home-made lentil and barley soup! I felt sorry that she had used her precious rations. I did enjoy the cream cheese bagels. I didn't have to worry about calories. Chasing sheep sure was a metabolism-raiser.

I liked Herbert. He was kind and thoughtful, and treated me with respect. But his kisses were wet and I found that distasteful. I did not like it. Not wanting to embarrass him, I did not offer that as my reason when I told him that our relationship was at an end. He took it very badly, and I was genuinely sorry and miserable too. All his friends at the camp were aware of our friendship, and they 'sent me to Coventry'. That is, none of them spoke to me if we met in the YM. Herbert never went there again, and our previous conversation was our last.

Some months later I heard that Herbert had volunteered for a dangerous mission abroad, and there was to be a farewell party at the camp. I was sent an invitation but I felt uncomfortable and did not accept. It was probably best for him too. He was a good and lovely man. I hope that he returned home safely when the war ended.

I did meet a few men who I particularly remember. There was a young Jewish soldier from Glasgow. His name was Charles and we called him Charlie –

I can still hear his broad Glaswegian accent. One day he proposed, and said he wanted to marry me. He was quite serious. I thought it was a 'hoot'.

I met another Jewish soldier on the train coming back from London. He was stationed in Durham, but I can't remember his name. His initial should have been a B! We arranged to meet half way between Durham and Grantham, at Nottingham, one Saturday evening. I bought my railway ticket and booked a bed for the night at the YMCA. He met me at the station. It was late and dark and the station was deserted. There was a kiss and a hug and he began to fumble in his pocket, withdrawing a condom. I was flabbergasted and very angry and told him what I thought, in no uncertain terms. I was mature, but sexually innocent, and I certainly did not envisage a rendezvous to undo my strongly-held principals. I left him there and then in the deserted railway station followed by a miserable Saturday evening in the Nottingham 'YM' reflecting on that episode.

Next morning, Sunday, I got an early train and went home to London, unannounced and unexpected, to the astonishment of the family. I did not give a reason. I returned to Grantham that afternoon. I was upset that this man thought that I was that kind of young woman, and annoyed that I had the unexpected outlay to purchase a return railway ticket for a journey to London that I did not expect to take. Oh well it is all part of life's rich tapestry!

The routine of the Land Army was one of the reasons why I opted to enlist, and to become a member of it. In a normal round of work requirement you did five-and-a-half days each week. You were free on Saturday afternoon and Sunday. You did not have that option in the forces. Of course, in seasonal urgency, like the harvest, and the spring planting, you worked long hours every day of the week.

So Land Girls did a vital job in their contribution of bolstering the food supply. And I loved it. Born and bred in the East End of London, unlike many children living in that area, I did know that milk came not from bottles, but from cows! There was a dairy run by a Welsh couple situated halfway between our house and Aunt Millie's, and when we walked to pay her family a visit, we always had a glass of warm milk straight from a real live cow, which was kept in their back garden, at a penny a throw. Most East End youngsters had never seen the sea or a green field. I have already mentioned our trips to the seaside, and I once went on a school journey to rural Devon, so I reckon to have been well educated in that regard.

Life in the country as a Land Girl, and the sudden transformation of finding myself pitched into a communal environment, was a moment of regeneration for me. It gave me a brand new insight, and I learnt things that changed my outlook and some things that I carry with me, even today.

* * *

A Letter from Somerset

I recently came across a copy of a letter written in August 1918 by a then serving member of the Women's Land Army to her mum and dad. It is a long letter describing her arrival from home and giving details of her working day. I did think of presenting it in full, but there is much of it and minutely detailed. I am recording the relevant parts, and I am including it because of the stark contrast between the land girl's life then to the one that I experienced in 1942.

She was sent to Crewkerne in Somerset, along with 69 others. After a two-and-a-half hour train journey, then being cramped together in a lorry, they arrived at the living quarters, a camp of 70 tents, each being the new home for a group of eight. Her first supper menu consisted of unskinned potatoes, cabbage, beans, rice pudding, bread and water. She writes that the luggage had not yet arrived, so they had to share "crocks" which indicated that they had to supply their own dishes, brought with them. They ate in three huge tents, which leads me to think that several hundreds of people were housed in that camp.

Before bed time she needed to make up her bed and she used the hard items from her now arrived kit bag as pillows. They were issued with mattress covers which they filled with straw and which they sewed for closure. They were woken up at 6am, and needed to scramble for a place in the wash tent, and roll up their mattresses before breakfast at 7am, which consisted of porridge without milk or sugar, bread and marmalade and tea doled out from large pails, using the same utensils for everything. They were paraded at 8am before "nabbing some grub" to take to the fields for lunch. Allotted to each was half a loaf, potted meat, biscuits and cake and loose tea leaves which they made up with cold water with their meal. They walked two-and-a-half miles, up and down dale, to reach the farm.

They rested at 11am for 15 minutes and they ate their food. The young woman writes that she was still very hungry. They carried on till 3.30pm, and stopped for their cold tea giving them a 30 minute break, and restarted until 5.30pm, "walking the two-and-a-half mile plod home singing *'It's a long way to Tipperary'* and other patriotic songs, to keep up our spirits". She tells her parents that her arms, face and hands are burnt as red as a lobster, and wouldn't like to say what they will be like in a few days.

At 6.30pm, they were fed, mostly vegetables, some ham, suet pudding with watered-down jam sauce. She writes that their eating arrangements are such that she wonders if she will ever be fit for civilized society by the time she returns home. By 8.15pm the women are able to relax, reclining on the grass, but she is using a mac and the cover of her stationery box to keep off the flies. She asks for a sun bonnet and a mackintosh sheet as some of her things have to be left outside the tent at night at the mercy of the dew and marauding livestock. She sends her letter with love to Mum and Dad.

So I now know that, by comparison to this girl's experiences, my own Land Army existence was, to coin a phrase, 'A life of Riley'.

Myrtle, aged 18. 1943

Chapter 7
Changing Fortunes of War

The Tide Changes

In 1942 an event took place in North Africa that changed the course of the conflict. We were fighting there to safeguard our lifeline to the Commonwealth Countries, India, Australia, New Zealand and Burma. We were in North Africa to protect the Suez Canal.

The war was not generally going well in the areas where we were engaged. There were some naval battles. There were times when we did well, sometimes we did not, and suffered heavy losses. We sent bombers over Germany and often many did not return. We lost men and aircraft. We attempted a few landing raids on coasts of mainland Europe. Mostly they failed, again with the loss of men and material.

Suddenly, in North Africa things changed. It happened in a place in Libya in the Sahara Desert. We fought a battle at a place called El Alamein. It began on the 23rd October 1942, and continued until the 5th November. It was our first real and decisive victory of the war. The British fought under the command of General Bernard Montgomery, and the tide of the war turned in our favour. The Germans fought under their Field Marshall Erwin Rommel. He was beaten and driven out of North Africa. Tens of thousands of dejected Germans and Italians were taken prisoner.

The Sahara was not an easy place in which to fight. The terrain is mostly flat, except for the dunes. It is sandy with perhaps an uncertain degree of firmness underfoot. There was no normal cover, no vegetation to give protection or to support the operation of a surprise attack. Both sides fought using tanks. An ex-Army Major I knew from Cardiff, Sandhurst trained, Bertram Brown, was the commander of one of those tanks. He is no longer with us but he lived to tell the tale. On his return home he did much good work for the community. In stature he was tall and slim. Wearing a black coat and sporting a bowler hat, and carrying a black rolled-up umbrella or a black walking stick, he was very much a military figure, and in a very professional military manner he led the Annual Parade on Remembrance Sunday in that fair city, every year, until his death many years later.

At this time, Mr Churchill, President Roosevelt and Marshall Josef Stalin, the Russian leader, met to discuss the progress of hostilities. They were known as 'The Big Three'. Stalin, who was now fighting the Germans in Russia, required, nay, demanded that a Second Front be opened up in Europe. It was sensible reasoning. If Hitler was confronted by an attack on mainland Europe, it would be necessary for him to withdraw forces from his Eastern Front, to meet the emergency in the west. This would lessen the strain on the Russian Command. But Churchill and Roosevelt refused, much to the chagrin of the Russian leader. They explained that they were not ready for such an undertaking.

But the British did much to help Russia and this is how they went about it.

* * *

Strangers in a Friendly Land

The aid we gave to Russia came in the form of ships bringing them war supplies. The undertaking began in August 1941 and continued until May 1945. Overall nearly eighty convoys made the perilous crossings.

The Merchant Navy service, crewed by extremely courageous men, some just lads, undertook that operation. The part played out by those crews is grossly underrated and, by comparison with other branches of His Majesty's Services, is hardly remembered today. Near the Tower of London there is erected a majestic memorial to the memory of the many who died, but in my opinion their gallantry and dedication has never been fully recognized and acknowledged.

The ships sailed in convoy formation; the smaller vessels being protected by an outer ring of larger battleships. They sailed in freezing Arctic temperatures, 20–40 degrees below zero Fahrenheit. They could expect to be torpedoed by German U Boats at any time, day or night. Conditions were horrific. Men on watch, on deck, suffered as their body parts froze as they stood. If eyes watered or a nose dripped you were in trouble. As ships were attacked and disappeared under the heaving waves, they drowned in the icy Arctic seas. It was later revealed that often one could hear their cries. Grown men calling for their mothers. These men were the bravest of the brave. The endeavour became known as the 'Russian Convoys', and that is how they are remembered.

Gradually, since the American entry into the war, large numbers of American personnel and war materials began to arrive here in Britain. There was a plan in the pipeline for an eventual Allied invasion of mainland Europe. This influx was a prelude to a massive build-up to this end.

The American servicemen arrived in smart uniforms, well paid, and having access via their PX (general supply source) to luxury items, some of which we here at home had not seen for years, and some items that we had never known at all, for instance, ladies nylon stockings which young women only dreamed about. Nylon had only just been invented. Until now ordinary lasses such as I wore stockings of a heavy lisle material. Perhaps the affluent had stockings of silk. Tights were a thing of the future. The Americans had chocolate and chewing gum, which the children clamoured for and received. "Got any gum chum?" was a cry bandied about by all the youngsters in the neighbourhood, whenever a benefactor was spotted.

And they soon arrived in very large numbers. One of them, a first cousin Eddie, arrived and introduced himself to the family. He was the son of my father's sister, my Aunt Bea. She had met and married an American who had come here as a serving soldier in the First World War, and she had gone to America as a World War I war bride. Life is strange. The wheel had spun full circle.

These young men from across the sea were very popular with the young ladies who were so happy to be presented with that nylon hosiery. The men were not shy in character and had lots of money to spend. They were far away from home and their folks, and they knew how to have fun, and to enjoy themselves. Often open rivalry sprang up between the GIs (as they were called – from the 'General Issue' items that were given out by the army stores), and our own serving men, who were perhaps home on leave. The young misses had much to be gained by giving their favours to the visitors who were a novelty and who were generous, with lots of 'goodies' on offer. Sometimes in a small local town or village dance hall open fisticuffs would erupt, especially after an alcoholic beverage or two – usually beer for our lads and whiskey for the GIs. The general opinion of these fellows was, and people said: "They are overpaid, over sexed and over here".

* * *

Letting One's Hair Down

I often went home at the end of the working week. I would go to work on Saturday in my working clothes, taking my official uniform with me in a small case.

After work, I would change under a hedge and walk a short distance to the main road. I was fortunate to be located where I was. In the pre-motorway era, Grantham lay on the Great North Road. It was a direct route into London. When I arrived at an unratified meeting place, I joined a queue with other travellers hoping to get transport. We met by way of an unspoken tacit arrangement, and we queued in a calm unhurried manner.

Hitch-hiking for lifts was normal at that time, and road users were very willing to stop and take on a passenger, especially one in uniform. That was the way I travelled home and I did it most Saturdays. It was an adventure in itself. On one occasion, I had a lift straight through to London, and that kind driver drove me all the way home, in the luxury of his posh car, to Stoke Newington where I lived. My Dad had a shock when he saw my arrival. Another week I did the trip in three stages. The first lift took me as far as Bedford, then on as far as St. Albans, and the last pick-up to London. The journeys home were always exciting. One never knew in advance where you had to hop off and wave down another vehicle. It was all part of the scene; and a lark, with a bit of adventure, sure enough.

I would get rides in lorries, climbing in over the side, sitting on the goods being carried in the back. Sometimes a lorry driver already had a passenger in the cab next to him. If it was a fellow, he would be politely asked to travel in the back, and give up his seat to me. If it was another girl she would move up and we three would squash in together. It was a caper and good fun. Drivers were good company too, and we would chat away like old friends. We would usually stop along the way for refreshments and I was always prepared to pay. Some drivers accepted but the majority absolutely refused and treated me instead. There was never any worry or fear that it was dangerous for a young miss to be hitch-hiking alone.

People in that time of war were only too happy to be helpful. And I had an extra safeguard. I wore breeches – tight fitting with very secure fastenings. Who knew about breeches and where the fastenings were? I always caught the train back on Sunday afternoon, in time for supper, and to get ready for work next morning.

One week end was special. It was the eve of the Yom Kippur Fast. My great grandma was staying with us for the festival, and I hurried and hoped to be there in time to start the Fast at sundown with the rest of the family. I managed to get a lift without delay. I stood in the queue as usual. There were about eight airmen before me.

A car stopped and the first in line stepped forward as was customary. The driver leaned out of his window and pointing at me said: "I'll take you". Some drivers preferred to offer a lift to a female. Better company. I was sorry for that fellow but had no qualms. We were all there for the same reason. Eventually everybody would get a ride, but I was not so lucky after all. We were delayed by traffic congestion en-route for hours, and I got home very late, distressed and apologetic. At home, everyone understood. Great grandma was a sweet kindly person who was sympathetic and consoling. My meal was quickly served even though the Fast had already started.

I am aware that this little anecdote which I have seen fit to record, is a triviality. This project which I have chosen to do, namely, to set down my memories of the war, and my involvement in same, emphasises the importance for me as a recollection of those days long ago. I decided to use this inconsequential incident to portray the very old lady, the grandmother of my mother, and the great-great grandmother of my own first child, born many years later. Aged nine months old she was the recipient of a cuddle from this grand old lady before she passed away. From the oldest to the youngest, it registered five generations. I grasp the opportunity that presents itself.

Before I return to my commentary concerning the war, and whilst musing on the minutiae of my past, I begin to analyse myself as the person I was then from the perspective of who I am now. I think that I was a nice respectful individual. In retrospect, I mark myself as being happy and carefree, always prepared to enjoy myself; interested in meeting new people, and having the spirit of adventure imbued within me. And of course I have to remember, as I have previously reminded my readers, that I was still in my late teens. I am wondering how much of that ethos remained within me through the years.

Not quite five generations, but four is a worthy picture - Myrtle with her mother, Hetty, daughter Sheila and granddaughter, Rochelle

The Weekend Battery-charger

Sometimes on my weekend visits home, I would go to one of the ballroom dances that were very popular years ago. I would change from my uniform into 'civvies' and toddle off to my favourite venue. The famous Covent Garden Opera House in London had 'shut up shop' for the duration of the war. The seats had all been removed and a new floor had been laid. The opera stage had been partitioned off, and a smaller one erected to house a live dance band. Some of the bands were famous, and very popular in those years. And the 'house' accommodated the young and 'fancy-free' for ballroom dancing.

I was never very good at it but I got by, and was always ensured of an enjoyable evening. It was always crowded. Young ladies went in posh frocks, and there were loads and loads of young eager fellows looking forward to a great evening, and the hope of meeting someone special. I too had the infrequent opportunity to change into 'mufti' (civilian clothes). Remembering all the trifling data which I have seen fit to chart, I can add to the list by remembering that I had two dresses, one black and the other the colour fuchsia, either of which I would don for the frolic.

I met young men from all parts of the world. There were Londoners home on leave; some who were stationed in London or other parts of the UK, who had travelled into the capital for an evening out. And there were many others who were very far from home and family, and who wondered if they would ever be re-united with their kith and kin. I met interesting young men from everywhere. During the war there were young people from all nations here in Britain. Some were refugees from Europe. They hailed from France, Holland, Belgium, Norway, Poland and Czechoslovakia. They came to fight alongside us. Each was recognized by the name of their country worn as a 'flash' on the epaulettes of their uniform. They came from under the yoke of Hitler to fight for freedom from tyranny. They were members of their own particular army units or squadrons, but all serving under the Union Jack.

We had our Commonwealth lads here too. They had arrived in Britain from India and Burma, and the Aussies and the Kiwis from 'down under'; and the Canadians and the Gurkhas from Nepal. They all flocked to Covent Garden. There was no shortage of partners for us girls. I had an Irish boyfriend, Davey from Belfast, and Andre from Belgium. Amongst the many I became quite friendly with, was a Canadian, who I got to know well enough to take home to meet my Mum and Dad.

Sorry, I've forgotten his name!

I met a handsome young man from Berlin, who had escaped from Germany and Hitler, just before the start of hostilities. He was Jewish and fortunate to leave. His name was Robert Zettler. On arrival here, he was classified as an enemy alien, and sent with people in similar circumstances, to an Internment Camp in the Isle of Man, set up for that purpose. After a period of interrogation and inquiry, he was released and he joined the British Army. Approximately 10,000 Jewish refugees, who had fled to Britain for succour, were similarly placed. They served in the Alien Pioneer Corps and in the Intelligence Services. Being fluent-speaking German, they played a vital role after the war when it was the enemy who were to be interrogated. They became 'listeners', based in Trent Park, Enfield, in Hertfordshire. They listened in to conversations between the German prisoners of war who were here in the UK, using hidden microphones, to try and pick up any useful information for us and our allies. Proving their trust and military potential, they were transferred to esteemed units and battalions. Some progressed as paratroopers and commandos. They earned commissions and decorations. It was their 'Thank you'.

Before they were recruited into the British Armed Services they were advised to abandon their given German names. This was considered as a precautionary measure, should capture by the Germans be the unfortunate fate of these now serving personnel. My friend Robert gave himself a very Anglicized name, John Green, but his friends and I always called him Robbie.

* * *

Robbie and Me

Robbie and I became, as one would call it today, an 'item'. And it remained that way for a long time. He was stationed here at home at various locations, and it was quite interesting because I was able to visit areas that I had not before. We saw each other in London and he was a regular visitor at home.

Soon after D Day, when the Allies landed on the shores of Normandy, Robbie was sent to France and our correspondence flourished. He was articulate and educated, and I would send him publications of note – The New Statesman, and others of that ilk. His spoken English was fluent, but he had not quite mastered the intricacies of English spelling. "My darling angle" was how he addressed me in his long and loving letters.

And he sent me French perfume, and would you believe it NYLON STOCKINGS!!!

My mother was not happy with the way as she said 'the wind was blowing' with this relationship. I hate to admit this, but ever since I started to chronicle my history, the notion has entered my head that my mother steamed open and read Robbie's letters. In all the passing years, this thought has never occurred to me before. I am certain that she reckoned that this was for the best. Considering this further, I think of my progeny and it was for the best. I did not think so at the time. She was rather old fashioned in her views and disapproved of the fact that, although Robbie's dad was Jewish, his mother was not, so that rendered him 'not suitable'. I was 19 years old and still did what I was told to do. I wrote to him that our relationship was over. I had letters from his friends, begging me to change my mind. They told me that my photograph was still attached to the tent pole. I don't know who was the more heart broken – Robbie or me.

I met lots of Yanks, as the Americans were known, at the dances, and I was introduced to the 'jitterbug'. I never underwent the torture of those gyrations, and I never dated one from across the Atlantic. Later on, I did meet the best person and in mother's opinion, 'very suitable', but that is a sequel for recounting later on in this story.

* * *

A Change of Scene and a Shock to the System

Personnel of all the Services and other vital sectors, were subject to transfer. You were sent where you were needed, and that applied to the WLA as well. I was assigned to a market-garden holding in a village, Laleham, on the outskirts of Staines on the River Thames. Market-garden produce was taken on a daily basis to the wholesale markets of large towns, where it was bought by buyers who sold it on to retailers for purchase by the general public. It sounds complicated but on the face of it, in reality, it was a straight-forward business. Except of course there was probably much in the way of form-filling, and war time regulations to be considered and adhered to. The Ministry of Food was in charge and you complied.

I was directed to a private billet in Ashford, Middlesex, two or three miles from the farm, on the Saturday after my departure from Grantham. I introduced myself; obviously I was expected. I unpacked my bag and handed in my ration book, and went to Laleham to see the farm and its owner Mr Bishop. He said: "You start at eight am Monday, and you will need a bike". "Sorry Mr Bishop", I replied, "I haven't got a bike, and in any case I can't ride one." "That's okay", he answered, "I can give you one now which you can pay for on a weekly basis, which I will deduct from your wages. Mind that you're here at eight sharp on Monday. Good-bye".

Following that enlightened and intriguing conversation, I wheeled the bike back to Ashford where I deposited it, and caught a train to London. I was pleased that I would be living and working much closer to home. I returned to that billet on Sunday at tea-time. I was horrified, and very angry at what confronted me. My left luggage had been examined and closely vetted. "You are a Jew," I was told. "We don't want you here." This was 1944 and racism was not yet considered illegal.

I had lived in London all my life, in a mixed community. Jewish and Christian people lived in close proximity with each other. I went to school where my Faith was recognized and respected. We had separate assemblies and school hours were adjusted to synchronize with the onset of the Sabbath on Fridays. I had just arrived from living in a hostel where the same principle of respect applied. I had spent hours in shelters with people facing the prospect of danger, and death, with no thought of difference in religious belief. And at the age of 19, this was my first experience of anti-Semitism.

I was shocked and shaken to the core.

I gathered up my belongings, (by virtue of its 'going-over', in a rumpled condition), which had been left, heaped on the stripped bed. I asked for my ration book back, which I later discovered to be denuded of its sweet and clothing coupons. And I made my way back to Laleham. I am not sure how I managed it with my bike, which I was not able to operate, and with my case. I obviously did.

I had the address of the billeting officer in Laleham and informed her of my plight. No convenience yet of mobiles. I brought her to her front door late on that Sunday evening. Just as well she was back from church. I was settled into a house a mile or two from Mr. Bishop's, which became my home for the rest of the war. They were an elderly couple, a Mr and Mrs Davies. They had one son who was serving abroad, and I suspect that the fact that he too might have been taken in by strangers, gave them the impetus to offer me bed and board.

* * *

'On Your Bike Girl'!

The next morning, Monday, was my 'start day' in my new job. But I had to get there.

Wearing my dungarees and feeling refreshed after Mrs Davies' plate of porridge, I looked at the bike and thought: "Think that I'm going to walk." "Never fear" said her husband: "on you get". And on I got. He gave it, and I, a hefty shove, and I wobbled away, yelling like an incarnated 'banshee'.

The journey took me down narrow lanes, and I nearly had a fit, and almost fell of it, when I saw a horse and cart coming towards me. Honestly, this is not one word of a lie, I shut my eyes and kept peddling and wobbling. When I opened them, I found myself past the cause of my panic. I often wonder if that poor old gentleman recovered from his heart attack, if he suffered one.

After that first ride, I made good progress. I loved it, and would cycle everywhere when free from work. I cycled for years afterwards. I carried my children on a seat behind me, and my shopping in a basket in the front. As a family we cycled as a foursome. I would cycle with one child, and my husband with the other. We carried the picnic baskets and other items between us. Thanks to Mr Bishop, AND to Mr Davies.

The river tow path runs directly into Staines. I cycled that path so many times. If only I could I would do it again. Staines was a busy little market town, with its shops and cinema and small friendly cafes. Sometimes during the week end, I would spend my time there instead of going home.

* * *

Market Gardening

The work at the market-garden was a lot easier than it had been in Lincolnshire. There were no acres of corn fields to thresh, no harvesting of a barley crop when ones' fingers were pricked by the barley ears, and no large acreage of sugar beet to bash. 'Bashing' was the term used when one walloped the vegetable to free the ice from it. Sugar beet was harvested mid-winter. And a shepherd, not required!

Here we grew salad vegetables and soft fruits, rhubarb, and other similar produce. I think there must have been some animals because one day there was a minor incident concerning some hay. A local boy would come after school to work.

He kept rabbits, and the owner saw him leave with a few bits of hay. He stopped him and asked the boy for 6 pence, (old money). He was a very rich man, and a very prominent and generous benefactor to the Laleham Church.

Everything was on a much smaller scale than I had been used to. Six or seven land girls worked there. They were a friendly lot, and I spent much of my free time in their company. It was a pleasure to cycle along the tow path on a balmy summer evening; sometimes alone, and sometimes in the company of my work mates. Many times I strolled alongside the river with a gentleman friend who had come to pay me a visit. Often I walked that mile with Robbie, when our romance was still flourishing, and had not yet died.

I was very happy and content when I lived in Laleham. The only 'fly in the ointment' as the saying goes, was Mr Smith – Smithy as we called him. He was an elderly gentleman who worked on the farm in the position of overseer. That is, he worked alongside us girls to ensure that we did our work and were diligent. I think that he originated from some northern county; he had a gusty accent.

One day, we were harvesting carrots. We were putting them into sacks for weighing; after which we would secure the sacks with string. We were all issued with lengths of string which we had attached to our dungaree fastenings. I had used my quota and I needed more. Smithy was working quite a distance from me so I had to yell to get his attention. In a loud Cockney voice, deliberately evocative to emulate his speech timbre, I shouted: "Have you some string on you, cock?" It was not meant to be rude or derogatory. The girls thought it funny and they all laughed. But dear old Smithy thought otherwise. He singled me out after that, and often arranged it so that I was isolated from my friends.

Many years later, I would often have a day out on a Sunday with my growing children and we would spend many happy hours in Laleham. You can probably detect from this narrative that I have strong nostalgic memories. Perhaps this summer I might take a train and go and visit. Bit long in the tooth to find a bike though!

One day, I was working in a row with the other land girls. We were planting lettuces. It was 8.30am on a bright sunny morning. The date was the 6th June 1944. The foreman of the farm went into the farmhouse for his breakfast, and to listen to the early morning news. We had all started work early at 6.30am. There was much to do that day. The foreman came out from his break and said: "I have something to tell you".

His cat was poorly, we thought that perhaps poor pussy had died. But that was not the case. "We have landed in France", is what he told us. Well we all stood up from our bent stance and we just cheered like mad. It was, as we called it D Day. To bestow upon it its full title, it was Deliverance Day. We had invaded mainland Europe. At long last perhaps the end of the war was in sight.

But not quite; here at home we had two more hurdles to face.

* * *

The Last Throw of the Dice

The Germans had developed an unmanned flying bomb. Officially it was called the 'V1' – an abbreviation of the German 'Vergeltungswaffe', which translated into English meant 'Retribution Weapon'. We called them 'Doodle Bugs'. They came. They were undetectable by radar and no siren sounded to warn the public to take shelter. They made a droning sound. Perhaps that was why we called them what we did, apart from other names. Unprintable! Their sound would stop, and they would fall to the earth killing civilians and demolishing property.

Later on a further development in aerial warfare, succeeded it. This was the V2. Again there was no warning, and these were even more deadly. They flew in, in silence. Unlike the V1 there was no ominous drone, and therefore, one was not aware that you were in danger. They just dropped from the sky, and the first you knew about it was the sound of explosion if it fell within earshot.

One day, during the period of the V2s, I was sitting on a window ledge drinking coffee. Suddenly, without warning, there was an almighty roar, like the noise of an express train. It was the sound of a very close rocket explosion and the window glass where I sat had shattered, and I was injured. Luckily my injuries were minor. I suffered a cut finger on my right hand. My finger still bears witness to that incident. It is bent from the first joint. I cannot straighten it. Considering what was happening, with thousands of people suffering death and serious injuries, I reckon myself to be extremely fortunate.

* * *

Let the Children Learn

1994 saw the 50th anniversary of the Normandy landings. I received a message from my daughter, Simone: "Mum, Jamie's school (primary) are looking to set out a memorabilia table for the event. They have requested bits and bobs from grandparents, to supply the same. I have told them that you have no such items but you will come up to Harrington, near Workington, Cumbria, to tell the children about the war." "Oh, thank you very much", I thought, "Who needs an agent?" Well, I never turn down the opportunity to visit my family, so in due course, off I toddled. It was a most interesting experience. Sixty or so, well-behaved 8–11 year-old nippers parked in the school hall, a bevy of young teachers in attendance, and myself established on a low chair.

Briefly, in easy English, I told them the story of war time life in London. I gave them an unvarnished truth, but a bit easy on the gory bits about the blitz. Finally, I lifted my hand, and demonstrated my deformed finger. Wow! When my grandson arrived home from school that afternoon, he told me he was now the most popular of his peers: "We saw your Nanna's finger", was the topic of playtime chatter.

I have to end this little yarn, by recording my impressions of those under-twelves. There was an 'any questions' slot, and the queries I was bombarded with were incredible. I did mention "Bad man Hitler", and I was asked why the German people followed him. I told them that we, in England do what our government say, and the Germans did likewise. I was stumped only once. I could not tell a lad how many guns a Spitfire had. On my return home I perused my books, and was able to write to the school – it had eight. I had a lovely letter in reply and some flowers. That note rests with so much else, mainly cards from my grandchildren, in my 'treasure box'. I had my small share of fame. Incidentally, I have repeated that talk nearer home last year, and when I still lived in Cardiff, I confronted a hundred or so sixth formers in a large comprehensive school. No holds barred!

To rouse myself from my memories, it is as well to note that there were more than 30,000 aerial attacks from the combined V1 and V2 rocket launchers. I was, indeed, a fortunate young woman.

Well it took until the 7th May 1945 to beat the Germans. Together, with our Commonwealth and Allies, we won the war. It was a victory. If one gives a thought to the cost of winning a war, one wonders if it can be a victory for anyone.

But my personal story is not over yet. Churchill decided that although the Armistice was signed on the previous day, the 8th of May would be designated VE Day.

That is, Victory in Europe Day. It must be remembered that the war against Japan was ongoing. In truth the war was not over yet.

But here in Britain, the population were euphoric with joy and happiness. As darkness fell, the lights came on, after nearly six years of black-out. It was such a relief that now we could look to the future. Writing this, a shudder goes through my old body as I remember it all. I am not able to discriminate if the emotion is of pleasure, owing to the date, or of sorrow, because of what I remember about all the calamitous consequences of war involvement.

On that day, for a brief moment in time, people forgot the suffering and hardship of six years. So many people had died; so many had been rendered homeless, and a multitude of suffering the lifelong effects of sustained injuries. There was now so much to do to rebuild our lives, and everything around us. And perhaps those who facilitate conflict might learn from history. I doubt it!!

Chapter 8

After the War was Over

Meeting Fate at the Balfour

I have already said that my personal war time story is not over. Like everyone else on that VE Day I too celebrated. I went home to London.

During the war years, many social clubs were established in London, and around the UK, for the benefit of Servicemen and Servicewomen. They offered respite to those who were perhaps far from home. And those, who knew there was nothing to go home for. Family dead, killed through hate, and evil, and conflict. Apart from ordinary venues like the YM in Allington, where I spent so many happy hours, there were specialised clubs.

Each of the Services had their own. Those serving, who came from other countries, had theirs. One was not barred if one did not 'fit'. All eligible Service people were welcome. It was just special to that particular group. You could go to your club, converse in your own language, have a special meal common to your cuisine, and to meet your people. These clubs, set up by generous organizations and philanthropists, carried out a very necessary and worthwhile undertaking.

And so it was with The Balfour Club in Great Portland St. London. The club was set up for Jewish service personnel, and I was a frequent visitor. It was unique; it was a haven. It was an oasis of pleasure and happiness: "Hail fellow, well met". Even if you had never met before you 'knew' everyone. Everyone was your brother or sister. If your English was poor, you got by in Yiddish. If you were in London, unconnected to the town or family or friends living there, the Balfour was a godsend. You could even get a salt beef meal or a schmaltz herring (herring marinated in olive oil) sandwich, or if stocks held out, a freshly-baked sweet smelling smoked salmon bagel!

Young civilian ladies, like my girl cousins, (the munitions workers), had their names on a long waiting list of volunteers for the chance to help in any capacity. To wait tables, to cook, be a receptionist, even as a washer-upper; any opportunity to be there to help and you never knew, you could easily meet 'a suitable'.

Being in the WLA, I was an accepted and regular member. I always went there in uniform. It was the obvious place to be to celebrate VE Day. When I arrived the party was in full swing. It was crowded with happy and excited people. There was music and dancing and a presentable young man approached me and asked me to dance. I was pleased to do so.

Young men were not always well versed in the social skills of dancing. I remember once at the club I danced with an American – a highly-ranked officer, who should have known better, who thought it very British, old girl, to dance with me whilst smoking his pipe! "For cor blimey's sake, mate!"

* * *

Raymond Re-introduced

I arrived home very late that night. It brings to mind a little banality that I like to remember about that momentous day. As I have already confided many of my little anecdotes, I might as well record this one. One evening, due to the limitations of the war, I arrived home rather late. It couldn't have been too excessive as I relied on public transport, and buses and the London Underground system tended to cease operating earlier than an unearthly hour.

My Dad, who always waited up for me was not best pleased. He expressed his displeasure, and said: "When the war ends, you can stay out all night". So tonight was the night at the end of the day when the war ended. I did not stay out all night, but it was late, so what could be fairer than that?

As a matter of fact when I did get home, the house was in darkness. I knew that my parents had gone to bed. But because I saw that the lights were on at my Aunty Tilly's house, a few doors down from ours, I knew that she was still awake. She didn't mind a bit at having a late visitor. Her son, my cousin Harold, was serving away in the RAF, and she was so relieved to know that now that the war was over, he would be returning home, that she had been out celebrating too. She put the kettle on for a cuppa and looked at me to tell her what I had been up to on that wonderful day. "Oh Auntie" I said, "I have met such a lovely man."!"

And indeed I had. Raymond was his name. He told me that his home was in Cardiff. We had paired-up during the shenanigans earlier on. As a group from the Balfour, we larked about going down London's Regent Street to Whitehall and we waited with the heaving happy masses in front of the Home Office building; we knew that there was sure to be something interesting about to happen. And sure enough, it did. Our Winnie, appeared on the building's balcony exhibiting his fingers in his 'Victory' sign (two fingers upright in the shape of a V). Wow! Can you imagine the noise from that crowd? The cheers were deafening. And then the singing started. We sang "For He's a Jolly Good Fellow", "Rule Britannia", and "There will always be an England". What an end to that day!

Re-reading the events that took place on my arrival home after that wonderful day of celebration, I am wondering whether it is indeed an unnecessary item to record. I called it 'banal'. Perhaps I over emphasized the adjective. Let it be as a light dessert after a heavy meal!

Raymond and I made arrangements to meet up again. He was a sergeant in the Airborne Division wearing his, by now famous, (because of their war record), red beret, and his own-designed hat badge. He was stationed not too far away in Rickmansworth in Hertfordshire.

Myrtle, aged 21, eight weeks before her wedding to Raymond in 1946. With her parents and brother, and an aunt.

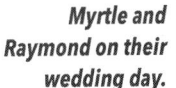

Myrtle and Raymond on their wedding day.

His last tour of duty, after serving in many theatres of war around the world was, if you could believe it, in a secret location on an upper floor of Peter Robinsons – a large department store in Oxford St. London. It was where the D Day landings were planned under the American General Dwight Eisenhower. I began to see a lot of this young man who asked me to dance the day the war ended.

Six weeks after the end of the war, a General Election was held here in Britain. Raymond, who was by now a frequent visitor at our house, had come for a late meal. My Mum and Dad went out to vote, and I was left to clear the dishes. Raymond asked me to sit on his knee and went on to say: "Would you like to spend the rest of your life with me?" Which of course I wanted to do very much.

"If Only ..."

On the 20th July 1944, ten months before the end of the war, an attempt was made on the life of Adolph Hitler, perpetrated by a group of his high ranking generals. It was code named 'Operation Valkyrie', and it took place inside Hitler's hide-out retreat – 'The Wolf's Lair' in East Prussia.

The enterprise was planned by a group whose objective it was to seize power and to control the politics of the state, and its armed forces. Operations on Germany's Eastern Front in Russia were in stalemate and failing. The dissatisfaction amongst these officers was high on their agenda, groaning under the weight of their leader's incompetence, giving rise to a lack of his understanding of military matters, and the psychology of future intentions. It was their aspiration that with Hitler gone, they would offer, and achieve, a peace settlement with the Allies. The plan was further supported by several groups of German resistant dissidents of the Nazi Regime.

The perpetrators placed a briefcase bomb under the conference table. They set the fuse, and left with excuses of 'bathroom needs' before it detonated. Some of the remaining occupants were killed, but Hitler managed to stay alive. The failure of the assassination led to the arrest of 7,000 people by the Gestapo, (The German State Secret Police), a vicious, brutal, butchering bunch, known by the initials SS. According to known records, 5,000 were executed, including the main plot devisors, some of whom chose to commit suicide. Hitler was not killed but injured. His trousers were singed and in tatters, and he suffered a perforated eardrum.

In 1967, a British film, 'Night of the Generals' was released; and in 2008, the Americans produced the film 'Valkyrie'. It is interesting to note that Hitler's favourite composer, of German nationality, Wagner, wrote 'The Ride of The Valkyries' in the 1850s. I wonder if the men of that liquidation plan attached some ironic gesture to the affair.

* * *

Dead or Alive?

I would like to add a postscript to this episode. I recently became aware of an interesting report emanating from our National Archives which lay hidden under The Secrets Act, but lately released. Hitler took his own life in his bunker hidden deep beneath the streets of Berlin; his body doused with petrol and incinerated on the spot, when defeat was obvious. His newly-married wife, Eva Braun, swallowed poison and died too. The Russians were already in Berlin, and were in fact, within a few hundred metres of that underground warren. The SS watched Hitler's body burn. For years afterwards, many are still not sure if it was the body of Hitler or a substitute; and in fact if Hitler still lived.

Recently-released documentation gives rise to some relevant information. Medical dossiers; x-ray reports; secret medical files; a skull and a jawbone were presented in an attempt to prove that Hitler did not die that night. The Russians were the first to suspect his fake demise. They scavenged the residue ashes of the burnt corpse, and set about scientifically investigating the possibility. Tight-lipped Stalin, a personality given to deceit and cunning and a liar to boot, guarded his secrets well, and as was his habitual trend, did not share the results of the findings with his co-partners in war. The discovery of the bones could have been proof that the cremation had not been complete. Bone is not easy to incinerate, thus providing further material to examine. The Russian scientific data gave a conflicting report. It was not confirmed, or denied, that the remains were unmistakably that of the German warmonger. The skull and the jawbone did provide evidence that there was a perforation of the eardrum, (that had occurred during the bomb blast), confirming Hitler's injury on the night of the assassination attempt; and the shape of the skull did tally with that person, and was indeed that which contained the evil brain of the tyrant. Skull shapes are akin to finger prints. No two person's are alike. The teeth of the second salvaged item collaborated the evidence. Hitler's jaw in life, held only five teeth, being the sum total of his natural molars/incisors. The rest were either the work of the dentist, on a denture frame or crowned. It was also noted, by not so flattering companions, that he emitted the result of halitosis (unpleasant-smelling breath), as a result of poor dental hygiene and decaying teeth.

So it was almost certain that Hitler had perished, even though many are mistrustful of Stalin's reports. The medical details, stored in all of the papers held by the British Archives, revealed other interesting secrets giving rise to hitherto unknown facts concerning the German despot, as a living person. It was proved that he was obsessional and of unstable and unsteady characteristics. He suffered fatigue and depression. He swallowed an assortment of 28 drugs on a daily basis.

If the reports are uncertain and Hitler did not die, then surely, based on the passage of time, he must be dead by now. Whenever it happened, I trust that his soul went straight to Hell.

A just punishment for him, who together with his cohorts, wrought a hell for millions word wide.

* * *

The Past and the Present - What Now?

It is important to look back and to review the situation after those ecstatic days of relief and joy of the VE Day celebrations. It is necessary to realize that it would take years to rebuild and reshape Britain, and in European countries where normality had ceased to exist. And it must be remembered that we were not entirely free from fighting a war. There was still Japan to deal with. But for now, peace in Europe was enough, and we basked in the rejoicing and freedom from fear and anxiety.

The first change occurred here at home, with the outcome of the General Election that was held soon after the cessation of hostilities. One cannot imagine that Clement Atlee, leader of the Labour party, would be elected to a post-war parliament as Prime Minister. What a shocking blow for Mr Churchill, treated in a manner so undeserved. He guided this country to victory. He did indeed save this nation. How could the country show its ingratitude in this way? I reckon him to have been the greatest Briton ever. I was not yet old enough to enjoy the franchise that would entitle me to cast a vote, (it was 21 back then), but I was old enough to know who I would have given my vote to. I was devastated by that result. But he did live to fight another day. He was re-elected as Prime Minister in October 1951, and remained in office until April 1955. I am willing to take the risk of repeating myself; I have an irresistible urge to stand up again and to shout: "Good on you, Winnie!"

What programme would the new Labour government provide for the recovery of the country? We were bankrupt. We had an enormous national debt. I have already recorded how many years would pass before we finally settled the money owed to the USA. We needed the men and women who had served overseas to return home; to pick up the threads of normal family life. Fathers, reunited with their families, met their young children for the first time. These youngsters only knew a dad as a photograph in a frame on the sideboard. And many did not take kindly to being usurped from the priority they had with their mums. It had to be shared now. It is a sad fact that many men returned home to broken marriages. Unfaithful wives are not an uncommon feature in war time. There were families whose husband or son or daughter did not return, and they had to rehabilitate without them.

Mourning their nearest and dearest, they did not celebrate VE Day. They stayed indoors, away from the singing and dancing in the streets, isolated from the merry-making laughing and joyous crowds.

The lives of women had changed. Many of them had married American servicemen and they, together with the children born of some of those marriages, left to start new lives in a strange country. There to meet unrecognizable new families and to acclimatize to a new way of living; perceiving their American husbands from a new viewpoint. It was the husband whose home it was now.

The destruction of property, owing to air bombardment, gave rise to a housing shortage, and where would these re-united families live? The 'Prefab' was born. Prefabricated houses, quick to manufacture and low in cost, literately rose from the ashes. One of my cousins lived in one for years. Her husband was demobbed after six years' service, and returned home to live with my cousin and her family, which they did for a lengthy period of time. As was to be expected, she became pregnant. Living space was already limited at home, so he took himself off to the council offices and stated his case, with threats, I have to say. My cousin and her husband soon moved into their prefab. And 'fab' it was. It even had a bath, plumbed in under the kitchen table! Wow! How many East End London homes had such a luxury? I patronized the public baths until I had my own home at 21 years old. These homes really were wonderful. Fitted kitchens, and each abode with its own garden. Their lifespan was limited, but they were lived in for years and years past their 'sell by' date, and people were so sad when they were eventually rehoused in some high rise block of flats.

There are so many facets to the list of 'recovery and regeneration'. I have only chosen a few. But it is so obvious that there was much to be done, to rebuild the war-torn, exhausted and weakened fabric of the infrastructure of our country, and there was much to do to galvanize the rebirth of a normal way of living.

* * *

Aftermath

And what was happening on the Continent? Germany lay in ruins. Hitler's senior underlings, and their families, took poison and died in Hitler's bunker, at the time when he reputedly shot himself. Arch-enemy Joseph Goebbels, whose history reads like a story out of Hades, were amongst those who did likewise, including his wife and their six children.

Goebbels joined the Nazi party in 1921, and from 1933 took the position of Reich Minister of Propaganda. Later on, he advocated and pursued a programme of 'Total War'. He was known for his virulent anti-Semite views, and unhealthy subversive attitudes against Christians. He was responsible for the murder of almost the entire European Jewry.

The concentration camps, those diabolical manifestations of Hitler's plan, where so many suffered and were murdered, were liberated. Camps for displaced persons were established for those who came out of such places as the 'Arbeit Macht Frei' gates of Auschwitz. Leaving those hellish places of the degradation of the human soul, they had nowhere else to go. Where was home now? What had happened to their families? How can they reconstruct their lives? Will they ever forget the nightmare?

Europe was drained. Borders were redrawn. The Russian army was in Berlin, exacting a revenge on the Berliners for the terrible Russian losses. Russia took over swathes of Eastern Europe. The plan that had been arranged at the Yalta conference in 1943 materialized. Germany was zoned into four parts, for each of the main Allied combatants. It was said at that time that Russia will always act as she thinks her own interests demand.

Raymond, now back in Cardiff, was thinking about his future. It was not easy. He had had no formal work-oriented training, or professional status. He had left school at the age of 18; three years prior to his 'call up', with no certificate of education, other than the many awards he received for his musical talent. He was a gifted violinist.

He later told me that he had contracted malaria whilst serving in North Africa, and had reoccurring bouts afterwards. Again as I write, my memory has jolted me back to 1945. I was engaged to Raymond when I received a message that he was ill with malaria in a military hospital in Newton Abbot, Devon. Without warning him, I decided to visit. I arrived early one afternoon, and walked into the ward. He certainly did not expect visitors. He was unwashed and unshaven; it was obvious that his hair had not been combed. Poor fellow! I left the afternoon visiting slot and returned later. Well, what a transformation. There he was sitting up in bed, looking handsome, and all spruced up. I took a B & B overnight, and saw him again the next day. He was so happy and I was too.

He had served in Italy and had landed, in a glider, on Sicily. He had fought, in the early days of the war, in France and was aware of his good fortune owing to a man sailing a 'Little Ship'.

My daughter Sheila, who has her Dad's medals for safe-keeping, tells me that 'The Africa Star' is amongst them. As Raymond hardly ever spoke of his combat duties, I was not aware at that time that he had fought in North Africa, but come to think of it, I have suddenly had a memory buzz from my brain, and I do recall that he once said, by way of explaining a small scar he carried on his forehead, that he suffered a minor injury when coming off a motorbike in North Africa when he was suffering the symptoms of an oncoming bout of malaria. So Africa can be added to the list of places where Raymond fought. Wow, it must be all of sixty years since we had that conversation and never once since have I ever thought of it until just now! He had been demobbed (demobilized) early. It was a system of 'first in, first out,' and he had served for six years. On leaving, he was given an ill-fitting navy blue 'Utility Suit'. A few pounds in his pocket and a travel warrant to take him back home to Cardiff.

'Utility' was the trade mark of all items, whatever the category, made here at home in a 'no-nonsense' system. All items were down-to-earth basics only – no frills or folderols. The Government had specific ministries to control everything, and everybody! They decided how many buttons were allowed on a jacket; how many door knobs on a sideboard; and everything else in between.

Raymond could draw and sketch. He had this amazing talent, and when he did manage to find work, he started a low paid job in the office of a friend who did advertising. I suppose in the language of today you would call it graphic designing. And he thought of me, working and living in London. Raymond and I loved each other and we wanted to be married, and in September 1946 we were.

When we were married, we furnished our house with all items 'utility'. It was all you could buy. Our furniture, all with its 'utility' logo, endured for years and years and years. Knobs and all!

* * *

The Blessed and the Damned

It has occurred to me that I have only casually enlightened my readers of the facts, appertaining to the lives of the wartime leaders. I have already mentioned the demise of Winston Churchill, and later on in my scribblings, I will bring to light the desolate news of the death of President Franklin D Roosevelt. Hitler satisfied everyone when he cowardly took his own life. Josef Stalin died 5th March 1953.

Perhaps, as I have the opportunity, I should fill in some of the gaps, elucidating the fate of Mussolini, the Italian leader. It was an omission which has a right to be amended. He was a crucial player in the events of World War Two, and I feel justified to impart his latter history.

Italy, in the face of the Allied advances from the south of the country, changed its allegiance to Hitler, and declared war on Germany. In any case, Hitler had already made plans to invade that country and to occupy it outright. As German troops advanced from the north, the general in charge of the remnants of the Italian army, and the King, Victor Emanuel 3rd, fled, thus provoking a civil war. Germany occupied northern Italy and pronounced it a 'Puppet State'. The Allied advance from the south eventually defeated the Germans and rendered Italy free. On the 28th April 1945, two days before the suicide of Hitler, Mussolini and his mistress, received fatal gunshot wounds from the hand of a communist partisan, in an Italian village. The bodies were taken to Milan, and Mussolini was hung upside down on the balcony of an important official building. It was an inglorious end, to a heinous aggressor.

Chapter 9
A Story about the War

The Bridge

The idea to write a book began purely by chance. I have never had the ambition to do so, nor did I think myself qualified or sufficiently erudite. But it happened. I handed the first finished draft to a friend, who had some experience in writing, and the immediate feedback wowed me; hence what you are reading now. My intention originally, was to write an account of my life as I lived it during WW2. To be honest, every person of my age can tell, even if they do not have the ability to do so on paper, a story of their life so far, especially if they have wartime involvement.

Gradually I realized that there was more to write about than just me. Why even on the very first page, it is not about me. I am but barely mentioned, and yet I think that it was interesting enough for people to turn to the next page.

So why you may ask, am I disclosing this now? I have good reason. The first half of my finished product, if my tale is the reason for writing it in the first place, should not have been the first half, but the whole. I decided that the story of my latter years, when I had a better understanding of the war from a different perspective, was of interest, especially when it was amalgamated with my travels. At the start of this book, I had felt as though I was a young person, actually writing as if it was all happening at that time. It was uncanny; as I was typing out the words I just could not believe it. I felt myself transported, as if in a 'back-to-the-future' time.

Gradually, as my work developed, I decided that it was an issue of not only my personal tale, but the story of the war. And I mean a story, not a history. What I set out to do was not to provide a text book for school children, nor to educate the general public. My intention was to whet the interest by offering a superficial, but accurate account, of what happened in certain war-time campaigns, using an approach to more or less present it in a story form. One cannot mix fact with fiction. I have not done that. This book is factual.

The second half of my venture is written from the stand-point of a person who has had many years of witnessing, and listening, and using all my other senses, to bring enlightenment, which leads to deep thinking and reflection. "What does war, any war, add up to in the end? How does it affect all of us?"

I have attempted to present some of the 'little things', and to break down some of the 'big things', to a level of easy understanding; we are not all expert historians. And of course in its raw state, I have tried to inject my own personality, such as it is.

The reason why I decided to write this particular explanation is because several people, whom I consulted, were of the opinion that my work should really have been split into two separate parts, each with its own theme. Specifically my autobiography, completely separate from the story of the war. In fact almost two individual works. I have given this much thought, and have come to the conclusion that I will continue with my original plan to write about my life, incorporating it into a potted saga of the Second World War. Be it as it may, I am not writing a book for financial gain. My original intention was to run off sixteen copies, one each for my fifteen grandchildren and another for my dear step granddaughter, Joëlle. Many people might be of the opinion that I should have left it at that. Nor am I expecting a Booker Prize for my humble endeavour.

* * *

Off on My Travels

My professional life had no connection with history of the war years, or any other historical period. History was my special subject at school, and as an adult, I have often regretted not having had the opportunity to study it seriously, in a more formalized regimen. So I class myself as a bit of a 'history buff', and I consider myself as being quite good at it. You might have noticed that I am adequately able to recall and record it. Also that modesty is not one of my strong points. The reason for this sequel, is to share my experience of later years, when I was able to travel to places connected to my story of the war.

Myrtle aged 63 - always with her head in a history book!

It was a habit to travel to various places in the UK with my youngest daughter, Simone. A bright youngster, then in her early teens, having gained a scholarship and bursary, and receiving her education in a renowned grammar school. We had our own transport, and would travel from place to place, staying overnight wherever we found ourselves to be. I decided that we would make a journey to Grantham, to visit the area of my Land Army days, which we did.

Obviously the town had changed much in those intervening years. The theatre where I had gone with the married officer, was advertising 'Bingo'. I had always thought that theatres and cinemas showing 'Bingo' must be giving that film or play, (whatever it was), a very good run. Must be a first rate production! I looked for the site which housed the NAAFI, but was unable to distinguish it from other buildings. I had arranged many a rendezvous there with a presentable young man. I was disappointed to think that maybe they were now showing Bingo too!

Our next stop was to the village of Allington. Not much had changed. We called at the house where our YMCA benefactor had lived. There was no reply. It was a long time ago, and he was quite old even then. We sought out the WLA hostel, where I had lived with all the friends I had made, and where Miss Perkins and her friend had so strictly ruled the roost. The hostel still stood. It was not quite as spick and span as I remembered it. It was being used for the storage of farming implements, and a farmer, who was in attendance, invited us in, reluctantly, but for 'old time's sake'. I was a bit upset to see it had deteriorated, but at least it still had some connection with the work we did, so I was quite pleased with that.

I briefly looked over my shoulder, to that place across the field, behind the hostel, where Herbert Lewis guarded the Italian Prisoners. I wondered if he, and they, returned home safely. I hope that they did, and that Herbert's mum was able to gift her home-made cakes and gefilte fish, (fish that has been filleted and minced), and appetising savoury-filled bagels to a much loved daughter-in-law.

***

Hayes

Whilst I am in that time zone of the Land Army, I would like to record, once more, the memories I have of the happy time spent in Laleham, which is not too far from London. I live in the north-west of the metropolis now. In earlier years I lived in Hayes

**Myrtle, aged 24. Cardiff 1948.
With Raymond and baby Sheila**

which was then in the county of Middlesex, now classified as Greater London. When Raymond and I were married in 1946 we lived in Cardiff until we relocated to London in 1955.

Those intervening nine years were not easy. We were a happy and loving family, but there were problems. Raymond's job was a curtesy offering from a friend and we lived in an emergency financial bubble. The type of work that the firm specialized in was advertising which was a far cry from the work needed to rebuild a post war Britain. Raymond and I also worked part-time to eke out our modest income. Even for ex-army returnees there was no government help forthcoming. We installed a Wall's ice cream chest in one of our rooms and he and I sold that product from shoulder-hanging trays at public events at week-ends, with just one child at that time, Sheila, parked in her pram at some convenient spot. (One could safely do that in those years).

In 1955 we made a life-changing decision. I was 28 years old and my Dad had just died. My Mum, living alone in London, approved of our plan and consequently offered Raymond a home until he could find work and resettle his family. We had two children by that time, Sheila and Diane. Raymond was in residence with my Mum for nine months, coming home once monthly for the weekend. He was now in regular employment settled in a clerical job in Greenford Middlesex, and had found us a house nearby in Hayes. It was there that our third daughter, Marian was born.

Life was good and a blessing. We were together and the future looked rosy. Until in 1957 when the Asian influenza struck. We were all ill and four of us recovered. Raymond did not. After having come through the war in the way that he did, he succumbed to the flu epidemic. He was 39 years old. The malaria that he had contracted in North Africa had damaged his liver, and he was not able to withstand the effects on that organ caused by the flu. He had survived the war, but its repercussions killed him in the end.

At 32, I was a widowed mother of three. Sheila was nine years old. She was the first to get better and nursed the rest of us. Diane was five, and the absence of a daddy manifested itself in anger and rage and frequent outbursts of uncontrollable temper as a young child. Marian was ten months old, and never remembering her Dad has, I think, affected her all her life. She is now sixty and a well-adjusted adult, but still talks of her loss. Diane overcame her trauma. She achieved a place in a top grammar school in Ealing, West London, following in the footsteps of her elder sister, Sheila. Both sisters have subsequently had considerable success in their lives. Diane, aged 64, now lives in Melbourne and is teaching; Sheila, at the age of 68, was recently awarded a doctorate. Me, their Mum, has neither scholarship awards or other degrees to boast about, but I 'kvell', (take pride in), my family of achievers.

Five years after Raymond's death I met and married Alfred Russell.

* * *

A Bit More About Me

Over the years, we would often traipse off west to Laleham for a day out in the sun. We went in anticipation of a happy carefree day, in a happy carefree group, with our children and their friends. With our packed-up food and petrol in the van, which was Alf's business vehicle, off we went. We never grew tired of it. We sat on the grassy bank along the tow path to Staines, where we would walk, or play ball, or just sit in the sun and chatter and enjoy ourselves.

It is obvious that as time passed and circumstances changed, my life pattern would too. I was widowed a second time when I was 50. My solace was my children. I have four now, then I had five. My only son died in 2000, aged 36. No matter the circumstance, life moves on and according to your situation, you move with it. I had no choice when my youngest two became fatherless; they were young, and they needed a supportive mum. I was 41 when Simone made her entrance. She was 9, and her brother Adam was 11 when their beloved dad passed away. Before our marriage he cared for his elderly father, and took me, and my three fatherless girls, when he was past 40. He never ever expected to marry and to have children of his own, and he adored his two. Tragedy it was, that he did not see them fully-grown. He was a good and loving man, and the world is a poorer place without him.

I was employed with a responsible job (a nursing sister), and we got by. I coped

Myrtle, aged 50, with Alf Russell. He died four months later, aged 55, after fighting a losing battle with lung cancer

and scrubbed up to my satisfaction. When I retired, and my youngest grown up, the world was my oyster and by crickey, I made the most of it.

I travelled sometimes solo and sometime with a friend. I went to those towns in the southern counties of England where the Americans had been based, in the beautiful and picturesque villages of Essex and Suffolk. I remember the name of just one, Lavernham, with its thatched roofed cottages. I am sure that those fellows had never seen them back home. These were the gentlemen who flew the four-engine 'Flying Fortress', and who carried out daylight air raids over Germany. The RAF had carried out sorties by night. I visited the museum, dedicated to the Americans, depicting the way they lived and where they died. So many returning in damaged aircraft and with broken bodies. I paid due respect at the cemetery where so many were buried.

* * *

Adam - A Difficult Decision

As previously mentioned, my son Adam died in 2000, aged 36.

When he was eleven, and his father Alf passed away, there were circumstances which made me reconsider the way in which I observed my Faith.

As with all of the three Abrahamic religions, Judaism has its sects. The Ultra-Orthodox, that is the Chassidic community, live by every word and literal interpretation of the Old Testament. They speak Yiddish as their first language at home.

They have large families, the outcome of restricted contraception, and live in large groups, perhaps as a security measure against infiltration. Their children are educated by gender separation, both physically and by curriculum. Chassids do not watch television. The women wear concealing clothing and wigs which cover their natural hair. Basically they live the lifestyle of Eastern European Jewish communities of earlier centuries.

Traditionally Orthodox, middle-of-the-road Jews, live their lives uncluttered by extreme religious practices compared to the Ultra-Orthodox. However, there are several differences but basically the level of their religious practices follow parallel lines. Observant Jews eat what is called 'Kosher' meat. That is meat from cloven-hoofed animals and only fish that have fins and scales. They do not work or drive their vehicles on the Sabbath or on Festival days. I was born and reared under this umbrella. I have twice been married in Orthodox synagogues. I was happy to subscribe to being a member of this community and this way of life until I was fifty years old.

In Germany in the 19th century, a new modern form of Judaism was conceived and delivered. It gave that religion, which was born over 5,000 years ago, a modern revival, an emancipation. It was identified, appropriately as 'Reform'. It did not change the basic foundations of a Jewish lifestyle – kosher food was the norm. Ordinary western apparel was worn by the women. The Sabbath and Festivals were observed but one was allowed to drive. If that was their religious calling, females could be trained and ordained into the Rabbinate, a feature unheard of in Orthodox fraternities. Unlike the seating arrangements in Orthodox synagogues, in a Reform House of Worship the gender restriction was lifted. Families sat together. Men could be with their wives together with sons and daughters.

Later, The Liberal Synagogue introduced more progressive ideas, liberalising the rituals and practices even more to the left, as their given name implies, and distanced the religion even further from the original Orthodox practices, whilst still maintaining the basic tenets of the Jewish Faith.

Whether all this information is of interest to my readers I am obviously not able to judge. As the name of this piece implies it obviously has a connection with my son Adam. I have presented it as a preamble to an episode which I think is part of my personal story.

* * *

Adam - A Dual Responsibility

My boy, number four in the family hierarchy, was eleven years old and rendered fatherless two years before his Bar Mitzvah; the occasion when a thirteen year old lad is regarded as a fully entitled male to take his place alongside his peers in the ritual obligations.

The Bar Mitzvah boy's initiation is orchestrated to take place during a Sabbath service when he reads, in Hebrew, from the Holy Torah Scrolls and wears a tallit (prayer shawl) for the first time. Nowadays boys of all ages wear long trousers; years ago a Bar Mitzvah boy proudly wore them for the very first time. That was really special and it was considered well worth a couple of year's hard swot, as well as worrying away at school homework. Well, Adam had begun to study for that occasion. As a family we would attend the orthodox synagogue where I was a member of the congregation. As practice decreed, Adam would sit in the men's section and me with my girls in the women's section, at a distance. I always positioned myself so that I could keep an eye on my son. It was soon after Alf Russell died and we were still a family wretched and in mourning after the loss of our husband and father. I needed to be as close as possible in all aspects to my two youngest, Adam and Simone. I would notice with irritation and disappointment that no-one sought Adam's company. Perhaps it was a sense of embarrassment at his loss that those grown men around him were not able to connect with a young lad at the time, when it would have been welcome.

When we returned home I called for a family 'pow-wow'. The children ceded to my suggestion that Adam would have his forthcoming Bar Mitzvah in our regular synagogue, after which we would change our membership to one of the Reform Movement. There was a large and respected Reform following in Edgware where we lived. And so it was that we attended services as a family, and seated as such, we became acquainted with a gracious and caring Rabbi who was the minister in charge.

The Rabbi, who was the Jewish Chaplain for the Edgware hospital where I was working at that time, and I often communicated regarding matters appertaining to various patients of our Faith. We were mostly concerned about the long-stay elderly who, for various reasons, had personal religious worries which needed to be addressed. We were, in addition, committed to bringing some aspect of our religion to them from the outside world. And so it was that every spring, at the time of the Jewish Festival of Passover, the Rabbi and his wife, (who took care of the cooking), and myself, were engulfed with plans to execute a Seder on the first or second evening of that special time. A Seder is the name given to a family gathering to re-enact the story of Passover; the time of the Hebrews' Exodus from Egypt after 400 years of being enslaved by the Pharaohs. It takes into account the story of the involvement of Moses and the crossing of the Red Sea to freedom.

Within the confines of that ritual it is the custom for the youngest child to ask, in a special format, four questions as to why and how the Exodus happened. At the hospital every year until I retired, Adam was the interlocutor on those evenings, and it was delivered in Hebrew with English translation. It was always an event to look forward to by us and especially those patients who so much appreciated it.

Adam and Simone would also come over to my ward on Christmas Day for tea. I would always arrange it so that my staff nurse, second in command, could be off-duty on that auspicious holiday. She was a mum with young children. As a matter of fact 25th December was Adam's birthday. Two of my children were born on that day – Marian was as well. And so Adam would don a white beard and an appropriate Santa Claus red hat, and wearing my nurses navy cape on its red reverse side he would saunter in with a: "Yo-Ho-Ho" and distribute the small gifts that children had donated their pocket money to buy. Everyone, my patients, and we three, had a great afternoon and a lovely slice of Christmas cake to partake of, as a bonus.

Myrtle, aged 54. At daughter Marian's wedding with son, Adam, and daughters Sheila, Diane and Simone

The Tragedy of Slapton Sands

Operation 'Tiger' had been the code name for a series of realistic rehearsals for the Normandy landings. The two exercises, which I am reporting, occurred on the beaches of the towns of Slapton Sands and Lyme Bay, both in South Devon, on the coast of the English Channel. Lack of communication resulted in 'friendly fire', (such is the name, I do not know what can be less 'friendly'), which resulted in the loss of the lives of fit young men in their prime of life, on the 27th April 1944. Slapton Sands was the chosen area due to its similar terrain to that of Utah beach, the planned target for the American landings, in France, a few months later. 30,000 United States troops prepared for the mock assault from Royal Navy ships. The friendly fire incident was enacted early in the morning of that day. It was arranged that the use of live ammunition would acclimatize those taking part to the sounds and sights, and even the smell, of battle. Obviously the firing would be high over heads. Custodians were stationed on the beach to make sure that safety precautions were in place. But a naval officer, for reasons I do not know, altered the firing time and this was not relayed to those on the shore. When the troops disembarked, the firing began, and the miscommunication was responsible for the death of hundreds.

The Battle of Lyme Bay took place one day later, on April 28th. A calamity arose of a similar nature but not quite identical. A convoy of 'follow-up' ships, carrying American soldiers, was attacked by nine German E Boats, 'Schnellboot', translated as 'fast boat' in English. They should have been designated D boats, for the devilish nature by which they could spew out death and destruction. The British ships took their share of loss, but the American toll was horrendous. The men drowned in the cold water of that sea, whilst awaiting rescue. Some, so untrained in the art of shipboard regime that they put on the lifebelts incorrectly, had no chance of survival when they leapt overboard. In total, the casualty count of both days was more than one thousand, who died for nothing.

The affair was covered up by the British and American Governments for years, and even now, they are anxious for not too much publicity. There is little documentation, and survivors were sworn to secrecy. To hide the truth, the casualty numbers were concealed, and added to those who succumbed in Normandy. There are countless unmarked graves in the fields of that English county. No efforts, by either of their governments, were put forward to recover their remains, or to install a memorial to those brave, ill-used men. In the 1970s, a Devonian beach comber discovered washed-up evidence on the shore.

In 1974 he purchased, from the United States government, the rights to a submerged Sherman tank, and with the help of local friends and a diving group, the tank was recovered, with the local authorities providing a plinth on the seafront. A memorial was finally installed, and tells that sorry tale. A replica was also erected to honour the fallen of Operation Tiger, at Fort Rodman Park in New Bedford, Massachusetts; and a third plaque, placed there in 2012, can be seen on a wall of a former German anti-aircraft bunker on Utah beach.

I have wandered over those sands of Slapton, and I have stood and wept by that memorial, meditating on the catalogue of catastrophic events that overtakes normal, sane, decent humanity.

* * *

Let the Children Go

As I have already mentioned at the beginning of this book, on the night of 9th–10th November 1938, 'Kristallnacht' took place in Germany, when synagogues, Jewish shops, schools and homes were vandalized. A hundred Jewish people were beaten and died. Old men were forced to scrub street pavements with tooth brushes. As an aftermath to that terrible night, thirty thousand were rounded up and sent to concentration camps. From 1935 to 1945, six million people of the Jewish Faith were murdered.

Shortly after the event of Kristallnacht, a delegation of British, Jewish, and Quaker leaders appealed in person to Prime Minister Chamberlain, to seek a permit to bring into this country unaccompanied children from areas now becoming increasingly vulnerable to the German atrocities. The British Colonial Office had already refused an appeal by Jewish refugee agencies, to allow children entry to British controlled Palestine. On the 21st November 1938, a day prior to a parliamentary debate to decide on this issue, Secretary of State for Air, Samuel Hoare, met a non-denominational group representing refugee organizations – 'The Movement for the Care of Children in Germany'. They promised to find homes for the children and to provide funds, thereby relieving the tax-paying public of the financial burden. In addition, every child would have a guarantee of £50 for his or her re-emigration, as it was expected that the children would only be temporary residents.

Within a very short time, that association sent representatives to establish the best, and quickest, route to initiate the programme. On 25th November 1938, the BBC broadcast an appeal for foster homes, and almost immediately 500 offers were on the table. No messing, when it comes to British help and generosity. Volunteers began a vetting campaign to ensure that the fostering conditions were safe. They felt it was in order to place Jewish children in Gentile homes. They did not probe into the character of the family, or their motives. If the house looked clean, and the family appeared respectful, it was enough.

In Germany, the volunteers worked tirelessly to list those children most at risk, teenagers who were in danger of arrest and others threatened with deportation, or those who had already lost a parent to a camp; and children from Jewish orphanages.

Once the listing was complete, parents or guardians were issued with a travel date and departure details. The children were each allowed to take one small sealed suitcase, with no valuables, and a few German marks for emergency expenditure. They were all issued with a numbered manila tag giving their name. Their credentials were as follows: "This document of identity is issued by the approval of His Majesty's Government in the United Kingdom, to a young person to be admitted to the United Kingdom, for educational purposes, under the care of the Inter-Aid Commission for Children. This document requires no visa". And it concluded with the name, gender, date and place of birth of the child, and full names and addresses of the parents.

The first 'Kindertransport' of 196 children left Berlin on the 1st December 1938. Most of them had lived in the Jewish orphanage of that city, which had been deliberately destroyed by fire weeks earlier. They arrived in the port of Harwich on December 2nd just three weeks after Kristallnacht. Just goes to show you, if the will is there, it can be done.

In the following nine months, 10,000 unaccompanied minors travelled to England as part of the scheme. In March 1939, when Czechoslovakia was annexed by Germany, transportation from Prague was hastily put into place, and achieved. It continued from out of Nazi-occupied Europe until the declaration of war in September 1939. The very last group left Holland with 74 children, on a passenger freighter in May 1940. It was the very last boat to freely leave that land until the end of the war. It was organized by a Dutch lady, Geertruida Wijsmuller-Meijer, who had arranged the first transport from Vienna in December 1938, and who had been active in this field since 1933, the year of Hitler's Chancellorship.

With a grudging compliance by the Germans, all the Kindertransports travelled by train to the Netherlands, leaving from the Hook of Holland, near Rotterdam; crossing the North Sea to Harwich; and on from there by train, to Liverpool Street Station, London. Here they were met by their new foster parents. Those with no pre-arranged foster families were sheltered in temporary holding centres at vacated summer camps, such as Dovercourt, a small seaside town in Essex, near Harwich, and Pakefield, a suburb of Lowestoft, in Suffolk. Between 1939 and 1940, 160 children without foster care, were sent to the Whittingehame Farm School in East Lothian, Scotland. It was the family estate and home of the late British Prime Minister Arthur Balfour.

Many Jewish children were left behind in occupied Europe. Ultimately they perished at the hands of the Nazis and their collaborators. Those who found a safe haven here in Britain were indeed the lucky ones. There were some children still not with private families. Ten thousand arriving here was, you will agree, a bit of an upheaval, and required a lot of reshuffling around. Those youngsters were still not in permanent places. Jewish Youth movements stepped in, and resolved the problem. They were instrumental in the running of country hostels, where these unplaced children found succour. The hostels evolved into centres of study, of secular and religious scholarship, as well as providing a home environment. The hostels were originally large family mansions that were made available by their owners, and funded by Jewish social and charitable sources, with a little bit of help from the British purse. They were run on a communal regime. Many of the older children maintained the farm, and they grew their own agricultural needs. They conversed in German, Polish, Czech, Yiddish, and Hebrew, and of course in English. Heck, well they all had a good opportunity to learn a foreign language!

At the end of the war, difficulties arose as Kindertransport children hoped to be reunited with their left-behind natural families. Agencies were flooded with claims from youngsters seeking to locate their parents, or any surviving family members. Some were able to do so, often travelling to far off countries, where a loved one had managed to escape to a safe haven. Most of the children were not so fortunate and learnt to mourn.

During the war years the older children made a considerable contribution to the British war effort. They served in the Armed Forces, the nursing profession, in food production, and war-related industries. Those who had nothing to go back to in their original homeland, stayed and resigned themselves to a new life. As adults they melded into the British community, and took their share in the responsibility in the rebuilding of a post-war era. They were involved with industry and commerce in education and the sciences, and the arts. They held positions in defence and welfare, and all manner of development programmes in their country of adoption.

* * *

The British Schindler

If you are a commuter, and you pass through the railway terminus of Liverpool Street station in London, or if on a fine day, you find yourself roaming round on the city streets, stop awhile and look upon that bronze just outside the station. You will never see its like, unless you travel to Vienna or Gadansk Glowny in Poland, or to Berlin, or even Prague, because at all of these above mentioned places, you will find a similar memorial. I am referring to the statue commemorating the Kindertransport. Go and see the London representation. Give yourself a treat. I go often. I never tire of it. It is unique in this country and was the first of its kind. The inspiration was later copied by the others that I have mentioned, and you don't need air miles. Our London model was unveiled by Sir Nicholas Winton in 2006.

I am certain that this gentleman's name needs no clarification from me, but how can I tell the story of the Kindertransport and not mention this illustrious person? Just before Christmas 1938, a 28 year-old British stockbroker was on his way to Switzerland, for a planned skiing holiday. He was diverted to Prague to help a friend who was involved in Refugee relief work. He became involved, and instead of whizzing down the slopes, he sat in a hotel room and set up an office on a table, to solve the problem of Jewish children caught up in the tragedy of calamitous German anti-Semitic repercussions in continental Europe. Isolated parentless children needed help, and Mr Winton was determined to arrange it. And he did – this man, born Nicholas George Wertheim, of German Jewish extraction. His parents changed their name to Winton, and they baptised their son in line with their integration ideal. They had arrived in Britain a few years before 1914, and I think that this worldly intelligent pair were aware that a war with Germany was brewing, and they acted accordingly by changing their name to something more British-sounding.

Nicholas was a humanitarian, and he succeeded in saving the lives of 669 children in a matter of 3 weeks. This became known as the Czech Kindertransport.

He arranged the travel, and he sought British homes for those poor friendless youngsters.

The story lay hidden for 40 years. His wife unearthed an account from its hiding place. It listed the name of every child and the families who had fostered them. When it finally saw the light of day, he was dubbed 'The British Schindler' by the press. I can vouch that all my readers know of the original Mr Schindler, (made famous by the film 'Schindler's List'), as the rescuer of many. Nicholas Winton received accolades. He was knighted, and awarded other honours. He said that he had approached President Roosevelt, and appealed to him to offer asylum to these children in need of it. Mr Roosevelt refused. Mr Winton added that 2,000 more could have been saved in America. Instead they were murdered at the hands of the Nazis. The last group of 250 children was preparing to leave Prague on the 1st September 1939, the day that Hitler's hoards marched into Poland. They were unable to depart and their fate was sealed. Only Sweden and Britain were saviours. They opened their hearts and their borders.

Before Sir Nicholas peacefully died in 2015, aged 106, he was interviewed by Stephen Sackur of the BBC. He said that he had become disillusioned with religion during the war. In which, by the way, he served in the capacity of Flight Lieutenant, in the RAF. He went on to tell Mr Sackur that he was not able to reconcile the fact that religious movements prayed for victory on both sides of the same war. He described his personal belief: "I believe in ethics, and if everyone did the same, we would have no problems at all. That's the only way out."

Kindertransport Memorial at Liverpool Street Station. With great-grandsons Matthew (13) and Jonathan (10)

In America, there existed an organization, 'One Thousand Children' (OTC). Its aim was similar to that of the European Kindertransport, but much less efficiently run, much smaller, and not as ambitious. It arranged for 1,400 unaccompanied children, between the ages of 14 months to 16 year-old teenagers, to travel to America. The OTC received no help from the US Government regarding entry, and efforts were deliberately hindered. A Bill was put forward to Congress for admittance, but it was rejected, and it failed to get Congress approval. They should have had a Nicholas Winton in their ranks!

* * *

Paying Tribute to Heroes

If you can find time on a fine day to stroll along White Hall, Westminster, in London, there are many very fine erections, in granite and bronze, depicting events and people of war-time years. I myself am particularly partial to quite a recent edition: of a group of women, from all the different branches in which they served, including my lot, The Women's Land Army. Well I would be; wouldn't I? Frankly, if you stopped to survey each monument, you would need to take a lunch break half-way along.

There is one I would especially recommend to be looked at, in Horse Guards Avenue, outside the Ministry of Defence building. It is an excellent facsimile of a Gurkha Warrior. I discovered it quite by accident, and as is my wont, I thought about that branch of the Services on the tedious journey homeward. London Transport buses ain't so frequent on a Sunday; and I read about that branch of the Service over tea when I finally arrived home. I have a veritable library, and can always pinpoint what I seek.

The dedicated lads from Nepal offered and gave service, and often their lives, to the British Army, in independent units or co-partnering their likewise brothers from India. They had a reputation for their fearless military prowess. A former Indian Army Chief of Staff once said: "If a man says he is not afraid of dying he is either a liar, or a Gurkha". A total of 250,280 Gurkhas served in an active capacity, in addition to training and garrison duties. They fought in almost every area of combat: in North Africa, Italy, Greece; and against the Japanese in the jungles of Burma; in North East India and in Singapore. Wow! They earnt their army rations.

Bravery and courage shone through their ranks, and they were the recipients of 3,000 awards, but their suffering amounted to the loss of 32,000 of their comrades.

In Remembrance

'Armistice Day', as it was once known, was originally conceived soon after the Great War. It was first acknowledged in 1919, when on the 11th November, at 11am, (the exact anniversary of the end of those contentious and bloody four years), the opportunity was made available to remember those who had fallen, those of the British and Commonwealth, who gave their lives. Commemoration services and parades took place at the hundreds of newly-erected memorial cenotaphs to be found in towns and villages throughout the land. The kith and kin here at home were able to recognize the names of their lost ones, set in stone. A silence was observed and poppy wreaths were laid, in remembrance and in farewell.

It was after the end of the Second World War in 1945, that Armistice Day became 'Remembrance Day' to include those who were lost in that second tragic epic which bears that title. Each year at 11am on the second Sunday in November, men and women who sacrificed their lives defending Britain and British values during the two World Wars and later conflicts are remembered.

As a child in school on two days every year at a special assembly in the school hall we would stand in front of a draped Union Jack standard. I say on two days. The first was to observe the ritual of remembrance, on Armistice Day; and the second was on the 23rd of April, St. George's Day. We would proudly declare allegiance, sing patriotic songs and a rendition of the National Anthem. It gave us children an enormous sense of pride, as young as we were, to stand before our flag and salute it in song. It was an emotional privilege to take part in those simple ceremonies, especially as we returned back to our classrooms marching to the music provided by a teacher playing us out with 'Land of Hope and Glory' on the old school piano. Perhaps we should revive this tradition today.

* * *

From the Tricorn to the Slouch

Over the years, I have made a particular effort to attend The Festival of Remembrance programmes, presented to the public on the eve of Remembrance Sunday every November. I went to them at the Royal Albert Hall when I lived in London years ago, and to those that took place in Cardiff when I resided in the Principality. The set-up is the same; the difference being when I proudly stood to sing the Welsh National Anthem – 'Cymru Am Byth' ('Wales Forever' or 'Long Live Wales').

I am, and will always feel, privileged to have those emotional ties.

So how does this tie up with the Gurkhas? I had better continue before I decide to buy a railway ticket and head off for 'The Land of My Fathers', as Wales is affectionately known. But that's a misnomer anyway; my Daddy was born and bred in the poorest part of London. But that phrase does apply to my two eldest daughters. Their Dad was born in Cardiff, as were they. True blue 'Welshies', but well, it should be green, white and red with a dragon to boot.

The Remembrance programme starts with a 'march in' of representatives of the British Legion, bearing aloft their individual Standards. They are followed by units of today's serving Forces and appropriate civilian groups: St. John's Ambulance; the WVS (Women's Voluntary Service); and the like, all to the accompanying stirring music of a military band. Following on in procession, come the entrance of invited serving personnel of other countries; from the Commonwealth and sometimes from France or the United States. A rousing cheer from the audience, greets 'The Boys of the Old Brigade', with the signature tune of the Chelsea Pensioners, played in slow march time, known as 'Old Contemptable'. The scarlet-uniformed 80 and 90 year-old veterans, in their black tricorne hats, and now, since the last few years, ladies too come from their home in the Royal Chelsea Hospital, London, an institution originated by King Charles ll in 1682, as a retirement home for ex-British army personnel.

Which brings me to the main reason for a run-down of this annual event: last of all, the Gurkhas, sporting their slouch hats, enter the auditorium, and the theatre vibrates in an almighty cheer and a standing ovation. It is an experience to tingle the hairs on the back of your neck! The programme ends with a two-minute silence, to honour and remember the fallen of war, and a showering of poppies from above.

I am not so good on my pins now and I do not go to these events any longer, but every year without fail, I switch on my TV set extra early, and I watch it now, with just as much emotion as I have, year after year, in the past. I hope to be doing it for a long time yet. I just love it!

* * *

From Flanders Fields

There is a history and a reason why poppies are the special flower associated with remembrance of the two World Wars. In the First World War, areas in Northern

France and Belgium were devastated and lay bare. The abundant landscape as it was once, became a ravished wilderness of mud and craters during the cataclysm of the Great War. The birds did not sing and the trees were broken and burnt, but every year the poppy flowered. It brought comfort and hope to all of those men who fought in that quagmire.

A serving Canadian doctor, Major John McCrae, was profoundly moved by the miracle of the annual flowering; the red blossom was in direct contrast to the flow of red blood seeping from the men he was there to care for. He was a man inspired, and he wrote the poem 'In Flanders Fields'. Today, a century after that conflict, that poem is still intoned on remembrance occasions, as moving to the emotions as it ever was. The doctor died in France soon after he had written it. It was picked up and published by a London magazine and it bought to public awareness the true environment of the battlefields.

After the war, with so many ex-servicemen who had suffered wounds or returned home unharmed, all in need of support, a way was triggered for their succour. An American teacher, Moina Belle Michael, together with a Frenchwoman, Anna Guérin, was greatly impressed by the poem and they sold poppies to raise funds. The Poppy remains the symbol of the Great War and that of the war which followed it twenty-one years afterwards.

I can recall two incidents that conjoin my spirit with the Poppy. I have already brought to light that I have toured the battlefields in those locations. The first impact when I arrived, was the sight of that genre of the flower family. I was taken aback. All of my self-taught education concerning the First World War rose to the surface. I was struck dumb, and rendered immobile. The sight of the growing poppies was unexpected and affected my senses. I will never ever forget it.

The second sighting was comparatively recent, (well two years ago in 2014), when I went to the Tower of London to gaze upon the 'River of Poppies' flowing from its ancient walls. I am sure that many of my readers were also witnesses to that scene. Again, as before, my emotions were overtaken by that unforgettable sight.

* * *

Canada in Yorkshire

I have a much-loved granddaughter, Alison. She lives in Harrogate, North Yorkshire. I was not aware until quite recently, (when I happened to come across an article), that in a cemetery near that town, two-thirds of its 1,000 plus graves are the resting places for Royal Canadian Airmen. It cited that many had died in the military wing of the Harrogate Hospital.

The piece was a report of that year's annual memorial service at the cemetery. I surmise that those buried there were of Bomber Command, returning home broken in body, and maybe, of mind. Or perhaps they were victims of the Germans, when covering Allied ships in the Battle of the Atlantic. Harrogate is situated in the north west of the UK, not too far from the coast that borders the Atlantic Ocean. So it was deemed to be sensible to site airfields and personnel quartering in that sector. It was the Royal Canadian Airforce who took up the challenge to monitor and keep safe the lifeline shipping convoys.

This area of Yorkshire gave hospitality to many Air Force bases, predominately those of the Canadian Royal Air Force (CRAF). Many of those who rest there were victims of German anti-aircraft fire, or from the machine-gun bullets of German fighter aircraft. The CRAF had flown over enemy land, and some had arrived back in planes still able to fly home from a bombing sortie, bringing their injured, and perhaps already dead men with it. And some died in training accidents.

I visit Harrogate often. I find its atmosphere pleasant, and I always look forward to my trips 'oop north'. For me, it is a double whammy, because it is always a treat to see Alison and her husband. Furthermore, I am in receipt of free board and lodging – and no hotel bill to settle. As soon as I perused that report, off I toddled to Kings Cross Station, London, and in next to no time I was in Harrogate.

I went to the Stonefall Cemetery, and as one always expects, it was never disappointing. The Commonwealth Graves Commission has made sure that this plot is beautifully maintained, in pristine condition, as they are everywhere. Not just here in Britain, but in every country in the world, wherever the need has arisen.

I was able to discover quite a lot of interesting data, which mingled with the sense of sadness and homage, which always overcomes me in the presence of the war dead. I did feel a sense of satisfaction that I had discovered yet another spur to gratify my insight into that era of time.

There is one particular story that I was able to elucidate which took me to a particular spot to verify. On one fateful evening a Wellington Bomber, after its four hour training flight, attempted to land through low cloud, and crashed into a hillside.

The crew were all killed. The aircraft remains were quickly removed, but the broken and burnt trees bore witness to that tragedy. As I stood there, I felt myself transported back to that time, and could feel the pain of those back across the sea in Canada, awaiting the return of loved ones, who did not come home.

* * *

The Righteous Smiths

I have recently found, from amongst the piles of papers and stuff unearthed from the depths of my very untidy and disorganized home contents, a leaflet relating to a visit I made to a venue in Loxton, Nottinghamshire. Immediately I was remembering how that excursion affected me, and I feel that I must unburden my memories of it onto paper.

I am referring to an organization, set up by the Smiths in 1995. A Christian family; mother Marina, and her two sons, Stephen and James.

They had visited the Yad Vashem Holocaust memorial in Jerusalem in 1991, and it had changed the way they understood the history of the Holocaust. Their father had served in a clerical capacity in the Church, and even at a very young age, the boys had been extremely interested in theology, and the relationship between the Abrahamic religions, Christianity and Judaism. One of the brothers took the subject as his study at university. It was a particular anathema to them, and they had deep feelings of regret that they had been deprived of some knowledge of the Holocaust. It had not been a curriculum subject in their early education.

Their visit to Yad Vashem remodelled their lives. It gave them the impetus to dedicate their time, energy and resources, to enlighten people of the importance of education and meaningful understanding, and to learn from it. Their aim was to teach that the Holocaust was not just a Jewish story. It should be seen as a stark lesson for all mankind and humanity to learn from.

The Smith family resided in a farmhouse in rural Nottinghamshire. Together with alterations and additions to the structure, they created the only dedicated Holocaust museum and education centre in the United Kingdom. They named it 'The Beth Shalom' ('House of Peace') Holocaust Centre. It has many facets to its purpose. One young member of our Royal Family was enlightened there after an incident when he publically appeared wearing a Nazi costume.

I went there for different reasons. I had heard of the centre, and I wanted to have a 'look see'. It was a very busy day with a full programme of events when I paid my visit to the Centre. It was just as well that I took an early train. It coincided with a school visit, of about 20 year 8 primary school children; a nice well-behaved bunch, seemingly so interested in what they were looking at and listening to. They especially liked the Journey Exhibition, providing a stimulating experience through the eyes of a young German lad, telling his story of how it was to be a Jewish child in 1938, living in Germany. I bypassed the regular visitor order of 'looking-seeing'; I was so taken up with these youngsters, musing on those of my own clan. I took a break for some quiet reflection, and a breath of fresh air in the beautiful landscaped Memorial Gardens, which sets the scene for its rose section. It gives one an opportunity to dedicate a rose; to commemorate a loved one lost to the gas chambers and crematoria. None of my family perished in that apocalypse, but that did not lighten the load of my own heart-ache as I thought of those who did.

One has the opportunity to partake of refreshments at this establishment, which I did indulge in, after which, I was held spellbound listening to a survivor's story, spoken first hand. It did not add a great deal to that which I already knew, but it impressed me greatly to bear witness to the fervour, and eloquence, and emotional input, of the speaker, and I noticed that I was not the only listener dabbing my eyes with a tissue. I wandered around The Holocaust Exhibition, which provides an insight into the historical events of that time. It is supported by artefacts, oral history, and archive footage. Due to some graphic images this exhibition is certainly not suitable for young visitors, and I was pleased to notice that it was well advertised as such.

Placed in its own museum collection and research area are a variety of articles on display, which provide a tangible link to the Holocaust events, and I expect that it will be a legacy for the future. I understood from a curator of the establishment, that they are in possession of many more, not on display, but which could be viewed by appointment. I rounded-off my visit by another refreshment break. They employ a thoughtful squad of organizers, who were more than willing to answer questions. Everything at that venue is so well presented, and a thoughtful understanding for their visitors was obvious. The printed poster menu, and prominently placed notices inform the public that they do not maintain a kosher kitchen. Well I imbibed cheese, not ham, so I was covered.

There were just two more areas of interest left for me to see. They maintain a Children's Memorial Garden, where thousands of visitors have placed stones in memory of the murdered children, in those dark catastrophic days under Hitler's regime of genocide. The Garden of Stones changes each day as more stones are placed in situ. Each and every stone, is put there because someone wants to remember, be it by a Jewish person or a Muslim, or one of the Christian or Hindu faith or of any other, be it another religion or an atheist; or just a person who is dedicated to the good of the world and all who dwell in it.

As is my custom, I always end my visit in the shop. Well it's compulsory unless you intend to take up residency; it's where the EXIT indicator is visible. I purchased a small souvenir and engaged myself in conversation with one or two of the assistants. They were very polite and knowledgeable, and willing to chat. That went down very nicely; I do tend to be somewhat garrulous.

That small item, a reminder of my day, is housed in a cabinet that is the home to many such treasured bits and pieces of my wanderings. When I have the time to have a quick browse, I handle that item, a replica stone, to recall the Stone Garden, lovingly, and with fond recollections of that day and that place.

* * *

Overlord Embroidery

On the 5th June 1994, I took a day off from my household chores and took a train to Hampshire, in the south of England. I had a special reason for doing so. The town of Southsea boasts a museum dedicated to the D Day landings on Normandy, 49 years and 364 days earlier. Well yes, it was one day short of the fiftieth anniversary.

The museum houses an extraordinary item, which was commissioned specifically for it. I should think that the idea was mooted by thoughts of the Bayeux Tapestry in Normandy. If you ever have the opportunity to look at that original, magnificent artwork, take it. I once did, and being an art and crafty person myself, I will never forget it.

And so I went to Southsea to satisfy my curiosity, and I did indeed stand and stare at this wonderful embroidery. The 'Overlord Embroidery', as it is called, is dedicated to the Service personnel who pledged themselves to a great cause, and that formidable quest. But there was a bit more to it than that. I was one among many thousands;

members of the public who witnessed a commemoration attended by the Queen, and at that time, the United States President, Bill Clinton, on Southsea Common. That too was something to remember.

* * *

A Missed Appointment

I am typing this on the 15th of the month of April. I have just listened to the news. I have been informed that on this day, 75 years ago, the Northern Ireland city of Belfast was devastated by German aerial bombardment, of the most diabolical kind. Hundreds of Luftwaffe bombers let fall their deadly cargo of high explosive bombs. It was the worst raid ever over the United Kingdom, apart from sometimes the Blitz in London.

In their wisdom, or rather lack of it, the local chiefs had considered the unlikelihood of a raid on their city. How much in error they were. Air-raid defences were almost non-existent. The Germans, without adequate deterrent, had a clear run. There were no searchlights or night-fighter cover, and only a fraction of tiny anti-aircraft capacity in operation. The government lacked the will, and energy, to deal with a major crisis of this magnitude. Specific targets were the military enclaves, manufacturing and the shipbuilding yards.

Belfast was a city with the highest population density, and the lowest proportion of air raid shelters. An earlier German reconnaissance over-fly reported it was the least defended city in the United Kingdom. So 'easy-peasy' here we go! The Victoria Barracks, housing military families, took a direct hit. That raid was one of four, in a very short time sequence. In the raid of the 15th April 1941, 900 perished and 1,500 were seriously injured. I have never visited that metropolis, and I was extremely distressed when I became aware of the tragedy. So why, you may ask, do I portray this interest?

When I lived in Laleham, and the Davies were my hosts, I returned from a hot day in the fields, late one afternoon; hot, dirty, and dishevelled. An unexpected visitor awaited me. It was a young fair-haired soldier I had recently met. Davey was his name, and his home was across the Irish Sea, in Belfast. I was blushingly embarrassed. Firstly, because of my unsightly appearance, but predominately because when Mrs Davies opened the front door to this unexpected visitor he announced his name.

So you may wonder why all the tizzy? Well, the Davies were not young, and their outlook veered towards non-modernity. They had only one son, and no daughter. Believe me they kept a beady eye on their female lodger, and I well and truly kept to the 'straight and narrer'. I was in some very minor relationship with a fella, and the Davies knew this. When I returned to Laleham the previous weekend from home, they were interested in my news, and I said that, (keeping my fingers crossed surreptitiously because I told them a fib), that I had met a friend, Harriet. When the front door opened for me, I was informed that 'Harriet' had come to call. Oh my! I was in the dog house!

Well, he and I thought it a bit of a giggle, and after a pleasant hour or two, we made arrangements to meet up again. We did not, because on his part it was 'no show' time. Maybe he had met someone better-looking than me. I was not terribly put out, but I did wonder why. Shortly afterwards, I received an apologetic note explaining that he had gone home to Belfast on compassionate leave. His mother and father had been killed in a raid whilst at home, and the wife of his brother who was serving abroad, and their two small children living in family quarters in the ill-fated barracks, had also died. I never knew these people but I was profoundly shocked as I read his letter.

When I listened to the news that morning 75 years later, I experienced a lightning flashback. All those years ago, when I was a flighty young miss and the world was my oyster, I did not ever think that one day as an old lady, I would be retelling this sad little tale.

* * *

A Double First

I must have been in my sixties when I nervously experienced my first aircraft flight. I decided with trepidation that I would give it a go, but I would need to limit flying time. I had never been to the Channel Islands, and as the 'ETA' was only 30 minutes after take-off, I reckoned that it would just about suit me. To add to my adventure, I had arranged a hire car, also breaking into my 'firsts'. I was delighted when I arrived. The sun shone; my hotel was fine; I found that the car was not difficult to handle; I enjoyed the delicious Jersey tomatoes; and I found the Jersey Zoo interesting. But there was much more connecting me to those Islands. I wanted to find out what it was like to live there, under German occupation, which they did for five years.

I did have one contact – a sort of distant relative through marriage, who was in residence, and I did accept her warm hospitality on a few occasions during that fortnight. She had survived the German presence, and I learnt much, very much. She gave a blow-by-blow account, and I almost felt that I was living it myself. But even without that source, the evidence was there, and was easily detected.

When the Germans invaded the Channel Islands in June 1940, after the fall of France, the British were not very interested. News of the invasion was muted, and just a press-release was issued shortly after it took place. The Channel Islands were not defended. Mr Churchill was not very happy that the oldest possession of the Crown was just surrendered up. It was considered that the Islands were of no benefit to the Germans, except for propaganda purposes. It would boost the morale of those back home, to the 'Frauen und Herren', and cock a snook at the British. They also thought of its strategic position when Hitler's invasion was in progress. They had a fruitless wait.

* * *

Under Occupation

At first, the Germans played it using a very soft pedal, unlike their conquests on mainland Europe. As time went on, increasing hardships and shortages took their toll, and Germans resorted to a much less 'friendly' attitude. The Islanders took a passive and non-aggressive stand. One, Madeleine Bunting, said, paradoxically using Churchill's words: "They did not fight on the beaches, on the fields or on the streets. They did not commit suicide, or kill the enemy. They just settled down to a hard, but relatively peaceful life". In my opinion, it wasn't so clear cut. Life became tenuous and morale fell. Wirelesses were confiscated, and deportations increased. From a population of 66,000, four thousand were sentenced for breaking German-made laws, and 570 were sent to continental prisons, and the dreaded camps. Many never saw those Islands again. The Jewish count was small, just 30–50 people. Church of England devotees with one or two Jewish grandparents were classified as Jewish, and subjected, along with the others, to the German edict of hate. Their businesses were closed, and they were restricted to only one hour in twenty four to be outdoors.

Many Islanders attempted to escape, either to England or to France. One such event, undertaken by three teenage lads in a small boat, ended, not only in their death, but the German prohibition of ownership of all photographic equipment, and the use, by the Islanders, of all small vessels. Regular raids by Germans, searching for 'verboten' (forbidden) items, included many things of normal everyday use, and also song sheets of patriotic songs, which further alienated the people.

Slave labourers were imported from all places on the continent. Thousands of Soviets from the Ukraine; French Jews; Spaniards who had declared against Franco; were a few of the many. They numbered 16,000. They were force-marched, every day, to and from their place of work. They were subjected to open public beatings, and the Islanders, now realizing the full force of the German ideology, became inflamed by what they were witnessing. Deportations in 1942 sparked the first mass British patriotic demonstration.

The slave labourers, in their wretched state, built facilities in some instances, where millions of tons of stone were needed to be hewn from bedrock. Roads, coastal pathways, gun emplacements and bunkers were built. Railways were laid to supply the German coastal defence forces, and deep and long tunnels were dug, to name but a few of the many assignments that were executed. They strengthened the so-called project of the 'Atlantic Wall' to such an extent, that it was said to be better defended than the Normandy coast. The Atlantic Wall was an extensive system of defences along the coast of continental Europe and Scandinavia. It was built to defend those areas against an Allied invasion. Hitler himself issued the order for its beginning and completion.

Those to be pitied victims, constructed four camps in Alderney; two to house themselves, and two that were used as concentration camps for Jews and Polish prisoners of war. During their internment, 700 of the camp dwellers died from the obvious-overwork, starvation and disease. I guess some welcomed death as a happy release. If you visit Alderney as I did, you will see that the island is still displaying those slave-labour erected monsters. If you raise your eyes to see them, it is almost that they too, are in an attitude of supplication: "Please, never again".

And the Islanders, as time went on, became more and more dissatisfied and restless. In 1943, a Royal Navy ship was sunk in the English Channel, and twenty one bodies were washed up in Guernsey. The Germans buried the British sailors with full military honours, and the funerals became a focal point for the Islanders to demonstrate their loyalty to Britain. Five thousand people attended; nearly one thousand wreaths were laid. That was it. Subsequent affairs of that nature were closed to the public, by order of the High Command, on the pain of death if disobeyed.

The Germans minted new coinage; well at least, new banknotes. Coins were being taken by the soldiers as souvenirs. New postage stamps were issued; both of these commodities bearing the German mark of Channel Island ownership. They were fretful of a sexually-transmitted disease epidemic taking hold of their men. They set up brothels and imported French prostitutes. Some female Islanders fraternized – they were nick-named 'Jerry-Bags', and 800 to 900 children were born to German fathers.

* * *

I Was There

Naturally, before I left that fortnight's sojourn, I did the tourist rounds. There was a plethora of places to 'look see'. In Jersey, I arrived at Noirmont, the site of a huge defensive wall, now sanctified as a memorial to all Jersey men who perished in the war. At la Hougue Bie, in an underground slave-labour dugout tunnel, one can only guess at how those so unfortunates lived. No not lived, they barely existed. The exhibition that portrays that time, and the slave workers, is a feature not to be missed. One can hardly think of it, it is a vision of hell, and I for one will never forget what I looked at, or how I felt. The shame that such brutality and inhumanity could have breathed in the same air from the same atmosphere that I did, not too many hundreds of miles away in England, at the same moment in time. I went to the underground hospital. I tried to make comparisons with the hospital in which I was employed during my working life here in London. Of course I could not. The institutions were there for the same reason, but they served a very different clientele. I completed my rambling around in Liberation Square. I understand that in 1995, an exciting sculpture was erected in the form of a monumental sundial. I was there in the 1980's, so it was a bit before my time. I will have to take that journey again.

In the course of a search for interesting sites to see, one cannot miss the myriad number of wall plaques, dotted here, there, and everywhere. They commemorate the heroes and the heroines. Those who died and those who survived. Those who remained and those who left. They detailed dates and places, and how many or how few. I was half expecting to read one: "Myrtle Russell was 'ere. Hope you had an enjoyable visit love, and that you found what you were looking for". I did on both counts.

* * *

The Republic of Ireland - A Story of Two Halves

Fighting did not materialize on the soil of the Republic of Ireland, but involved they were. Eire was not a strategic goal for German military aggression. Germany had planned a military operation, but it was for a divisionary device and not an expression of intent to conquer the Republic. Germany was more interested in keeping Eire neutral and using it as a tool to constantly worry and chip away at the British.

It began well before September 1st 1939. In 1922 Mr Churchill, in his capacity as the Colonial and Dominions Secretary, was responsible for dealing with the details of an Irish Settlement which the British government cabinet of those days, under the auspices of Prime Minister Henry Herbert Asquith, had devised. Churchill was dealing with the issue of the two Southern Irish ports, Queenstown and Berehaven, and the base in Lough Swilly. These ports were essential to Britain; they allowed supplies of food to be imported for our use and in naval defence. The Irish understood our need and were willing for them to be so utilized.

In 1938, fifteen months before the war declaration and after sixteen years of smooth running, negotiations were in place between the British Government under the leadership of Prime Minister Neville Chamberlain, and Mr Eamon de Valera, President of the Republic of Ireland. On the 25th April an agreement was signed whereby Great Britain renounced all rights of benefit from the two southern ports and the Lough Swilly base. The loss of these facilities were a drastic blow with the impending hostilities. The consequences were that there were no western ports for the refuelling of naval flotillas sailing the Atlantic; those vessels, hounding the German U-Boats, or baby-minding the convoys. It was also a dire turn of events which precluded the unloading of cargo-carrying ships bringing in food and supplies to a wartime Britain.

The Government of Nazi Germany, like all governments in war, relied on the art of intelligence gathering, and in 1938 they set up the organization known as the Abwehr (German Secret Service). Germans and Irishmen were active in the field. They collaborated and acted in unison both in the Republic and in Germany. Their aims were manifest, including co-ordinated missions with the anti-British Irish Republican Army (IRA). They set into motion communication links between the two countries and they directed military missions against British targets, especially naval establishments, and the reporting of incidental items of military interest.

In January 1939 the IRA declared war against Britain. In August 1939 they activated their 'S Plan', (Sabotage Plan), and with explosive devices swooped onto the towns of London, Manchester, Birmingham and Coventry, leaving the dead in their wake.

I had a wonderful three week holiday in Eire. I took the car and went across the Irish Sea. It was raining when I arrived at Rosslare. I B & B'd every night in a different place. I toured the country in a circular route. I kissed the Blarney Stone in Cork, although some might say it kissed me. I jaunted along the lanes in a jauntry cart and I stayed two days in Dublin, greatly impressed with the architecture and its gaily coloured house-front doors in some locales. I did an Irish event at their Jury's hotel, and I spent evenings in pubs with my feet a-tapping to the music of the local fiddlers. I 'circled' the Ring of Kerry and 'bantered about' in Bantry Bay. I drank Guinness with my breakfast: if it was not in a glass, it was an ingredient in whatever you ate. I counted the number of pubs and funeral parlours along one street, they were alternate premises. I 'dingled' in Dingle Bay and boated the River Shannon. I chatted to the counter assistant in a Cork post-office. I asked him what the rate of income tax was in the domain; he replied, "tirty tree and a turd"! Honest to goodness, he did. I brought home a lovely little clock from Waterford, a local product, and I dreamt every night of the myriad shades of green. It was uncanny, the sun shone from a blue sky, in Ireland! When I boarded the ferry to return to Milford Haven, it started to rain. Oh, I have forgotten to mention Tipperary; as I approached it, I stopped to read the sign, it informed me that I had come a long way. Yes indeed I had, I had come a very long, long way.

Tipperary, Ireland

Chapter 10
A Broader Perspective

A Directional Decision

I have come to a fork in the road in my efforts to submit this story of the war, and how it appeared to me, firstly as a young woman, and subsequently as a rather elderly one. The last pages of my written efforts reflect those differences.

It has probably been noticed that my latter reporting has not focused on a chronological order of events. This has been a deliberate ploy, and it did not happen accidentally. Whether it has been successful, it is for my readers to cast their opinion. I prefer to 'do things' differently, and to follow the conservative path does not inflame my passion.

The later pages of this book have brought to life my experiences, when doing 'my thing' in local areas. That is in London and further afield here in the United Kingdom. The war encompassed every country and nation on this earth, except the Arctic and Antarctic regions and some countries in South America, and I will attempt to embrace their entanglements in my journal.

A dilemma has arisen. Do I continue widening out from home to other places, which is perhaps circumspect, or should I begin where the war promoted its evidence, in faraway regions; and to gradually draw back to my starting point? Well, actually I have already decided, but I thought it respectful to offer my pre-thought resolve for your attention.

* * *

Prologue to Overlord

I am kicking off my gallivanting around the rest of the world with a debut into mainland Europe, and I am making an entrance with a flourish. The day is the 6th June 1944 and the location is Normandy. It was that date and location that ultimately led to the heart of Germany.

Crossing the English Channel for the purpose of invasion was first recorded as an event of that nature when the Roman Legionaries arrived in 431 AD.

William the Conqueror put in an appearance in 1066. The Dutch followed, bringing William of Orange to be King William 3rd in 1688, and that was the final count. The Spanish tried it in 1588 and Napoleon had a go in 1796. But we are not speaking Spanish or French. Hitler was waiting in the wings for his opportunity to have a crack at it and was somewhat put out by our RAF in 1940, so we are not conversing in his lingo either.

That day in June witnessed the largest seaborne landings in history. It led to the liberation of German-occupied north-west Europe, and it contributed in no small measure to the end of World War 2 and to ultimate victory. I hope to tell of incidents relating to the war that have perhaps not been as well publicized as the main facts, but is not always possible to do so. I will try in this instance. If one is hoping to present a full form of any picture or object, or articulate an account of a battle or even the exploits of an invading army, one needs a skeletal base on which to add the 'extra bits' to enhance it to give the whole thing its finishing touches so that it can be viewed as being complete. The skeleton is always standard; it's the 'extra bits' that give the whole its difference and originality. I hope that my narrative will throw light on what I am attempting to do on this particular day – D Day (as it was called), and on the occasion of all the other large scale military affairs. I have no regrets that my discourse drifts into a long and detailed account. It was, after all, one of the most important events of the war.

It is a fact that we do not learn the lesson; perhaps some small spark in the mind of a young person reading this might ignite into a flame that will bring to the fore the conception that war is bad, and should not be allowed to happen.

I intend to bring the Normandy invasion to life a year or two before it actually happened, and I would like to give a detailed account of D Day and to leave the rest safely in the knowledge of what I am sure you already know.

*　*　*

Where, Why and When?

As early as 1941, Mr Churchill and the other Allied leaders realized that the war could not end without an over-run of Europe's mainland and to achieve that we would need to invade its shores. Together with President Roosevelt, who Churchill frequently met, it was decided the code name 'Operation Overlord' would immortalise a future invasion.

Reliable and thorough planning was the key to the success of the operation. The enterprise required inspiration and imagination and I am certain that was achieved.

In May 1943, the Allied leaders convened a meeting in Washington – the Trident Conference. It was here that Prime Minister Churchill and the American President Roosevelt promised Joseph Stalin that a second front into France would be an eventuality within a year.

Studies were already in place and had gone forward in an ever expanding measure, taking into consideration every possible and conceivable facet. Where, why, how and when were the subjects of their meetings with all the commanders of the Forces. Mostly in their thoughts were previous failures when undertaking coastal raids in France and some insurgencies on the Atlantic coast of Norway. Later still, they remembered the discrepancies of reconnaissance giving rise to problems played out on the coast of North Africa. Prominent thought to maritime data was essential.

Mr Churchill decreed that the three arms of British military might must fight as one, and that the United Kingdom should be converted into an army camp launching the greatest coastal assault of all time. And new engines of war must be contrived and developed at whatever the cost. Top of the list to dwell on was where to land the invasion forces. There were several options. Holland, or the Belgium Coast, or at Calais or the Balkans; the South of France, Britany or Normandy? They weighed each one up very carefully. They could all notch-up pluses and minuses. Each one was considered under a set of different factors. Of these the principal considerations were the beaches; the weather; the tides; airfield sites; voyage mileage; accessible ports easily captured; the hinterland terrain for post invasion operations; enemy dispositions; their mine fields and their overall defences. My, they did have a marathon to sort out and woe betide anyone who got it wrong.

* * *

And the Winner is - Normandy

The choice narrowed down to Calais and Normandy.

It was decided Calais gave them the best air-cover but because it was the nearest point to England, the Germans would gauge it as being the obvious target, and had fortified it accordingly, but it did promise the shortest sea route – just 21 miles across the Channel.

It was taken into consideration, that in the event, the departure ports for Calais would be Dover and Folkestone, neither one having the capacity for a wholesale exit venue alone.

Normandy was the best hope. German defences were weaker, the beaches suitable and the nearby port of Cherbourg could be isolated and taken early on in the campaign. The hinterland favoured rapid deployment of large numbers and was sufficiently remote from the main strength of the enemy.

Although this area of the coast was implanted with concrete forts and pill boxes, there was no harbour to sustain a substantial German defence force in this 50 mile half-moon shape of sand. It was thought the Germans would not assemble a sizeable force to defend a position that they deemed only suitable for a low grade attack and not a full-blown invasion.

As far back as 1941, Mr Churchill knew exactly what was needed. He issued orders that troop-carrying landing craft were to be constructed with a side flap and a frontal drawbridge long enough to over reach the moorings of a pier. When the beach-heads were consolidated, piers were erected giving the facility for the unloading of men and supplies. His thoughts later moved on to the creation of a large area of sheltered water protected by a breakwater, based on old ships arriving under their own steam and sunk in position. It was the 'Grand-daddy' of the recycling innovation. Another break-water device was constructed of sunken concrete blocks. These were called 'Gooseberries'. Careful and innovative activity carried on unceasingly, and by August 1943 there were plans for a complete project for the manufacture, in two parts, of a full-scale temporary harbour. These synthetic structures were called 'Mulberries'. The construction would be executed in Britain and enormous masses of special equipment and material would be required, for example, a million tons of steel and concrete. The completed structure would be towed over by sea, liable to enemy attack, and subjected to the vagaries of the weather. But it worked and was on active service within a few days of the landings.

* * *

The Silly and the Sensible

Could we create a floating airstrip that was the brain-wave of a bod? Wow! That was a good idea. A base, for our aircraft to take off and land, on tap? So the notion was thought to be brilliant, and work began to bring it to fruition.

It was suggested that a structure of ice, large enough to serve as a runway, would be of ship-like construction, propelling itself at slow speed with its own Anti-aircraft defence, with workshops and repair facilities, and maintained by a small refrigeration plant for the preservation of its own existence. It was discovered that by adding a proportion of wood pulp in various forms, the ice becomes extremely tough. But, and there is always a 'but', it happened that as the ice sometimes melted in hot weather, the fibrous content quickly formed a furry outer surface which acted as an insulator and very speedily affected the melting rate so that the whole construction would become zero.

Another innovation was judged to be jolly a good idea. A pipe-line could be laid on the sea-bed to produce bubbles to calm wave action in high winds. Not surprisingly these two mad-cap ideas was well and truly submerged. If there are any motivated clever clogs out there, maybe those ideas can be resurrected in some sci-fi masterpiece on film.

Two conceptions did work, and both in their way contributed to the ultimate success of Overlord. Pluto was the code name for a sea-bed pipe line that kept fuel flowing directly from England. t alleviated the use of oil tanker surface ships, vulnerable targets for the enemy to aim for. There were other decoy devices, which I have described in the next piece.

* * *

Operation 'Now you see it - now you don't'

Operation 'Bodyguard' was the code name allotted to the plan of deception. It was an essential part of pre-invasion tactics. Its objective was to mislead the enemy concerning the date and site of an eventual landing and the strength of the forces that would be employed.

In 1944, a scheme was brought in to make the German think that the Allies were planning to win the war by extensive aerial bombardment, and that an invasion on mainland Europe would not be the route. A focus was put on the sudden escalation of the production of bomber fleets.

A fictitious British 4th Army saw a large gathering of troops in Scotland, giving rise to the assumption that Norway would be the way into Europe across the North Sea. This thought was supplemented by fake radio signals for the Germans to listen to.

A similar group in southern England led by the US General Patton, indicated that the route was to be to Calais. This inspired Rommel, a fan and admirer of the American General, into believing that Patton's pointer was the one to follow.

Operation 'Copperfield' was a decoy device just before D Day, aimed to mislead the German intelligence as to the movements of our General Montgomery, Commander in Chief of Allied Armies. A look-alike actor made public appearances in Gibraltar and North Africa. The Allies hoped that it would indicate a forthcoming invasion via the Mediterranean. Operation Bodyguard deceptions were implemented in so many guises. Double-agents were handing over misleading information. Allied intelligence was above par and from decrypted German radio transmissions, it confirmed that the German High Command believed what we were dishing out.

During the winter of 1943, the Allied leaders met twice, in Cairo and in Tehran, to decide on the strategy for the following year. That led the Germans to reckon that an invasion would not happen, when it was being discussed and planned as late as 1943. In their estimation, the assault would occur in 1945. So not to worry about it just yet. They thought that come the time, a small force would land on the Normandy beaches as a decoy. That being the case, the strengthening of the defences elsewhere was the German priority, whilst awaiting the actual site of an authentic invasion.

Visual deceptions were put into operation to give the Germans an opportunity to see for themselves. Dummy military hardware, manufactured in canvas and rubber, was stockpiled in places sign-posting the way across the Channel to Calais. Tanks and motorized vehicles, and in particular a large volume of landing craft, all caught the eye of the Luftwaffe reconnaissance planes.

The night before the invasion, a small group of the Special Air Services (SAS) operators deployed 500 dummy paratroopers over Le Havre. Each dummy had attached to it a noise-maker to stimulate rifle fire. They also carried a small explosive device timed to destroy the fakes which gave the appearance of a paratrooper burning its 'chute. This ruse led the Germans to believe this was a rehearsal and that the valid operation would follow at the same time in the same place. A squadron of the RAF dropped strips of window-metal foil to cause a radar return, which was mistakenly interpreted by the German radar operators as an approaching naval convoy. The illusion was further bolstered by a group of small boats towing barrage balloons. Ingenious!

Overall, Operation Bodyguard is regarded as a tactical success. It delayed the German Army positioned in the Calais area for seven weeks giving the Allies time to build up the beach-heads and ultimately marking the Normandy landings as a foothold to the main objective, victory. The foe did not expect Normandy to be the jumping off pad en-route to the Rhine. It was all due to Churchill's foresight and the brilliant minds of those who carried that mastermind planning forward.

* * *

Time and Tide Wait for No Man

A double enigma caused the planners to scratch their heads in consternation. One was the weather, and the other, the English Channel tidal system. The tides running against the Normandy coast have a play of more than twenty feet with responding scours along the beach. It was considered that the best timing for the landings would be between high and low tide with its flow incoming. This would offer the optimum visibility of the beach obstacles and those protruding from the water. It was imperative that the timing was impeccable. The weather is always erratic, and winds may whip up sharp play in a very few hours. Both of these problems needed detailed and precise study. It is not easy to predict uncertain conditions which can easily change, sometimes within minutes.

Only a few days in each month in the spring and summer of 1944 offered a favourable combination of tide, a full moon and hours of daylight, all of which was the necessary criteria to ensure a successful outcome. June 5th was the original day planned for this venture but meteorologists predicted inclement weather, and whilst the forecast was not much better for the next day, the timing would be satisfactory. It was thought that a delay of two weeks which would augur a similar conducive pattern, would entail the disbandment of all the forces ready to leave. They had been training and preparing for months on end and a let-down at the last minute would dilute their resolve. In that extra time lapse the Germans might twig what was going on. So far, the secret had been well hidden. It later transpired that a fortnight after the 6th of that month – on the 19th and 20th – delegated as the next two suitable days if the earlier planned dates had been postponed, a major storm battered the Normandy coast.

* * *

Time Off for the Boys

Allied air sorties over Germany had crippled the Luftwaffe. Rommel, in charge, was aware that he could not rely on air support. Germany could muster 815 planes to cover that vulnerable area. The Allies were credited with 10,000. Two weeks prior to D Day, air supremacy was vital to ensure the success of this pivotal project. To this end, the Allies undertook a bombing agenda entailing the targeting of German aircraft production, fuel supplies and airfields. It was a softening-up process. It was as if all the pieces of the jigsaw were finally emerging as a completed picture.

Allied control of the Atlantic had deprived German weather-watchers of reliable intelligence. Their Paris office predicted poor conditions on the few days before and after the 6th. Rommel estimated that it was not possible to execute a landing invasion and decided that it was a timely opportunity for some home leave. It was his wife's birthday and he was looking forward to the party. The weather was bad, no-way was anything interesting going to happen, and besides it was common knowledge that an invasion was not going to take place for at least another twelve months. His officers were given leave to take part in some war games and some Mongolian conscripts were left minding the shop nursing the unreliable captured equipment from the Soviets. Owing to heavy losses in Russia, Germany had no pool of young men from which to draw reinforcements. On average, the military personnel were six years older than ours. The darling of North Africa, the so called 'Desert Fox' Rommel, must have had a dreadful shock when he heard the news coming out of France. I trust he had a stiff brandy to hand. I don't suppose his boss was too pleased either!

* * *

Erwin

Field Marshall Erwin Rommel was an outstanding and experienced general in command of the area in North West France. He was under orders to expect that Calais was the kingpin link in the defence of that coast and he fortified it accordingly. In his understanding of coastal attack he did not think that Calais would be the site of an invasion. Privately he held a belief that Normandy would be where an attack would be mounted and he prepared for it.

It was he who oversaw the beach paraphernalia for obstructing and impeding an Allied advance. In addition to gun emplacements at strategic points, wooden stakes, metal tripods, barbed wire tangles and mega-large tank deterrents were installed.

He expected the incursion to be simultaneous with a high tide. Infantry disembarking from their transporting craft would become heavily congested on a narrow water-logged beach and more likely to be within range of the German machine guns. With this in mind and having military 'know how', it seemed laudable. Rommel gave orders for his deterrents to be sited at high-water mark. On his instruction, the number of mines previously laid along that area of coast was tripled. He was determined that those troops treading on German-occupied sand received a hazardous and dangerous welcome.

Even the cleverest of us come up with goofy ideas and Erwin was no exception. It has come to be known as 'Rommel's Asparagus'. It brought into play wooden logs, 13–16 feet in length. One million of 'em. They were placed in the fields and meadows of Normandy, behind the beaches. The purpose was to damage incoming gliders, and subsequently to kill and maim their pilots. The scheme proved inconsequential. It was a boo-boo. Don't we all do daft things sometimes? And that was his.

* * *

Dawning of a New Day

A few minutes into the new day of the 6th June 1944, Operation Overlord was heralded into world history. As a prelude to the Normandy invasion, 2,200 British and American bombers spewed out their deadly cargo onto the beaches and targets further inland, hoping to negate German defences. Mine sweepers began to decongest the treacherous sea and to forge clear paths in readiness for the large ships of war and the small boats waiting to depart from home shores. That cleansing purge carried on apace with no enemy interference. Was that a good luck omen or was it that the German military were abed? Whatever, it had begun and it was going to be a very long day.

Soon after midnight 24,000 American, British and Canadian airborne troops landed. American airborne landings commenced with the arrival of the pathfinders at 00.15am. It was not easy; the sky was overcast with thick clouds. Paratroopers were dropped at 01.30am, tasked with controlling the causeway behind the beach and destroying road and rail bridges. Some were killed on impact when their parachutes did not have time to open, the transporting planes flying in too low. Others were drowned in the flooded fields missing the beaches altogether. Gathered together in fighting formation was made difficult by a shortage of radios and by the boggy terrain with its hedgerows, stone walls and marshes.

Later units arrived around 02.30am. They captured the first town to be liberated. Can you imagine the joy and happiness of those town folk, in spite of the hullabaloo that was surrounding them? Reinforcements arrived by glider at 04.00am bringing additional men and heavy equipment. Many landed in unspecified sectors and even those that did land where they were ordered to be, found themselves in difficulties. The heavy cargo, (for example jeeps), had shifted on landing and crashed through the wooden fuselage, and in some cases crushing personnel on board. Other paratroopers were blown off course by the freshening wind and had no option but to set up navigational aids too far to the east, and it took hours, and sometimes days, to reunite with their parent units.

When the planners were planning, one of the essential musts had to be that the date would coincide with a full moon. The light would give illumination to the early pathfinders giving them the ability to ascertain their position. In such a wide over-spread, and complicated affair, there was bound to be pathfinder failures. When the drop zones were incorrectly identified it would result in regiment members finding themselves scattered, and not able to link up as a whole. Managing to consolidate into small groups was usually with a combination of men of different ranks and from different units. They were probably anxious to reunite with their original units. I suspect they felt more secure amongst those they were familiar with.

Naval guns opened fire at 05.45am that morning whilst it was not yet daylight, targeting the land beyond the beaches, hoping to engage defence forces. At a pre-arranged signal, as soon as dawn was beginning to break, the naval guns retrained their sights and the beaches were the chosen targets.

During the activity across the Channel one must think of the lads on the other side here at home.

* * *

Dunkirk in Reverse

A BBC war correspondent, Robert Barr, described the scene as paratroopers prepared to board the aircraft ready to go:

"Their faces were darkened with cocoa; sheathed knives strapped to their ankles. Tommy guns strapped to their waists. Bandoliers, grenades, coils of rope, pick handles, spades and rubber dinghies hung about them. They carried a few personal oddments, like a young lad taking a newspaper to read on the plane. There was an easy familiar touch about the way they were getting ready as though they had done it often before. Well yes, they had kitted up and climbed aboard often just like twenty or thirty or fifty times, but it had never been quite like this before. This was the first combat jump for every one of them".

At 06.30am airborne troops, infantry and armoured divisions arrived to seize key objectives, for example, bridges, road junctions and pertinent terrain features some distance behind the beaches. The strategic purpose was to eliminate or impede the event of German counter-attacks. By contrast, a secondary objective was to ease the egress of amphibian forces off the beaches later on when the battle would be in full flow. And whilst they were there, on the spot, they neutralized German coastal defence batteries, for good measure.

Only four percent of the drops landed on pre-arranged areas. Many landed in swamps with the resulting heavy losses. At the end of that day only 4,500 men were under the control of their original divisions; approximately one third of the forces who landed on terra firma. On the other hand, the wide dispersal confused the enemy and fragmented its response. They did not initially believe that a major invasion was underway. The Allied destruction of the German radar sites along the coast, carried out a week before, proved that the enemy did not detect the approaching fleet until 02.00am.

* * *

The Famous Fighting Five

The beaches of Normandy were sectioned off into five sectors. They were co-named Omaha, Gold, Utah, Juno and Sword. 24,000 men landed on Omaha that day from the sea. Strong east winds blew them well off-course and when their craft finally hit the shore, they discovered to their cost that it had been well and truly prepared for unwelcome visitors. They confronted a myriad of all the obstacles that had come about by Rommel's forward planning, and the beach was mined. High cliffs barred the way, and if it had been possible to advance from the beach, the situation was such that they would not have been able to do it.

Omaha was the most heavily defended of the five sectors. Delayed Allied aircraft support resulted in undisturbed and intact beach deterrents which the troops faced when they came ashore. Many of the landing craft came aground on sandbanks and they were compelled to wade in water neck-high whilst under fire to reach the sand.

A tank battalion was dropped, but too far from the shore, and 27 out of 32 tanks were flooded. Some, disabled, but on the beach, provided cover until the ammunition was depleted or were caught by the rising tide. Men faced gun fire from the cliffs above and 2,000 were killed. Exit from that strand was only possible via five heavily-defended gullies, and by late morning barely a fraction had reached the higher ground. By noon the Germans were now also low on gun fodder, and the Allies were able to leave their landing sites. They were able to clear the gullies of enemy defences so that vehicles could move freely onward. This tenuous beach-head was expanded over the following days: it was judged that the Omaha zone had achieved what they had hoped for.

The casualty total was greater than any of the other sectors. It was a purely American ordeal, and I think that by virtue of the heavy losses sustained, it is probably the site most visited today.

Men arrived at 06.30am by sea, landing on Utah Beach. They were also affected by high winds and their landing boats drifted southwards by strong currents. They came ashore 1.8 kilometres from the pre-ordained area. Bombers had previously dropped their loads from a low altitude, and mega damage had been inflicted against the set defences.

Brigadier General Theodore Roosevelt Jnr, son of the American President, led this detachment, and it was his decision that although this was not the intended target, stated: "The war will start right here", and ordered further landings to be re-routed to that place. Theodore Roosevelt Jnr was a man of 56 years old; the oldest to take part that day, and a veteran of World War I. He survived D Day but died in France after a heart attack one month later. He lays in that land alongside his brother, Quentin, a victim of the earlier conflict.

* * *

Business is Brisk in the Channel

The initial invading battalions were quickly followed by tanks and waves of engineers and demolition squads to clear the mined areas directly behind the beach. Gaps were blown in the sea wall for easy access for troops and tanks. The beach-head secured, these combat men began an exit, and they were ready to advance. The division at Utah did not meet all of their D Day aims, but they proved worthy of their salt.

21,000 troops landed with a loss of only 197 of their company. If one can describe any loss as 'only' it is a sacrilege. One loss in war is one too many.

Pointe de Hoc is a prominent headland situated between Utah and Omaha beaches. It was assigned to a Ranger battalion. Their chore was to scale the 30 metre-high cliffs. I guess that was a tall order, but with grappling hooks, ropes and ladders they located and destroyed the coastal gun batteries at the top. That incident left 65 men alive from the starting party of 200. The German machine-gunners with itchy fingers, held that position and gave rise to the high percentage of those killed. In desperation the residue of survivors, unable to take that site by way of a frontal attack, did so by way of a surprise appearance from the rear. War is a sorry tale and as I write of it, I need to take a few minutes away from its story to recover from my sense of utter helplessness, despair and frustration. How can anyone do anything to prevent it from happening again and again? Looking back in retrospect, since that time in 1944, has there been any time at all, with the exception of a few neutral states, when peace has reigned unilaterally, or trouble-free, in any place on this planet?

The first landings on Gold beach were timed at 07.45am, in variance with the other Allied sectors due to the differences in tidal times. The ensuing battle was a win/lose affair for the Allies and the foe, but finally a tank fired a large 'Petrad' charge into the rear entrance of an enemy gun emplacement. That, and the weapon therein, was rendered definitely out of action. Infantry began to clear the heavily-fortified shore-lined houses and advanced on targets further inland, capturing a small port as they went. A company sergeant major was the only Victoria Cross recipient on D Day for his actions whilst attacking two pill boxes. Their aim to take Bayeux did not happen, stiff German resistance prevented it. One thousand warriors from Gold did not make it home.

***

Hobart's 'Funnies'

In the last paragraph I mentioned the 'Petrad' charge. If that term is unknown to you, you will probably locate it in a dictionary of military terminology. It is an implement of warfare devised by an American, Major General Percy Hobart, and is one of a series of 'Hobart Funnies'. The gentleman was an armoured warfare expert responsible for the modification of tanks, converting them into categories for specialized purposes.

The Petrad was one of them. It was a forty-pound bomb which was designed to demolish steel and concrete and fired from a specifically designed tank. It was known as 'the flying dustbin'. Other unusual modifications came in the form of tanks that could 'swim' in water; some were fitted with ramps that could unfold – it was a Churchill tank with a foldable ramp in place of a turret. They were driven into a gap which needed to be breached. It unfolded its ramps, creating a bridge that other vehicles could cross.

In World War One, a 'Funny' was in service to fill in trenches that were too deep or too wide to cross. These types of armour were available and utilized on the Normandy beaches. They did the chore of scaling high cliffs; of breaking through sea walls; and in all manner of jobs clearing the debris and providing a path for the troops to advance from their original landing place. It was one of this series that was used on Juno beach. A converted tank unrolling from its structure; the covering for the crater that needed to be filled with the so called 'facine', a composite mixture of wood and other material that was rolled off that armoured vehicle in layers.

I heard of Hobart's 'Funnies' at a talk some years ago. I have been, and I still am, a member of various historical societies, and I learn all matter of stuff, but this one impressed me and I particularly remember it. I am intrigued by the bizarre; I think that I am a bit on the quirky side myself! I am always amazed when I hear of the ingenuity of these so brilliant minds. Tanks a lot!

* * *

One Tank Going Cheap

Because of choppy seas, troops arrived on Juno beach ahead of their supporting armour and because of it, casualty rate was high as they disembarked. Most of the early morning naval softening-up bombardment had missed the German defences in that region. Several exits from the beach were created with difficulty but with imagination – a large crater in the sand needed to be bypassed. Seaside bucket and spade appurtenances were hardly adequate. It was filled in using an abandoned tank and several rolls of facine which was then covered by a temporary bridge. Golly it must have been some large cavity. (That tank remained in situ until 1972 when it was removed and restored by members of the British Royal Engineers.) The beach and nearby streets were clogged with traffic for most of that day, making it difficult to move inland. Major German strong points manning heavy guns, machine-gun nests, concrete strong holds, barbed wire and mines were located at three nearby towns. The houses needed Allied clearance, and hand-to-hand combat was the manner in which it was procured.

Soldiers on their way three miles inland discovered that the route was well covered by machine-gun emplacements. It was necessary to outflank the road before they could proceed. By nightfall, the contiguous Juno and Gold beach-heads had advanced to an area twelve miles deep. Juno accounted for the loss of 961 men.

Twenty-one out of twenty-five tanks of the first wave made it safely on shore on the sector marked down as Sword. They were able to provide infantry cover when they began disembarking at 07.30am. The beach was densely mined and peppered with obstacles making the beach-clearing labour difficult and dangerous. In the windy conditions the tide flowed in quicker than expected so manoeuvring the armour was no easy occupation. The beach quickly became congested. A concrete impediment and control tower at this emplacement needed to be bypassed and was not captured until several days later.

* * *

Coming-home Warriors and the Backroom Specials

The first Free French to arrive in Normandy attacked and cleared a solidly fortified strong-point at a small town casino. I hope they brought cash with them to have a go at the tables. It would have given any one of those fighters a bit of light relief. The infantry began advancing on Caen on foot, coming within a kilometre of the town but were forced to withdraw. At 16.00pm a German Panzer (tank) division put up a counter-attack between Sword and Juno and almost succeeded in driving them back to the Channel. It was the determined resistance from a British division that reversed the situation and it was back to square one. Allied losses at Sword left one thousand families without their menfolk.

The French Resistance did a superlative service for the Allied cause. They provided intelligence of the German defences and orders of battle. They planned and co-ordinated, and executed acts of sabotage on the electrical grid, transport facilities and telecommunications network. They fought besides the Allies after the landings to liberate their cities. They carried out operations on the orders from London. Messages were passed via the BBC French Service in the weeks leading up to D Day.

Authentic orders were communicated enveloped in a welter of fakes. They listened to random sentences, poetry scraps and literary quotes, but they knew how to sort it out and they got the message. The orders were carried out regardless of the danger. They can be considered as the fourth arm of the three branches of the Military.

The Commonwealth can be rightfully proud of the support and service it generated that day. Overall, the British and Canadian contingents numbered 83,000 men. By nightfall it was the latter who were the first to fulfil their objective. Air and naval undertakings included a high percentage of the Royal Australian Air Force taking its share in a good day's work. Other RAF squadrons were manned by mixed overseas air crew. Hats off to all of them. They did good!

* * *

Overview

To sum up the Normandy landings operation, it was the most concentrated seaborne incursion yet to be recorded into the archives. The invasion naval fleet was drawn from eight different navies, comprising 5,000 landing and assault boats, 1,200 warships, 280 escort vessels and 270 mine sweepers. Seven thousand ancillary, and 900 merchant vessels took their share. 196,000 naval personnel sailed in them.

Forty Allied Army divisions were committed; 22 American who fought on Omaha and Utah, 13 British who took charge on Sword and Gold; and 3 Canadian divisions who operated out of Juno. In addition, the Poles and the Free French each gallantly contributed, making up one division each. The manpower totalled 160,000, and to cap that, one lady crossed the English Channel too. (I hope to find the opportunity to tell her story.) The numbers fighting in Normandy rose to 875,000 by the end of the month, and in the middle of July, the count reached the one million mark. That figure was more than doubled by the end of August.

By the 11th June, within just five days after the initial Overlord crusade, tons of supplies were shipped over from the UK. It was astounding that in spite of this mammoth undertaking, there was never any shortage of necessities.

Allied casualties on the first day totalled 10,000. German losses were 1,000. We were the attackers that day and could have expected that our losses would be higher in comparison to the defenders. Despite those early losses, the morale of those doughty and lion-hearted squaddies, fliers and matelots remained high. It was no easy task to fulfil the mission and to witness the slaughter of those who fought besides you; your mates and your friends.

Barely a few of the planned objectives for that day were achieved. The five bridge heads would not link up for another six days by which time the Allies held a front sixty miles long and fifteen miles in depth. The German command had ordered French civilians, other than those considered to be necessary for their war effort, to evacuate potential combat areas in Normandy. Civilian casualties on the 6th June 1944 were registered as 3,000. In spite of the losses and the heartache that would follow, and the destruction and of the suffering of the local population and the financial outlay, we had to do it. It was not a feasible proposition that we could allow mainland Europe to rot under the heel of German oppression.

On the 26th June the port of Cherbourg fell to the Allies, and the Canadians captured the town of Caen on the 21st July. To the jubilation of the French, Paris was once more their capital city. It was loosened from the German aggressors on the 25th August. They retreated across the Seine on the 30th of that month. The light was shining at the end of a very long tunnel. General Dwight D Eisenhower, commander of the Supreme Headquarters Allied Expeditionary Force (SHAEF), and General Bernard Montgomery, who commanded all the land forces involved in Operation Overlord, had done their job well.

The Allies advanced on, sometimes winning a battle and sometimes not, but Normandy showed us the way and we were on that journey to the Rhine.

As I sit here at my PC typing this work on sheets of A4 and dwelling on the men that fought in that battle of Normandy, thoughts have incongruously crept into my head of my one time, (so very long ago), first love Robbie, who had been part of this story. I know that he survived. I am not able to record the fact as to how I acquired the information, but I did learn that he did not return to the United Kingdom. Post-war he settled in the States.

* * *

Mission Achieved

Victory in Normandy can be accounted for by virtue of many factors:

1. The defences provided by the Atlantic Wall were not yet completed.
2. The Allies achieved and maintained air supremacy.

3. The organized deception programme was successful. It led to the German reaction of preparing for a defence of a widespread stretch of coastline. They were unable to fathom out the siting of attack when it happened.

4. The allied bombing, and the work of the Resistance, severely disrupted the German transport and infrastructure, causing their inability to bring forward reinforcements.

5. The monumental and astonishing manner in which it was all planned; and of course all credit to those who activated them.

* * *

Make-believe v. Reality

The 1962 film 'The Longest Day' depicted the story of D Day. Do not regard it all as a valid account of the actual reality: it does not portray the 'nitty gritty'. We are presented with an image of those well celebrated actors in their neat un-creased uniforms, revealing their beautiful white-toothed smiles and issuing dialogue in perfect grammatical English. Have none of it; on film it is a production to entertain. In real life it was men wading metres deep out of the water, of drawn anxious faces as they waited their turn to leave the craft that had brought them there. Of the cries of pain as they lay dying in their blood-soaked clothes, and the screams as they became the targets of exploding hand grenades. Use your imagination and put aside the two hours you sat in a cinema seat.

In any case, a film once seen in the comfort afforded by a darkened cinema easily fades from memory. The real-life story of the Normandy campaign is perpetually enshrined in the minds of the interested and those seeking understanding.

In all honesty I cannot end my account of this representation of the colossal event of the Normandy landings on a facetious note. It is all very well being funny but I am not one of Hobart's and I do not consider Operation Overlord a joke. I have said earlier that I have had no desire to visit that one-time war zone. Having expounded on it I might change my mind. However, I have a friend who has taken an excursion to that scene, and she gave me a snippet which I would like to pass on. At a war cemetery where the British lay, there is an inscription on a memorial edifice. It is inscribed in Latin but I have the translation: "We, once conquered by William, have now set free the Conqueror's native land".

A Lady of Merit

Earlier on in this chapter, I made mention of the only female who crossed the English Channel to Normandy on 6th June 1944, and I would now like to tell her story.

Martha Ellis Gellhorn was an American novelist, travel writer and journalist and is considered to be the most esteemed war correspondent of the 20th Century. She was on hand to report on virtually every conflict during her career of 60 years. She was born in St. Louis, Missouri of a mixed background. Her maternal grandmother came from a Protestant family while her maternal grandfather was of Jewish origin. Her father was German born. He was eminent in the medical world as was her younger brother whilst another had become a noted professor of law.

In 1930, after having her first articles published, Martha went to France working as a foreign correspondent. In 1934 she wrote her first book, 'What Mad Pursuit'. In 1936 she travelled to Spain to cover the Spanish Civil War and it was here that she first met Ernest Hemingway. Later, from Germany she reported on the rise of Adolph Hitler, and 1938 found her in Czechoslovakia. After the outbreak of war she described the events in her novel 'A Stricken Field'.

She reported on the conflict from Finland, Hong Kong, Burma, Singapore, and from England. Lacking official press credentials to witness the Normandy landings, she hid in a hospital ship bathroom, and upon arriving she impersonated a stretcher bearer. She later said that she followed the war wherever she could reach it. She was among the first journalists to report on the liberation, by Allied troops, of the Dachau concentration camp.

She was Hemingway's fourth wife. After four years of a contentious marriage they divorced. The 2012 film 'Hemingway and Gellhorn' is based on these four years. Later she covered the war in Vietnam and the Arab-Israeli conflicts in the 1960s. At the age of 70 she continued to work, and during the next decade covered the civil wars in Central America. Approaching 80, and showing signs of slowing down, she still managed to report on the United States invasion of Panama in 1989, and finally retired one year later. An unsuccessful eye operation left her with impaired vision and she admitted that she was too old to cover the Balkan conflicts in the 90s, although she did a last overseas trip to Brazil in 1995 to highlight the state of poverty in that country.

At the age of 89, ill, and almost completely blind, she died of an apparent suicide. Apart from the fact that she was the only female to arrive in Normandy on D Day, I decided to present a cameo of this lady to express my admiration of her courage and tenacity to pursue the work that she did. She personifies my ideal. She was a woman after my own heart. And I say "three cheers" for that lady with a pen, and for the personality that wielded it.

* * *

Operation Market Garden - Not a WLA Story

The epic story of The Battle of Arnhem will be remembered in the annuls of British history in general, and as an example of the national spirt of its fighting men during World War 2, written into its military archives in particular. The end result was an Allied defeat, as with the failure in France in 1940, which culminated in the Dunkirk Evacuation. I remember a Churchillian quote that comes to mind. There was no connection between our withdrawal in France and the affair at Arnhem, except of course that instead of success, it was a failure. But our PM linked the two in this way. He said, on both occasions: "This was their finest hour". No doubt he was referring to the courage and spirit of the British and the Allied fighting resolve.

The battle fought in Arnhem and the surrounding towns in Holland happened during nine days in September 1944, just two months after the Normandy landings. During that intervening eight weeks Allied forces had broken through the German lines liberating areas in France and Belgium and were preparing to advance onto Dutch soil via the region of the lower tributaries of the River Rhine.

An operation was mounted on the 17th of that month, code named 'Market Garden'. The objective was the capture of key bridges marking the way for river crossings penetrating deep into that country bordering Germany itself. The plan was for those sites to be taken and held awaiting reinforcements by the main body of troops coming up behind them. It was to be achieved by men of the 1st Airborne Division of the Parachute Regiment, a Brigade of the Polish Parachute Regiment in addition to men of the Glider Pilot Regiment.

It was expected that the phalanx of the main units would link up with the original force of airborne warriors within two or three days. It did not happen. Several reasons were brought to light to explain this failure. In the first instance most of the original landings were not exactly where they were planned to be.

Secondly German resistance was far heavier and more concentrated than intelligence had predicted and reported. Only a small group of those dropped had actually reached the bridge at Arnhem; the rest found themselves in outer areas of the town held by the enemy and unable to relieve those still awaiting their arrival, which they could not.

* * *

No Good News Coming out of Holland

Four days passed without a change in the situation and the men still holding the bridge were overwhelmed by the Germans. Those who landed, but not on target, were trapped in a small pocket north of the river. In between the nearby towns of Nijmegen and Eindhoven minor bridges were taken by the Allies in the early stages after the landings, but this was offset by the failure to capture the main road bridge at Nijmegen, which carried the road across the River Waal, and this contributed to the overall disappointing outcome. By the 26th of September the shattered remains of the airborne forces were overcome. The failure of the operation was put down to the poor intelligence and an under-estimation of enemy strength. It was a victory for Germany and a bitter, disappointing and major disaster for us.

Subsequently the front line advance into the Netherlands was delayed until after that winter. The end result dashed the expectation of the Allied leaders of ending the war by Christmas of that year. It was the opinion of military and historical experts that the operation in total was a gross mistake and the result of bad planning. Despite it being a demoralizing failure, the Battle of Arnhem has become synonymous with the bravery and the fighting spirit of the British military. General Montgomery claimed that: "In years to come it will be a great thing for a man to be able to say – "I fought at Arnhem". Those words remind me of the Battle of Agincourt which was enacted in 1415, when King Henry V uttered almost identical words about his bowmen fighting for England in France.

The Battle of Arnhem defeat drained the life blood of the 1st Airborne Division from which it never recovered. Three quarters of its formation did not come home. The Glider Pilot Regiment suffered the highest proportion of fatalities and it was phased out after the war and eventually disbanded. The Polish contingent suffered the loss or wounded numbering 92 and 111 missing, with a safe withdrawal of 1,500. In total 1,500 were killed or died of sustained wounds; 6,500 were captured or reported missing.

Of the 2,000 who survived 59 were decorated, including five who were awarded the Victoria Cross, the highest British honour for gallantry in the field: four went to men of the Army and one to a Flight Lieutenant of the RAF.

* * *

Extra Bits and Pieces

Raymond, a serving sergeant in the Parachute Regiment, was busy in another ongoing theatre of war. He could easily have been part of the Arnhem story. In 1945, the year the war ended, a certain Louis Hagen, a Jewish refugee who had fled from Germany seeking refuge in Britain, and who was a British Army glider pilot fighting at Arnhem, wrote 'Arnhem Lift', believed to be the first book published recording the event. In the same year the film 'Theirs is the Glory' went into production, which featured some original footage and used 120 Allied veterans as extras. In 1977 the film makers presented 'A Bridge Too Far'.

With the telling of the Arnhem story my memories came flooding back of this historical time. The names, Arnhem, Nijmegen and Eindhoven are consolidated in my brain, and I recall so vividly the news of these named places coming over the airways on our wireless set at home. I feel as if the years have hardly moved on. Having written this account I think that it was indeed a 'bridge too far', and I would not be surprised if most of my readers agree with me.

South Holland and Belgium 1944

Chapter 11
The Balkans

All Change in Central Europe

The downfall of the ruling powers in the Balkan States occurred with the defeat in 1918 of the Ottoman Empire and the Austro-Hungarian Empire. Albania was one of a group of countries comprising that land mass, together with Greece, Yugoslavia, Bulgaria and the island of Crete. Albania sought cover for its protection from the kingdom of Italy. Benito Mussolini, dictator of Italy, did consider the proposition and listened to Albania's plea but decided, in the 1920s, to dominate it instead. In 1928 Albania was a country under the rule of King Zog 1st, remembered for his failure to stave off the Italian greed, and in April 1939 Mussolini's troops marched eastward and sailed across the Adriatic Sea. They overthrew King Zog and Albania was occupied and annexed to the Italian empire.

Having secured his initial objective, the appetite for more ascended sharply in the digestion of the Italian Fascist. His hoards invaded Greece in October 1940, which was an integral part of World War 2. The Battle of Greece was in evidence from the 28th October 1940 to 30th April 1941, with Germany's appearance on the field in March 1941 to stem the Italian failure to succeed in that country.

Next in line for being swallowed up by the Axis, (Germany, Italy, Japan, and now with Hungary hanging on), was the kingdom of Yugoslavia, a newly created state which emerged with the re-drawing of borders in line with the treaties and peace plans arranged by the victorious Allies after the Great War of 1914–1918. The invasion took place on the 6th April 1941. The news of that event is fresh in my mind; it was my brother's birthday! That debacle ended with the surrender of the Royal Yugoslav Army within 11 days, giving Germany and Italy the opportunity for the cohesion of their newly-appropriated Yugoslavia with Bosnia, Herzegovina, and tit-bits of Croatia; bestowing upon the whole the title of the Independent State of Croatia. (Independent, my eye, it was not!) Under German control a puppet government was put into place; the Government of National Salvation, (please refer to my recent remark in brackets – salvation it was not). The area of Montenegro was now under Italian occupation and Bulgaria joined the fray for its bit of the pie and was permitted to annex already affected areas in eastern Yugoslavia, with the inclusion of what we know today as Macedonia.

The island of Crete was drastically involved in this heady and toxic brew. In succeeding chapters I am recording the events which were enacted in that place together with a more detailed and precise story of what was happening in its neighbour, Greece.

Despite having officially joined the Axis powers, Bulgaria, at the onset of the war shindigs in those Balkan States, was not a participant at the feast. It appeared as an interested on-looker. But late in April 1941 the Bulgarian Army did rouse itself to occupy most of Western Thrace and the Greek province of Eastern Macedonia. They also took much of Eastern Serbia, sharing those spoils with the Italians.

Such was the war-time story of the countries situated in central Europe. What a complicated area it was and what a complex story it gives rise to.

I have been a tourist in that part of the world. I have travelled around those countries, Croatia, Slovenia, Montenegro and most of the others in the Balkan zone already mentioned, headquartering in Dubrovnik and Split, and Zagreb. I did the museum rounds and learnt much of its WW2 history. I also came to understand the causes and outcome of the troubles that beset that area; the hostilities and bloodshed and inter-religious disharmony and political upheavals of the 1980s and 90s. But enough is enough and my telling of the early forties will suffice.

* * *

Wartime Machinations in Greece

On a number of occasions Greece has been my holiday destination. I had 'done' the tourist rounds, including the quaint spectacle of the changing of the skirted guards outside the palace, and the Tomb of the Unknown Soldier, both in Athens. I was aware of that country's chequered history during World War 2, both of internal politics and in battle. The Allies and the German forces fought not only in Greece but in Crete.

Greece entered the war in October 1940. The Italians, led by Mussolini, had been the aggressor since 1936 when they invaded Abyssinia (now Ethiopia) and filched it from its Emperor Haile Selassie, the peaceful ruler of that country.

I was 11 years old at that time, and I can clearly recollect listening to the news item on the wireless at home, and how excited I was that I could follow the gist of it. The Italian advance in Greece was slow, and when it appeared to falter, the Germans made it their business to help. And just for a bit more land grabbing, in April 1941, they had a good old 'nosh up' in Yugoslavia as well. Within one month Greece was overrun; the conquest of that land was complete and split three ways. Germany, Italy and Bulgaria all had a slice of the cake. The latter was now in cahoots with the other two having joined in the war on their side. The Greek King George ll and his government exiled themselves and fled to Egypt. They organized themselves into a fighting force and fought alongside the Allies in the Middle East, North Africa and Italy. The Greek navy and its mercantile mariners did their share with the help they gave in the fight against the usurpers.

As I pause for a moment to decide on the choice of words to continue this gazette, I spontaneously remember having met Greek sailors whilst waltzing around the dance floor in those far back Covent Garden heydays. They wore the flash 'Greece' on their hat bands. And funny sort of hats they were too. I am indeed lucky that the computer in my head is still able to retrieve such memories.

* * *

British Interference

The Allies did have a finger in the pie during the factional bother in Greece. In April 1939, five months before our war with Germany, the Greek Prime Minister, General Metaxas, invoked from our own incumbent PM at that time, Mr Chamberlain, a guarantee of aid if it were ever needed. When Italy attacked that help was needed and we were duty bound to honour that pledge. Mr Churchill, who succeeded Chamberlain, was invited by the Greek government to send Allied Forces to Crete. It was a very strategic move. Churchill was a master of his trade. It was vital that the best Cretan harbour at Suda Bay lay in British hands and not in those of the enemy. Should Germany or Italy attack Egypt, a British Protectorate, we would be on hand to defend it.

Britain sent several missions to Greece. In 1941, when that country was in the grip of a severe famine, it was partially relieved by British arranged Red Cross shipments. Britain parachuted in men to destroy German supply lines. Bridges, viaducts and main-line railway networks were destroyed. Axis shipping in the port of Piraeus was obliterated.

The success of these operations encouraged us to repeat them and we despatched specialists with supplies of explosives and arms. The destruction of sites vital to the enemy continued. The activities which I have described in this paragraph were not carried out by the British alone. They were aided and abetted by guerrilla fighters of the Resistance who, as patriotic Greeks, submerged themselves into the Allied cause. They wanted their homeland to be free. The movement has its own story to tell during this war.

It was the Greek Resistance who thwarted the Italians in the early part of the Greco-Italian war, as it is called. They attempted to do likewise when the Germans intervened, but the might of Hitler's forces out-weighed them. Gradually their numbers increased, especially when famine struck and they were better supported by being together in a united group. By 1943, the movement had developed into a considerable body of men and women, and they were able to liberate huge swathes of land in the mountainous interior and tying down enemy numbers. But political tensions arose between different factions of the Resistance, leading to an outbreak of Civil War which continued until 1944.

* * *

Greece - a Battle and a Defeat

The British did more than contribute arbitrary support for the Resistance in Greece during the early years. They were building a force to oust the Germans from their hold on that country. On the 6th April 1941 a force of British, Australians, New Zealanders, Cypriots and a contingent of the Palestine Pioneer Corps, in all numbering 62,000, had taken their place, and the Battle of Greece was initiated.

The hoped for victory did not materialize. It was an ill-fated expedition. It underwent a tragic setback which in the end necessitated an evacuation of the survivors by sea. In my opinion, and from the logic of that situation, I am left with the unsettling feeling that the process of that evacuation was not as organized as its predecessor Dunkirk, where under bombardment they patiently waited for the rescuing boats. In this instance I feel from the narrative that it was a kind of 'hotch-potch' set up. An array of small individual craft mopping up men in a disorganized fashion from the land and even from the sea and from small islands dotted there about.

Mainland Greece was liberated in October 1944, after Hitler withdrew his forces in the face of the advancing Russian army on his eastern front. He needed the resources to deal with it. A German garrison continued to hold out in the Aegean islands until the end of the war. Greece was devastated by the conflict and the occupation. The infrastructure lay in ruins. The economy had sunk to rock bottom. Greece had sustained the loss of 400,000 souls, and the country's Jewish community was almost completely annihilated in the Holocaust.

* * *

Crete - a Battle and a Defeat

From an Allied perspective a successful defence of Crete was an important factor in the defence of Egypt. The ensuing Battle of Crete was the first large-scale airborne operation in the annals of war. On the 21st May 1941, ruthless, fire-branding, highly trained hand-picked young men, full of Teutonic fervour landed and an assault was unleashed onto the main Cretan airfield. Vast numbers of gliders and parachutists preceded by heavy German aerial bombardment followed by murderous machine-gun fire confronted the Allied defenders. The continuous flow of the German troop-carrying aircraft landed onto that space in the vicinity of Maleme, in the north west of the island, coinciding with a naval battle.

It was estimated that the casualties, which resulted from the shipping losses during the naval exchanges, were 4,000 men, who died from drowning. These included those wounded by the Germans, who in their fearless, unbridled disregard of those who landed, and attempted to land from the troop carriers during the night of the 21st June 1941.

A land-battle commenced two days later and fared no better. The overwhelming numbers of the invaders, and the conditions in which our forces found themselves caught up in, and were committed to fight in; the debris of hundreds of crashed gliders and planes and the bodies of the dead, proved to be an uneven playing field for our boys.

It can be recorded that the Allies were alerted to the fact that an enemy invasion of the island was imminent. It was the first time that Mr Turing's code-breaking machine was used to pass on intelligence picked up from German sources. It is regrettable that in spite of it, the Battle of Crete was an Allied disaster.

Goring's Luftwaffe victory, resulting from the delivery of airborne troops, did at least give Mr Churchill some thought to dwell on. The enormity in numbers and the fierce patriotic attitude of the Germans who played a part, was an ideal which he admired and aspired to.

Airborne landings were an inaugural event. It had never been done before and our PM decided that it was a good policy to imitate, and he did just that. He realized that he had been taught a good lesson, not in spite of the violent struggle, but because of it, even though it was the shocking loss of life that had brought it to his attention.

Thinking back from my view point, that time-lock seems to tally. When after Dunkirk the lads were back home and camped on Salisbury Plain, they were asked to volunteer for a new and original regiment that would be formulated to train and utilize airborne personnel, and for an insignia design, bringing to mind that young fellow Raymond, who, like Winston Churchill, did just that. To me the wheel had turned full circle. Churchill's brainwave guaranteed many future victories as armies benefitted from the strategic use of airborne invading techniques and assaults in difficult circumstances. Mr Churchill found himself thus engrossed in a second line of contemplation whilst over-viewing the war in Crete. The loss of life on both sides resulted in a diabolical ending but with a favourable sequel. It did divert the enemy there and not, in his forward thinking mode, to more vital areas, for example Syria and Iraq. We were very busy in each area, and we would rather not have had too many of the German adversaries to keep us company at those sites.

I feel obliged to add a little bit of gossip to this epic. Australian Forces were in attendance in the Greek machinations, but a couple of the 'Big Boys' back home were not too happy for them to go there. The Prime Minister, Mr Mackenzie, and a General Blamey felt that a foray into Greece was too risky, but they were won over when the British Government provided briefings under-stating the chances of a rout. The hope for a success was further compromised by inconsistences between Greek and Allied plans. In the event they proved right, but it is an interesting point about this little whiff of tittle tattle.

* * *

Cretan Repercussions

The Battle of Crete was over. But their story was not, in fact, far from it. The Cretan Resistance movement fought an undeclared war on the German and Italian occupiers from the spring of 1941 to the autumn of 1945. It was a long haul. During the war civilians picked off the German paratroopers using knives, axes, scythes and even their bare hands, and they managed to inflict wounds on many of them. Later they banded together under their name, the 'National Liberation Front'.

In the early days their objective was basic and of minimal ambition. They boosted the morale of the occupied people and they distributed food at that time of German imposed deprivation.

As they developed and became confident and better armed they became more daring and aggressive, and they raised the stakes. The Cretan resistance and the British worked closely together. It was after all, in our interests; they were fighting our enemy. They communicated with Egypt by boat; it was a useful tool by which they sent back straggling Allied soldiers trapped there after the defeat, and supplies were transported in on a reverse trip.

British intelligence agents were active. The Germans used Crete as a launching pad in readiness for their hoped-for invasion of those lands not too far away over the water, Egypt and North Africa. They always had an eye out for a little bit more. The Resistance and their British buddies organised numerous cells isolated in the mountains and they engaged 'runners' as messengers to pass information. Attached to these units one could discover Greeks who had no affiliation with the main body but they were a useful ally. They were all in it together!

Most of the venues had radio communication facilities with Egypt, useful to pass intelligence back to interested and dedicated sources. It was also a handy method of requesting supplies of food and clothing and weapons which arrived by parachute. German scouts were constantly on the alert to locate the radios, and their owners were compelled to change their locales on a frequent and regular rota. Together these two tightly-knit groups of people were responsible for some daring exploits including the abduction of a prominent German general and the sabotage of airfields.

But this was not a one-man show. There was no free lunch. There was a terrible price to pay.

The aftermath of the Battle of Crete is a tragedy in itself. Orders were issued by the German general in charge. He earnt himself the title 'The Butcher of Crete'. The civilian population had worn no identity armbands or insignia during their resistance against the enemy invader, and the German admission that because of this fact and the rules of war laid down by The Hague Convention, no blame can be attached to them. They accepted it as their right and claimed a 'not guilty' plea for their post battle actions.

Since when did the Germans act according to any rules anywhere, anytime, anyplace? Did they ever adhere to the rules of The Hague Convention or the Geneva Convention? Not in my book. In Crete they carried out a series of collective punishments; indiscriminate mass shootings, burning of villages, wholesale looting, and repeated year-on-year destruction of the harvests. What kind of emotion does it arouse as you read this? I know what I feel as I write it, and I know how I reacted when I went to Maleme in Crete.

It was a small village at the time of the battle but a bustling tourist resort now. I read its story, and contemplated the memorial stone telling of it. There are many more remembrance edifices in that island, but none have impressed themselves on my consciousness more than that one. I grieved for those who suffered, and I was overwhelmed with loathsome, and dare I say it, hate, for those barbarian inflictors, no matter whatever the reason, for resorting to inhuman brutality.

* * *

Resistance

I feel that at this point I should enlarge upon the history of the Resistance movement. It played an important part, even though in a minor role, in the progression of the war. The movement was comprised of groups of civilians, men and women, living in their countries under German rule. Not in the Armed Forces but fighting the enemy in their own land in their own way. They carried out 'under-cover' exploits. They used the tactics and strategies of a guerrilla war.

They dynamited trains transporting military personnel and military hardware. They ambushed vehicles on the road, killing and maiming the occupants – often people important to the enemy's cause. They aided men of our Forces. In particular the men of RAF air crew, who, having been shot down over enemy territory, parachuted to earth and landed in a foreign field, sometimes not knowing exactly where they were. They would hastily bury their landing gear and would very quickly be located by a Resistance member. Sometimes a bewildered airman would find his way to a farmhouse or cottage. If he was lucky he would be welcomed, and soon a member of the Resistance would be contacted and he would be hidden in a 'safe house' until arrangements could be made for his clandestine return home. If he was not so fortunate, the reception he would receive would result in the arrival of Germans and he would be interrogated by the SS, that vicious and brutal organization, the German Secret Service, capable of the most terrible types of torture to extract information from their victims.

The Resistance was a vital tool for the Allies in other ways. They possessed secret radios and were able to pass important information that was so necessary when plans were formulated for future military manoeuvres. This was of special importance when 'Top Brass' discussions were taking place to set into motion plans for the D Day Landings in Normandy. The data that was sent regarding enemy numbers, location and fortification details were invaluable. This particular information was relayed by the French arm of The Resistance. When the British needed to contact them they sent out a pre-arranged signal. It was the first few bars of Beethoven's 5th Symphony. It sounded, if I can describe it in words on paper, like 'dardardar (pause) dar'. It represented the letter 'V', which is, of course, V for Victory.

It was an extremely dangerous occupation. These amazing people of the Resistance literally walked a tightrope with death and torture. If detected and captured they would suffer the most savage brutality, and if they did not die under torture, they would be dragged out and shot. And a great many were. The SS were clever and they carried out their work with dedicated proficiency and competence. Sometimes 'double agents' were employed, traitors to their country. Betrayal was rife.

The British recruited suitable applicants; those who were physically and mentally able and fluent in several languages, and trained them in the art of subterfuge. In addition, they were taught the mastery of parachuting, and when fully prepared would be dropped over a designated site and would contact and work with the Resistance there. Many of these extremely heroic individuals were caught or betrayed, and suffered and died for their country in the cause of freedom, at the hands of the SS fiends. Many of the inhabitants living under the Germans worked for them and fraternized. Young women who did so, with men of the enemy, were punished by the faithful when the war finally ended. They were publicly exposed and taunted, and under restraint their heads were shaved by jubilant captors. It was a mark of shame that they carried until their hair grew back.

Such is the sorry legacy of war. But it has to be recognized that the Resistance, from whichever country they operated from, can have the satisfaction of knowing that they played no small part in achieving the victory when it came.

The Balkans – South-east Europe

Chapter 12
A Middle Eastern Tale

The Melting Pot of Europe

The region classified as the Middle East was untouched by war for the first few months after the declaration in September 1939. In 1940 Fascist Italy declared war on Britain and France shadowing their Nazi German pals. Perhaps it was a case of basking in reflective glory brought to light with the German advance into France.

From that event, the Middle East evolved into a major theatre of hostile activity and thus remained so for the next two-and-a-half years, until the finale of a future confrontation which resulted with the victorious British 8th Army under the exalted General Montgomery, (Monty as he was affectionately called), crossing the border from his happy hunting ground Libya, into Tunisia.

On the 1st of July 1940, Italy dispatched its bombers to the British-held mandate of Palestine. Tel Aviv, Haifa and the coastal towns of Acre and Jaffa were attacked. Two hundred people died and many were injured. There was no unanimity amongst Palestinian Arabs. Some signed up for service in the British Army. Some akin to the Grand Mufti of Jerusalem formerly declared a jihad declaration of war against the Allies. Jews attempting to escape their persecution in pre-war Germany were barred from entry by the British, placing them in detention camps or deporting them to other places like Mauritius or Cyprus, if they dared to defy. Jewish people in residence fought alongside the regular British Army, in spite of the shabby decree which was suggested in a British Government White Paper publication named after the British Colonial Secretary Malcolm McDonald in 1939, with the blessing of the then Prime Minister Chamberlain, that hindered and prevented immigration into that land. In total some 30,000 Jews living in Palestine fought alongside British Service personnel, being named the Jewish Brigade.

One would not expect any Middle East country to be implicated in a war when the news was saturated with the goings on in France and in Russia, and the U-Boat onslaught in the North Atlantic and in the Pacific with the Japanese. In a much less dramatic turn of events, a number of Middle Eastern countries were involved, and operations were acted out in various ways and to various degrees.

The Allies secured the upper hand which counted towards a final victory, balanced unfortunately with the customary casualty lists. The stories manifest themselves in sundry guises. I hope you will find them interesting.

* * *

Battleground Syria - 1940 not 2016

Pre-war Syria was one of many overseas territories of the French Empire. Post the fall of France in 1940, it was now in the control of the Vichy Government, with Marshall Petain in charge. Syria's position in the Middle East was of strategic importance.

The Ottoman Empire was in control of most of the Middle East for nearly 400 years. During the Great War it was allied to Germany. In 1916 the Anglo-French Sykes-Picot Agreement allocated to the British Empire the present day areas of Jordan, Israel, the Palestinian Territories and Iraq. By 1917 the British had succeeded in defeating the Ottoman-Turkish forces who were in control and occupied the Palestinian region which remained under British military administration for the rest of the war, until 1918. Arthur Balfour wrote the Balfour Declaration in 1917. In 1920 a conference was held in San Remo in the USA, endorsing the 1916 Anglo-French Agreement. To France, in victorious partnership with Britain, went Syria and the Lebanon. They were the spoils of war. In 1922 the League of Nations formally established the British Mandate for Palestine and Trans Jordan. All of the land east of the River Jordan was assigned to the Emirate of that country, ruled by the Hashemite King Abdullah. The remaining part of the west of Jordan became Palestine.

During the time hostilities had been in progress in those lands, the British needed help from the Arabs living there and the Jews who had fled from the religious hatred in their homes in Russia. The British made promises of land acquisition to both of these ethnic groups. They were already sowing the seeds of later enmity with Britain, which developed into the violence between all three groups in the inter-war years and afterwards, leading up to the subsequent United Nations vote to sanction the birth of Israel in 1948. When the Second World War began, the Palestinian Grand Mufti sought an allegiance with the Axis powers for help in expelling the British from the Middle East. The British response was to banish him, and he consequently spent much of the war years in Italy. He aided the formation of the Muslim SS Division in the Balkans.

This history of that region is important. I think it is a necessary tool for understanding how it connects to the events that took place there during WW2, and why certain countries within it took the actions that they did. Hopefully it is easier now to comprehend why the emphasis that wartime Syria, in the grip of a German 'fall guy', placed on the priority to maintain a 'no-holds barred' attitude in their efforts to prevent the dribbling of cross-over adherents from that country to Palestine under its British control, and of those preferring to serve their own master, namely the Fuhrer of the Third Reich, Adolf Hitler.

By the end of 1940 Syria was a hive of activity for Anti-British and Anti-Zionist propaganda, encouraging Hitlerites and the local Arab population to take part. By the end of March 1941 the Luftwaffe was attacking the Suez Canal. The Allied lifeline to parts of the free world further afield was under threat as German aircraft were flying in from Dodecanese bases. They had the opportunity, if they had wanted to, to operate from Syria with a possible German take-over. The British protectorate, which held sway in Egypt, together with the responsibility for the Suez Canal and the oil refineries in that locality, could find themselves in dire danger of German intervention and attack, notwithstanding the British vital land-lines to Iraq and to Palestine.

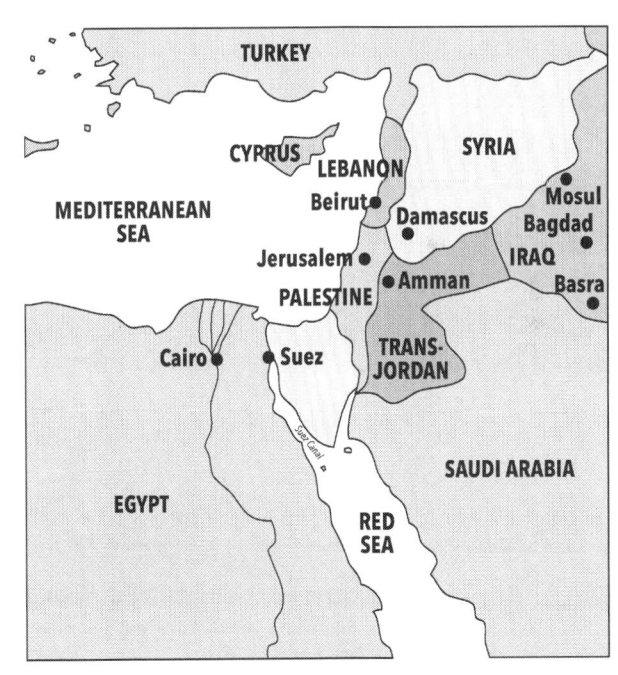

The Middle East 1940 - showing the vulnerability of the Suez Canal and beyond

* * *

Churchill's Headache

In May of that year Axis aircraft assembled on Syrian airfields. Our forces in the Middle East smelled trouble. Crete at that time was in the throes of battle – our forces fully occupied defending it; with Malta under siege pleading for reinforcements, an Allied defeat and evacuation from Greece; Iraq facing a troop shortage and needing more; and Palestine having only one division with which to defend it. Heck our PM was in for a big headache which even aspirin couldn't cure!

Mr Churchill in his wisdom, made a deal with General Henrik Dentz, Commissioner and Commander-in-Chief of the Vichy High Command. The offer was a promise that if he would organize a resistance to a German sea or air attack on Syria, British forces would be available to aid him immediately. Even with this plan in the pipeline, the situation looked unsafe and threatening. It depended on how far the General could be trusted. Probably as far as one could throw him, which ain't very far!

The RAF was authorized to act against the German aircraft amassing in Syria and Allied Forces were held on standby. It fell to Australian Forces to leave North Africa where they were currently serving, redeploying to Palestine. It was part of a plan to prepare for their advance into Syria. The British General Wavell, in charge of this operation, mustered a force of British and Indian service personnel, and any available Free French. Air support was limited. The RAF had other fish to fry as already mentioned. In any case the struggle in Crete was still ongoing and that was their priority. In the event a Navy force would be in attendance. The task objective was the capture of Damascus and Beirut as a preliminary action to a final occupation of the whole of Syria.

Battle commenced on the 8th June 1940. Vichy opposition was scant in the early days, but the British-controlled forces had no great success either. The Free French were held ten miles short of the targeted Damascus; the Australian Division on the coastal road made slow progress over rough terrain. Seaward, we fared little better than we had on land. General Wavell, with difficulty, conjured up reinforcements which turned the tide. Damascus was finally taken by Australians after three days of severe combat aided by British Commandos who executed a daring raid, a seaborne landing behind enemy lines.

In the first week of July 1940 a Vichy collapse hovered into immediate perspective. Vichy envoys arrived to sue for an armistice which was sanctioned. Syria passed into Allied hands. General Dentz and other highly placed officers were taken into custody as hostages. When the war finally ended in 1945, Marshal Philippe Petain, the takeover authoritarian for Hitler, and the governor of Vichy France, was convicted as a traitor to his country and sentenced to death. However his sentence was commuted to life imprisonment, and he died in 1951, aged 95.

* * *

My Connections

Reading over this piece which I have just recorded, I realize that in some instances I have somewhat verged on the 'vulgar'. Unfortunately it is my vernacular. And I can tell you how that came about. To start with, I was born and bred in Cockney London. That is, in the true East End, not what one watches daily on BBC TV, and as is said, within the sound of Bow Bells issuing forth from a church sited in the centre of the district. So my upbringing did not bring me into contact with the 'genteel'. I was never shy or bashful, and 'what you saw is what you got', and I have always stood by that mantra. And now in old age I have neither the ability to change my ways and neither do I want to. So sorry if I have offended you, make of it as you will. What you see is what you get, so there!

Syria was not to be outdone by so many other countries worldwide. It too had a World War 2 history. It is a worthy story and I felt compelled to tell it. That region is entitled to its recordable tale and I have my own personal reason too.

It is of interest to me, even though I have never set foot there. It is because of its siting. It is the gateway to Egypt and the Suez Canal, and I have fridge magnets on a magnetic board on a wall in my kitchen to prove that 'I was there', and memorable times they were too. Their history recedes into the past much further than the 1940s. And the afore-mentioned Arthur Balfour is prominent in my thoughts having met Raymond at the service club which bore his illustrious name. And because I have alighted at Tel Aviv airport and journeyed on to witness the golden-coloured stone of Jerusalem, reminding me of the British Mandate. It was their authority that forbade the use of any other than that stone that fronts that city's buildings. Perhaps that is why it is called 'Jerusalem the Golden'.

With an ache in my heart I think of Syria today, in 2016 devastated by civil war. I abhor war of any kind or for any reason. It gives me cause for distress and sorrow for those who suffer because of it.

Chapter 13
Mediterranean Action

France and Spain

I toured localities of World War I activities in France, which, incidentally, I would heartedly recommend. I travelled with a group in a minibus, and we had the best of guides. He was a fount of knowledge. He knew and could recount and explain it all: the First and the Second World Wars. At one point, as we were returning home, we were approaching Calais to board the ferry to Dover. Our guide stopped the bus and pointed to a particular road and said: "That was the line of retreat when the British were driven back in 1940, towards Dunkirk". I went into shock. To think that dear Raymond trod that path. Many Americans and some British visit the areas in France where we landed on D Day. The Normandy beaches are a priority to see. I am not able to fathom out the reasons why, but I had never had the inclination to go there.

Earlier in my story, I mentioned the fact that Spain was officially neutral – well it professed to be. It was not. Madrid was a hot-bed of German spies, and so incidentally, was Lisbon, Portugal, which also professed to be neutral, which it was not. In 1936 Spain was in the throes of a Civil War. Although that war cannot be considered as part of WW2, there are implications and connections. I feel obliged to offer a brief history of it.

Spain was a country beset by unrest and was ripe for an anarchist revolution. The Communist faction was set to overthrow the government, and the army, under General Franco, took charge to oppose it. He was a fascist, and Hitler's 'side kick'. Hitler took the opportunity to utilise the Spanish Civil War as a rehearsal for what he knew was the coming storm with Britain and her Allies. And that was three years before it actually happened.

So Hitler used his Luftwaffe and bombed 'the living daylights' out of the little defenceless Spanish town of Guernica. Hitler had set up that raid as a 'dummy run'. It happened in April 1937, on a market day when thousands were out in the streets. Thirty-one tons of munitions rained down, razing the town to the ground. It lasted for hours and was considered to be the worst atrocity of the war.

Spain under Franco

The systematic persecution of the Jewish people under the auspices of Adolph Hitler in Germany since 1933 spread in its many treacherous forms of detention and murder to all of the countries that were under the Nazi heel during the Second World War and before it.

The first anti-Semitic measures in Germany brought about the exodus of thousands of Jews seeking a safe haven. A few thousand managed to escape from the barbarity by crossing the Pyrenees, first officially through border controls, and later secretly over the mountains in amazing escapes. Many settled in Spain.

Regarding the attitude of General Franco, some are of the opinion that he tolerated the Jewish communities in residence giving sanctuary to the Sephardi community, that is, the Jews of Spanish and Portuguese origin. However, some say that in the early years of the Spanish Civil War, Jewish communities were aware of his animosity.

Some Jews left and others converted to the religion of that country, Catholicism. Early in 1939 a synagogue was ransacked by Franco's supporters and the community went into hiding. In some towns collective solidarity existed, and help was forthcoming from sympathetic townspeople for those who were escaping from France via the mountains. Valleys provided isolation, especially in winter, hidden from the police and the ensuing deportation back to France.

Escape networks set up by Allied services in France and Andorra were collaborating with anti-Franco adherents. The escaping refugees were led on the difficult and dangerous journeys across mountain ranges in the cold and snow, and in foggy conditions. Unable to obtain official permits, people entered Spain illegally. An American reporter saved hundreds of those fleeing including many of the famous. Such a one, was Marc Chagall, the artist.

Consulates of many countries in Spain undertook the care and protection of the refugees, including America, Britain, Holland and the Belgians, and the honorary consulate of Poland. The priority of the aid organizations was to rescue the children. They were sheltered and hidden until moved onto Spanish or Portuguese departure ports bound for America or to Palestine.

* * *

From Sidney to Roger

As is my established format in these stories I have my own little bit to relate in connection with the above. As well as being given an English forename, Jewish people often have a biblical one. I am called Myrtle; my Hebrew name is Miriam. My Mum was Hetty on her birth certificate, her Jewish name was Esther. One of my sons-in-law, Roger, has the name of Rueben, a son of the biblical Jacob. Jewish history tells of the Twelve Tribes of Israel, and Rueben is one such group.

When my daughter, Sheila, married Roger I was at a loss as what to give them for a wedding present. Both partners had established homes and it presented a problem. I had a brainwave. Marc Chagall had painted a depiction of each of the Twelve Tribes. The originals now hang in the Hadassah University Medical Centre in Jerusalem. I decided to work a tapestry of the one dedicated to Rueben. By coincidence Sheila's Dad, Raymond, also bore that name as his birthright, and so my prezzie would be as a double whammy both to Sheil and Rog.

Trawling the craft shops in the UK was a 'no-go' for a pre-printed tapestry. I eventually located a canvas in, of all places, Sydney, Australia. I have a rider to add to this tale. Approaching Easter and busy on the needlework, I discovered that I had run short of black embroidery wool. Again I scoured the local shops but I was not able to match that colour, which might come as a surprise to you as it did to me. After all black is black, no matter how one sees it. It is not so, black can look greyish in many degrees. I resorted once again to the supplier in Sydney. The parcel was posted on a Thursday, the day before Good Friday, and I had it delivered to my door the following Tuesday. It had taken five days with the Easter holiday in between. How about that?

Tapestry of Marc Chagall's Reuben window

I worked feverishly on the project. I had five months in which to complete it before the wedding and it was necessary to allow time for framing. It hangs on the wall of my daughter's home facing the front door, and I have an exact photographic replica hanging opposite the front door of my flat. I have recently become a great grandmother for the seventh time and the name of the new baby is Rueben. I intend to offer that picture to my granddaughter for her little boy. The photograph is remarkable, every stitch is visible, and I am very pleased at the outcome of both the original and the copy.

So if Marc Chagall had not been rescued over the Pyrenees Alps my daughter Sheila and her new husband Roger would have a wedding present of a vase or a dish stuck away in some corner or cupboard.

* * *

Meanderings and a Haircut

I was on holiday in Madrid, and as I always do, I visited famous museums and galleries. In the National Art Gallery, the Prado, I stood and looked for a long time at the painting by Picasso of his depiction of the attack on Guernica. It was worth going to that capital if for no other reason than to have the opportunity to gaze upon that masterpiece.

Whilst I was there in Spain, I visited Franco's tomb and memorial. He had ruled Spain until he died, when the monarchy was reinstated. He was a dictator: he instigated a war with massive loss of life, and he aided his pal, Hitler. He was no friend of mine. I went purely as a tourist and because I like to 'look see' places and objects that I have never seen before.

Just as a fact of history, many young men from around the world went to Spain to support the Republican cause fighting Fascist Franco. They came from America, Wales, Ireland and many other developed countries. Many volunteered from London. They were members of the Communist Party which was quite the 'thing' to be in in the East End of London where I lived. Banded together, these courageous activists came to be known, and remembered, as 'The International Brigade'. Although I was a youngster of eleven, I was quite interested in the affair and I knew many of the men who left. Some never returned home.

The Ernest Hemingway book, 'For Whom the Bell Tolls' presents an intimate insight into that Spanish tragedy. It was later adapted for cinema audiences. The female lead was Ingrid Bergman. She had an accusation thrust upon her, and she is punished by the loss of her hair. I have previously described my trendy hair style of the 40s. Having seen the film, I decided that I would have my hair cut short to emulate Miss Bergman. My locks had a good curl when I was young, and I thought that that style would suit me. It became the 'thing to do', and was followed by all the young ladies.

I was engaged to Raymond at that time. I had arranged to get my tresses shorn on a weekend when he was not expected. Well, expected or not, he was the one who opened the front door on my return home. Seeing him, I refused to remove the headscarf I was wearing until I was finally coaxed to do so, and the "New Me" was revealed. Happily it was well received. In all of the intervening seventy years, until now, I have never worn my hair long again.

It is not curly now and the colour is somewhat changed, but short it still is.

* * *

A Man to Remember with Love

Alfred Russell, my late spouse, was a demobilized RAF serviceman when I met him. Like so many others, he was reluctant to talk of his wartime experiences and I did not insist that he did. Nevertheless, I was aware that he spent some of those years in Basra, Iraq. In the 1940s, I had no idea where Basra was. I was a Land Girl then and did not have a bedroom door on which to attach my war map. But if you read the middle newspaper pages or listened to the tail-end of the wireless news, you would get an inkling that something was going on in that place. It did not rate 'big time' attention. I reckon that I was too busy digging up spuds or embroiled in the high jinks down at the YM to have too much time for news-scanning.

There were two main bases in World War 2 Iraq – Basra and Habbaniya. One was used as an RAF outfitters, converting training aircraft to planes ready for normal air force activities. I am not sure if Alf Russell was one of the spanner or pincer operators. He was a talented trumpet virtuoso. He did not blow the 'wake up' bugle, and he was not a follower of Bach; nor was military music his forte, although I am sure that he could have tackled either. Popular music was his tune. I can imagine the local ladies fox-trotting to his playing as I did all those years ago, or perhaps they did not in Iraq.

Nevertheless, entertainment was bound to have been organized for the pleasure of those serving abroad, and I dare say his music was much appreciated when there were less vital matters to see to. And maybe his band did play for dancing. When he was back in civvy street he organized a dance band of his own as a hobby, and they played for free for various local events and charities. After we met, I would accompany him and I realized how brilliant and versatile he was. It's a sorry tail piece to this little bit of my story; dear Alf, a good and loving man to his own and extended family, is no longer with us.

I wonder if he is amazing the angels with an 'obligato'.

* * *

Iraqi Troubles 20th Century - What's New in the 21st Century?

A Treaty with Iraq in 1930 provided the British with peace-time air-force bases near the towns of Basra and Habbaniya, and the right to transit military forces in a time of war, in addition to facilitating cover for the usage of the railways, rivers, ports and airfields.

When war materialized, Iraq broke off diplomatic relations with Germany but refrained from an actual declaration of hostilities. Italy entered the arena and the Iraqi government was not inclined to go even as far as to sever relational links with Mussolini's lot. The Italian Legation in Baghdad became a hot bed of intrigue and propaganda, fermenting anti-British attitudes, encouraged by the pro-German Mufti of Jerusalem living there under asylum.

In March 1941, Rashid Ali, a collaborator of Hitler's, became Prime Minister. The pro-British regent, Emir Abdul-Ilah fled. It was vital that Basra, the main port of Iraq on the Persian Gulf, was accessible and available to the British. Reinforcements arrived from the Commonwealth including India. The Indian Brigade landed on Iraqi soil on the 18th April. Later in my story I will tell of an Indian general – one Jack Jacobs. I came to hear that one of the engagements he was involved with was in Iraq. 'What goes around, comes around', as they say!

When Rashid Ali was informed that further transports were expected, he refused permission. He was hoping for German assistance to exploit his decision. When German aid was not forthcoming he took matters into his own hands and acted. The first hostile act was directed towards Habbaniya, the British air-training post in the Iraqi desert.

British women and children had been evacuated there from Baghdad to ensure their safety. The British encamped on that site numbered a total of 9,000 civilians and 2,000 fighting men. Iraqi forces arrived and took up positions on a plateau overlooking the cantonment less than a mile away. Early in the morning of that 2nd May 1941, the Iraqis attacked.

The constant worry back home was that Egypt and the Suez Canal should stay stable, and that any matter of trouble in the Middle East was dangerous. From the time of the outbreak of war in September 1939 right through the 1940s, that was the paramount priority of Mr Churchill and the Allied military. Iraq was not too far away in distance from those two vulnerable locations, and the truculent 'naughties' needed to be dealt with pronto, especially when the Iraqis expected reinforcements from neighbouring Falluja. The RAF squadrons took charge and quickly put an end to the Iraqi insurgents. It transpired that the Iraqis were extremely nervous, especially when the RAF planes appeared, and their now deserted unmanned guns could not be fired! By the 7th May, the siege was brought to a satisfactory conclusion. The women and their offspring were flown to Basra; 400 prisoners and some captured military hardware gave proof of a job well done.

* * *

It Ain't Finished Yet

The tale of the 'how-d'ye-do' in that part of the world was by no means over. May 18th 1941 saw the arrival of yet additional numbers of the British to resume operations. By that time the Germans had arrived in opposition and were established in the town of Mosul. The remit of the RAF was to attack and to prevent supplies from neighbouring Vichy Syria reaching them. In the long run, British ground forces were required which finally scuppered the German objectives.

The British advance moved upon Baghdad on May 27th, giving forward troops scope to reach and achieve the target three days later. Rashid Ali and his acolytes did a runner to Persia (Iran) with the rest of the rabble rousers, taking with them the ex-Mufti. An armistice was signed the following day and the Iraqi Regent was re-installed.

That country was now under British control, and was in occupation forthwith.

Do any of the named places mentioned in this saga ring a bell? Cast your minds back thirteen years ago to 2003 when the American coalition entered Iraq:

they had hoped to topple the regime of Saddam Hussein. Back-track the years to that British invasion in 1941. In the reckoning of my elementary powers of arithmetic, I deduce that the answer should be sixty-two years. That is if my limited mathematical prowess proves me correct. Sixty-two years had elapsed between those two invasions. The point I am attempting to stress, as I have tried to do many times before in my account is, do they ever learn? And is it any better today in the Middle East in 2016? I have today, 8th November 2016, just channelled into the news. They are fighting in Mosul. Will they ever, ever learn?!

* * *

Not Quite a Gamble or a Boat Ride

Operation Dragoon was the code name allotted to the Allied invasion of the coast on the Mediterranean in Southern France. It took place on August 15th 1944, just two months after the Allied Normandy landings in Northern France in June. The campaign is not well known or remembered; the interest and excitement of the earlier offensive rather overshadowed the latter.

Preceded by aerial and naval attacks, airborne and glider detachments followed. It gave the Allies swift entrenchment and success. The Germans speedily abandoned the area. It was a rapid assault and the Germans had no real interest in the south of that country. They had too much in hand in the north-west. They could not retreat fast enough. They did retreat however, through the Rhone Valley to the low-range Vosges Mountains in eastern France, near to the German border.

The planners of the operation were correct in their assumption that Hitler was in no mood to deploy his forces in that area when he had more important worries to fret about, even though he must have expected such an attack on that Mediterranean coast. He was beset by the recent news from Normandy; he was involved in trouble in the then Yugoslavia; and most urgent of all was the fact of the advancing forces of the Russian Soviet Army.

The reason and purpose of an onslaught in that vicinity of the Mediterranean was to eventually capture the strategic and important ports of Marseille and Toulon, situated in line with the towns pinpointed for attack. It was a well thought-out manoeuvre. It was considered vital and essential for the Allies to have a reliable and easily accessible supply-line to maintain the expanding Allied Forces now so enmeshed in activities in that country.

Of course I was not witness to the occasion, but recording this episode I have a strange instinctive notion that Mr Churchill's vibrant brain conceived and gave birth to the endeavour.

Raymond never recounted his wartime adventures, and thinking of that now, I wonder if he was one of those taking part.

It must be obvious to my readers that I have enjoyed a much travelled history. Of latter years I have come to a reluctant acknowledgement that I am now a bit too 'long in the tooth' as the saying goes, to venture too far from home. I am now reduced to browsing with envy through the holiday brochures I receive unsolicited in the post. Whilst feeling relatively cerebrally fit, I must admit to a degree of physical immobility which proves to be a handicap to a roving 'wannabe'. However, last year I did feel some of the old wanderlust, and summoning up a bit of 'Dutch Courage', I opted to review my 'Bucket List' and decided that I would travel to the South of France. I left London and travelled on Eurostar from St. Pancras Station to St. Raphael, St. Topaz, Nice and Monte Carlo. I was not much taken or interested in casinos and yachts, but I was keen to explore the history and effects of the involvement of those towns which were involved in World War 2, particularly the first two I have mentioned. Pillboxes, erected for defence against an enemy, were still standing and in view. My imagination working on all four cylinders, almost brought me face-to-face with the ghosts of those fighting men. I read the accounts of that time on the various plaques and inscriptions. I was there standing on the same soil in that same place. The years had rolled away and it was the 15th August 1944.

* * *

The Agony of Malta

In 1940, the struggle began for control of the Mediterranean island of Malta, situated in a strategically important position, where success or failure could affect the entire balance of the war itself. In my opinion, it was a 'win or lose' toss-up. And I mean not just Malta but the whole unmitigated shindig. But this is not the time for jokes. Malta was a serious matter and not many of the Maltese made fatuous comments at that time. Believe me, I do not regard the Second World War as a lark. If I was not able to interject a few of my ludicrous remarks into the recording of it, I would not be able to tell of it.

The combined air and naval forces of Germany and Italy were pitted against the RAF and the Royal Navy. The battle that was fought in North Africa increased Malta's already considerable value and strategic importance. British air and sea forces based on the island were in a position to interfere in the Axis' ability to transport vital supplies and reinforcements from Europe. General Erwin Rommel, commanding the Axis military in North Africa, aired his views and implied that Malta was the 'king pin', and that if they were not able to grind Malta into submission, and to hold it, the North African tussle would witness an Axis defeat.

Malta was one of the most intensely bombed areas of the war. The Axis flew a total of 3,000 raids over that tiny island in a period of two years in an effort to destroy the RAF defences, the ports, and the morale of its people. By 1942, Rommel had lost the war in the deserts of Libya and Egypt, and the process of hostilities were concentrated in Tunisia. Attacks on Malta were rapidly reduced, and in November 1942 the Siege of Malta lifted. A month later the Axis chickens came home to roost. The British air and sea capabilities operating from the island sank 230 enemy ships in 164 days.

I have enjoyed the pleasures that a vacation in Malta can provide. I was comfortable amid the friendly natives; I basked in the sunshine; I was interested in its 'Knights of old' history, and I did trips on its surrounding blue waters of the Med. There was not a vestige of evidence that the island had suffered so much during the war years.

In that tiny but densely populated island, nearly 6,000 private dwellings were destroyed and almost 10,000 were damaged. One hundred and eleven churches and fifty institutional buildings, including hospitals, banks, clubs, government offices, theatres, factories, flour mills and other commercial buildings took hits and were rendered out of action. Their Royal Opera House and the famous Clock Tower and Government House were obliterated. Thirteen hundred citizens of Malta perished.

In 1942, King George VI bestowed upon the island of Malta the George Cross: the citation was "To bear witness to the heroism and devotion of its people". How well it was deserved. The symbol of the cross is woven into its national flag, and that history should be remembered whenever and wherever that flag is observed.

* * *

From London E1 to the Med and Back

Some years ago, when my mobility capabilities were better than they are today, I did a voluntary job as a tour guide at the Jewish Museum in Camden, London.

I did a Sunday afternoon stint and I loved it. Having an interest in history, of all dimensions, my particular niche is on the first floor where the history of the Jews in Britain is laid bare for scrutiny, and I was around to enlarge upon it.

I would take my visitors through the gallery from the time of William the Conqueror, who brought Jewish physicians with him from Normandy, right through the ages. Queen Elizabeth 1 also had Jewish doctors; King Charles II decreed freedom for all religions; and so on, until I reached the Great War and introduced the substantial Jewish contribution to that conflict, and on through history to the Second World War, when the service given to King and Country was again matched by the former. And I would tell them the story of the 'King of Lampedusa'.

I am apologizing now because I am leaving my subject to get an item off my chest. It has been a source of indigestion for years. Sometime ago, an Honourable Member of the House of Parliament, (I wish I could remember his name), stated that he was not aware that Jewish people had fought in the war. Was he kidding or just plain stupid or a total ignoramus!

Right, I'm back on track. I continue now with my story of the King of Lampedusa. On 10th June 1941, a young RAF pilot was on sortie duty over the Mediterranean Sea. His name was Sydney Cohen, son of a tailor, and his home was the East End of London. His engine began to splutter and he needed to land. Where? Below him lay the Italian-held island of Lampedusa. The name of that island had been long forgotten for more than 70 years. Last year, 2015, it had a dusting down and its name revived by the advent of the refugee migration into Europe. So Sydney managed to land his plane on Lampedusa, where some of the 4,300 Italian troops garrisoned there rushed out waving white handkerchiefs shouting: "The British have landed", promptly surrendering that domain. He was handed a note of surrender which he delivered when he returned to his Malta base. That long-forgotten newspaper, The News Chronicle, headlined the news next morning: "London tailor's cutter now King of Lampedusa". War news was not encouraging at that time and public morale was low. The Chronicle report was a 'feel good' item.

* * *

Germany's Business and a Follow-up

The news even reached Germany. During the war German propaganda programmes were broadcast on our wireless network by a man nicknamed Lord Haw Haw.

His real name was William Joyce and he spoke with a perfect upper-class English accent. The programmes began with a call sign: "Germany calling, Germany calling"; we treated it with derision. He was American born and grew up in Ireland; he became a member of the then National Union of Fascists. He got himself to Germany before the war and became a naturalized citizen of that country. He voiced the German views regarding Sydney Cohen in their usual spurious, virulent cultish mode. The Germans used him to discourage and alarm, but we laughed and thought it a good joke.

However my tale has an epilogue. In the East End of London there existed a 'Yiddish Theatre'. It was conceived after the Jewish exodus from persecution in Eastern Europe: in the late 19th and early 20th century people not yet able to manipulate the English language, sought entertainment in their own tongue. Not Hebrew in which they prayed and used in worship at their synagogues, but in the lingo that they had used in their former home. They could meet up and have a good night at the theatre. It produced all sorts, even Shakespeare. I have actually seen a handbill advertising King Lear, in Yiddish! I once met a very elderly lady, Anna Tzeinker, who as a child, acted on that stage with her Dad, Meier, a leading doyen in that venue. And a play was produced – 'The King of Lampedusa'. It was a hum-dinger of a wow! The word was circulated and the crowds arrived from everywhere. Even the 'nobs' from the posh West End sought tickets. But a cloud appeared on the horizon. Another local theatre was in dire straits. Business was bleak and it took to dirty tricks. They put it about that Mr Churchill was arriving on a certain date to see for himself this phenomenon. As they had expected, the entire population of East London and beyond crowded onto the streets awaiting Winnie's arrival which did not materialize. Everybody was very disappointed and nobody, but nobody, had bought tickets for the 'The King'. Lord Haw-Haw broadcasting from Germany, advised us that the theatre playing the Lampedusa story, The Grand Palais, would be visited by the Luftwaffe. It was all spin and alarmist rubbish, and it didn't work.

***

A Russian Demand - the Iranian Dilemma

In the summer of 1941, after Russia entered into the war, they desperately needed supplies, particularly of oil. Goods were already arriving at the ports of Murmansk and Archangel from Britain, but capacity by that route was limited and subject to enemy action. Supplies were also dispatched from the United States to Vladivostok and since America was still a neutral country, the transporting ships sailed under a Soviet flag.

The Russians faced a long haul in their fight against Germany and large quantities of war material was needed. The obvious solution was to seek an additional source and a route to match, and Iran, once Persia, was the answer to that problem. However, the Shah, King Reza, was deemed to be Hitler's pal and blatantly refused to relieve Russia of her dilemma. He denied free access. The British, who were involved in this 'Cat and Mouse' game, and the Russians, cast envious eyes on a recently opened Trans Iranian Railway, and surmised that would be a very handy gizmo to move the spoils.

Well they did what they all did in the war: "We want so we will 'ave it, thank you very much". Churchill's and the Soviet troops invaded Iran on the 25th August 1941, and the enterprise of 'getting it' ended on the 17th September. They arrested the monarch – they deposed him in favour of a younger brother and shoved him off with a 'flea in his ear' to South Africa, in exile; they took control of Iranian communications and the coveted railway, to boot!

Iranian resistance was of little matter to the aggressors. They had no allies, only a small army which had no time to organize itself into a viable fighting force to face a surprise tactical incursion from two overbearing and power-house war experienced machines. That episode was the final military operation of the war in the Middle East but not quite the end of the story. The Russians and the British remained in Iran, in occupation, until 1946. The British left in March of that year, seven months after the cessation of hostilities with Japan. The Soviets were reluctant to go. They took their case to the United Nations on the pretext of being, under threat, security-wise.

It was the United Nations first complaint to be filed by a member country. It tested its ability; it took no steps to pressurise the Soviets to leave. They did, however, leave for home later that year. We now know that Russia has good experience in 'take-over' deals. They later land-grabbed mid European States, for example Hungary and East Berlin. Perhaps they had ambitions for a return encore to Iran one day. As I write this account, they are in the Ukraine which isn't theirs. So where next?

I cannot admit to any connection to Iran except one. I knit sophisticated teddy bears for charity. I do exact replicas of players of all the football clubs. I do popular characters, like Batman and Dr Who, and I knit teds incorporating national flags, such as Wales – reminiscent of my Cardiff days. A lady asked me to do one of Iran which I did.

The red, white and green made up in correct colour order pleased her, and I was satisfied too. It is a bonus because white, green and red are appropriate colours for Christmas and any stock of the Iranian model is a good seller at the craft fairs I do in December. Well I did manage to get my commercial in and no fee attached.

* * *

Operation Torch

A British-American invasion of Vichy France territories in the North African coastal countries of Algeria and Morocco, was decided upon as a sop to the Soviet Union's insistence for the opening of a Second Front which would

One of Myrtle's hand-knitted teddies depicting Wales

relieve the pressure on Soviet forces. German military would be required to transfer its strength from Russia to face a new onslaught elsewhere. It was condescending lip-service to Stalin, but it was to the Allied advantage to do so in any case. It would clear the Axis Powers from North Africa and it would give the Allies greater control of the Mediterranean Sea, and thereby prepare for an invasion of southern Europe.

The Allies landed in Morocco on the 8th November 1942, and thus Operation Torch materialized. It was planned that three amphibious task forces would seize key ports and airports of Morocco and Algeria, simultaneously targeting Casablanca, Algiers and another less-known but just as important, Oran. The latter invaded by airborne paratroopers.

It was also an affair staged for propaganda purposes. It was made to appear as an all-American onslaught for the winning of French hearts and minds. The French were still a bit upset at British action in Meres-el-Kabir with the resulting loss of French lives.

The operation was in reality a combined American and British operation, with a difference – Royal Navy ships flew 'The Stars and Stripes' and the British Fleet Air Arm planes displayed the US 'star roundel'. Mr Churchill suggested in the planning stage, that British 'tommies' should wear US uniforms, which was turned down. If it had happened, I think that they should have put in a request for the inflated GI pay equivalent.

This ploy of misinformation reminds me of the sometimes German dirty tricks of hoisting a neutral flag from a ship's mast to bamboozle an Allied vessel and replacing it with a Swastika when it was too late for that ship to adequately defend itself. It is said 'all's fair in love and war'. I have no argument about the former but there is nothing fair about war. It is an unwarranted and undeserved arbitrary state of affairs that affects everyone.

Another device conceived by the planners of this operation was to entice German U-Boats prowling around the eastern Atlantic to deliberately attack a passing convoy sailing at a far enough distance away from the site of the Torch action. I hope that these convoy ships were manufactured in plywood and seamen-less automatic steerage. The master brainwaves of the 'Big Boys' did throw up some crafty capers.

The Allies were not able to latch on to the adverse intelligence afoot in Vichy French circles, made available to the defenders, by which they were able to bolster their coastal defences, to the disadvantage of the Allied landings. There were a few other hiccoughs. At one point in the action, the inclement weather was a feature against them. In another, troops were uncertain of where they were. A newly-arrived transportation of Americans directly from home bases, unlike the others who came via the UK, were untried; recently trained, with no experience of battle. This would be their trial by fire ordeal.

Some damage to landing craft came about because of the unexpected shallowness of the water. No previous reconnaissance had been put into place to monitor local maritime conditions. The lesson was well learnt, and sea landings in a later coastal onslaught in Normandy bore the fruits of Operation Torch mistakes. The beaches of Normandy were fully investigated and charted beforehand. A further unexpected incident occurred when a French convoy appeared during an Allied mine-sweeping routine, clearing a path for the landing parties. Amid delay and confusion, two Allied invasion vessels were attacked and destroyed, and an exchange of fire resulted in the sinking of most of those sailing under the Vichy flag; the remaining ones still afloat, scurrying back to shore.

Operation Torch was our first Allied major airborne assault. To join the engagement, aircraft of that regiment transported paratroopers from Britain, flying across Spain. The flight was hindered by bad weather over that country, exacerbated by communication problems and by the long-haul travel arrangements. The formation was forced to scatter and 30 of their start number of 37 were compelled to land in the dry salt lake west of the objective.

* * *

Algerian Patriots

In the early hours of the 8th November 1942, four hundred French Jewish Resistance fighters staged a coup in the city of Algiers. They seized the telephone exchange, the radio station, the governor's house and some army headquarters. At another time coastal batteries had been neutralized by Resistance members, and one French commander openly welcomed the incoming Allies. With the help of these people the French Commander, General Giraud, was surreptitiously smuggled aboard a British ship to nearby Gibraltar where General Eisenhower, in command of Operation Torch, had set up his headquarters. He was offered a position in Dwight Eisenhower's set up, but Giraud refused. He wanted the boss's job. The Frenchman remained in Gibraltar. He decided to stay there and remained a 'spectator' in the affair.

Eisenhower, with the support of President Roosevelt and Mr Churchill, entered into an agreement with the Vichy French Admiral Darlan, recognizing him as High Commissioner in North Africa in return for his compliance in ordering a cessation of all resistance. Apart from those taken prisoner, the population submitted to the Allies and joined them. They would see much action under the Allied banner and fought for us against Italy in a future Italian campaign: 60% of the soon to be part of Free French forces were mostly Moroccans.

When Adolph Hitler got wind of Darlan's deal he immediately ordered a German invasion of the Vichy French territory of Tunisia. On the 24th December a French local, of obscure allegiance, assassinated Darlan giving the French North African government leave to gradually immerse itself in all of the Allied war efforts.

* * *

Me in Fancy Dress

I have seen fit to write about the exploits of this part of the world, and there has to be a twist in the tail. So here goes. A few years ago one of my daughters was due to be married. I had arranged a holiday to Algeria and it coincided more or less with her wedding date. In fact my arrival back home would be in the region of a couple of days before her nuptials.

To travel to my destination I left on Eurostar and did an overnight trip across the Iberian Peninsula. It was rather an experience and a lark to take a 'sleeper'. It was not a straight run. I took the advantage of several stop-overs, and I remember how taken I was when I stayed a few days in the Spanish town of Ronda. When I lived in Cardiff, I would often shop in the Welsh Rhondda, with an 'H' and an extra 'D'. I finally arrived after crossing the Straights of Gibraltar.

I had a very good holiday. I went to Casablanca, Rabat, Marrakech and Tangier; topped by a trip into the Atlas Mountains, all the while keeping a very strict eye on my calorie intake. I had a new dress hanging in the wardrobe at home for the special function on the horizon, and I hoped I would be able to get into it.

Waiting on the jetty, arriving at the meeting venue to board a boat back to Spain, I was becoming more and more anxious about any increase in girth and more and more worried about how I would fit into my clobber back home. I espied a stall holder offering mementos of those tourist resorts, and I seized upon the idea of taking a replacement garment home with me, just in case. So I purchased a djellaba. It looked quite a bit out of the ordinary but I thought its loose folds would hide any extra inches, and the colour suited me. It was certainly a lot less expensive than purchasing another Brent Cross, (a shopping mall close to my home – very up market), garment. So I tucked the item into my bag. I still have it. I did not need it for the wedding. The original garment looked fine. And that late acquisition is sometimes given an airing for a fancy dress do, or I don it just for a laugh in front of my great grandchildren.

Tunisia, a land mass lying due east of Algeria with a partial coastal border, was held by Vichy France. Hitler's threat to invade it was fulfilled. The initial German operations were weak but they succeeded. Allied forces met the challenge. Under the command of General Eisenhower and General Montgomery victory was finally brought about.

The combatting troops were a unified band of brothers, even though they were far from their peace-time homes, and living long distances from each other. They were of course British and American. Others had left homes in India, New Zealand, with a few Free Frenchman in the mix. Sadly 76,000 never saw home again. But they scuppered the Germans and their mates the Italians, and in May 1943, six months after the bugle blew for battle to commence, the action ended with a feather in the cap for the 'good guys'. The fall of Tunisia signalled the ejection of the 'baddies' from North Africa which would in due course become part of Free France.

* * *

Me and the Foreign Office

Years ago, while I was still at work, I did a European trip. It was very early on in my wanderings. My holiday allowance in those far-off days was not as generous as that given today. I needed to do as much as I could in a short space of time. I plumped for a 'Tuesday – Belgium; Wednesday – Germany; Thursday – Spain; in seven days', type of vacation. I remember I had wanted to see Gibraltar at the southern tip of Spain, and was told by the booking staff that was included in the itinerary. Two days later that company informed me that 'Gib' was off the books, with no forthcoming information as to why.

Well I have never been a 'Mrs Muggings', so I telephoned the Foreign Office to elucidate why. The conversation went as follows:

"Mrs, the frontier between Spain and Gibraltar is closed". I asked: "Since when?" They replied: "Since General Franco's Spanish take-over many years ago." I asked: "When will it re-open?" They replied: "Mrs, when Franco is dead.".

If the Foreign Office retains old telephone recordings you can check this conversation for accuracy. I was jubilant when I won my court case against the holiday firm for misrepresentation. I hope they have learned to be a bit more honest with their travel promotion now. I refused their offer of a freebee holiday – (how could I trust them?), and took the cash instead. When Franco rested in the nether world, I revived my plans and crossed that frontier. I had arrived!

* * *

The Apes and the Tunnels

I really enjoyed my stay on the 'Rock', as Gibraltar is affectionately known, and apart from the apes perching on my shoulders as I ate my sandwiches, I felt thoroughly at home, what with M&S and the Co-Op in view. Naturally I did all the tourist things that were to be done in that location, and I left with my mind buzzing with what I had learnt of its war-time history.

Gibraltarians enjoyed a peaceful few months at the beginning of the war, apart from increased activity on the Rock itself. Things changed when in May 1940 Germany invaded France and Italy hitched onto the Axis coat-tails two months later. In 1941 the British went feverishly into action and undertook a 'make-over' of the 18th century excavation of 30 miles of tunnelling within the Rock itself.

The siege of Gibraltar at that time, (1779–1783), had activated the building of the tunnels. Tons of limestone were blasted out to fashion a huge man-made system of caverns. The British Army Royal Engineers carried out the renovation work in 1941. It developed into an underground city comprising barracks, offices and a fully equipped hospital. Water and electrical supplies, sanitary arrangements, a laundry, and all else to accommodate personnel for normal living, were installed.

The geographical position of Gibraltar served as a vital role in both the Atlantic and the Mediterranean campaigns. It presented a strongly defended harbour from which ships could provide escorts for convoys to and from the besieged island of Malta. It suffered aerial attack from Vichy France and the Italian Air Force. Spaniards and some home-grown Gibraltarians were recruited by Germany as undercover agents and active saboteurs.

Following the successful Allied engagements in North Africa and the turn-coat resolution of the Italians in 1943, Gibraltar's role shifted from a forward operational area to a rear-guard position and supply base. The harbour continued to maintain its dry dock activities. Convoy routes through the Mediterranean relied on its depots for servicing and maintenance and for its crucial supplies and requirements.

I have a granddaughter, Helen, living and working in Gibraltar. She offers beautician services and operates two salons in the main areas. Her business is called 'Aphrodite', and if some travellers should happen to find themselves on the Rock, call in and say "Hi" from Nana. You might get a freebee too.

The Colours of Italy - Red, White and Green

A holiday in Italy gave me the opportunity to visit a particular town, traveling north from Naples, halfway on the road to Rome. Inadvertently, I have not mentioned the campaign fought in Italy apart from the fact that Raymond landed there taking part in a British offensive. That is remiss of me, and I intend to rectify that mistake at this juncture.

During WW2 Italy lay under the dictator, Mussolini. He was a fascist and Hitler's friend and ally. After a series of operational setbacks in 1943, Mussolini surrendered to the Allies and Germany took over the fight. Mr Churchill and President Roosevelt planned to drive the Germans out of that country.

The Americans and the British made landings on Anzio and Salerno in Southern Italy on July 3rd 1943. Their objective was to reach Rome and capture it, thereby freeing Italy from German subjugation. It was a tough campaign – extremely hard fought and very costly for the Allies. Indians, New Zealanders and Polish reinforcements were also engaged.

They had reached a point halfway up the leg of Italy and were held at the town of Cassino. There atop a very steep cliff was perched a monastery; Monte Cassino. And here the Germans dug in and were in an advantageous position to rebuff any attack that was attempted. By now Polish divisions were brought in as reinforcements, and together with the British, they sought to fight their way up that treacherous cliff, being shelled and mown down in a continuous hail of mortars and gunfire. It was a slaughter. The Germans had the upper hand and not just in the literal sense. Eventually we succeeded. We had such a very costly victory, but were able to advance to Rome. We had reached our objective and cleared Italy of the enemy.

That was the reason why I decided as I was already in Italy, I would go to Monte Cassino. I climbed to the top of the cliff and wandered around inside the rebuilt Abbey. I looked down from that cliff top and tried to imagine the carnage that happened there from the 17th January to the 18th May 1943. From my standpoint I could see the lie of the land. I could see so much of that beautiful Italian terrain which was designated to be the resting place of so many dead. Acres and acres of white lay before me. It looked like huge swathes of settled snow. It was the white of the sea of gravestones that I looking at. Men from many parts of the world, buried where they fell. I left in tears.

Travelling On, the War Continued

Leaving Cassino, I travelled north-east to the Adriatic coastal town of Ortona. It was here that the Moro River campaign was fought, 4th to the 26th December 1943. The British and Canadians faced the German Panzer Divisions and it resulted in a fight from hell. Eight thousand men sacrificed their lives in the space of a few weeks. Not much of a Christmas present for those at home waiting for news of their kith and kin.

Carnage reigned in that town. Throughout the week 11th to the 18th December the narrow streets, filled with masonry debris, became a nightmarish maze. The Germans had prepared well for the ensuing confrontation. Major thoroughfares were mined and booby traps were implanted throughout the town. Vicious house-to-house warfare was the mode of combat. Eventually the Germans abandoned the action. The Allies did make gains but were denied an outright victory. Their objective had not been achieved. The Allied operation commander aborted the battle, probably owing to the winter conditions.

I duly paid my respects to those heroes, the war dead, in the Moro River Canadian war cemetery. It is located on high ground near the sea. In situations of that nature I always feel that the men buried in their graves facing outwards to waterways are somehow reaching out for home.

I think that it is mandatory here to add a post script to the Italian story. I must confess that although I lived through the war, and I knew that some action had taken place in Italy, it was remembering that Raymond had been awarded the Italian Campaign Medal that encouraged me to visit this war arena and to impart these episodes.

I very clearly recollect him telling me that he had landed in Sicily. He gave no details of his life 'in the field' and I did not press him. I surmised that if he wanted to talk about it, he would have done so. I researched the history of the Sicilian invasion and I have discovered that it started on the 3rd July 1943, and the Airborne Division, under whose command he fought, landed in gliders near a town called Syracuse on the east coast of the island.

They landed as planned, beyond the beachheads to seize key points to aid the invasion troops coming ashore. Leaving that once stricken area it occurred to me that it represented the colours of the Italian flag. Green for the beautiful landscape, white, the colour of the tombstones under which so many of the brave and committed lay in eternal rest, and the colour that seeped from them as they lay dying.

The Sands of the Sahara

I spent some time in North Africa. I went there specifically because I wanted to go to El Alamein where our tank corps gave us the first sweet taste of success. I wandered over the dunes to the flat sandy ground, and in my mind I could hear the rumble of approaching tanks. Major Bertram Brown (from Cardiff), leading his column.

It is ironic. On post-mortem, after the German defeat, it was thought that the German in command, Rommel, had lost the battle of the tanks because of the depletion of oil. Little did he know that he and his army were standing on top of it. A huge reservoir of that commodity has been discovered right under the Sahara desert.

When I visit war-time sites I always visit the war cemeteries. I always pay my respects to the fallen. Until you do you cannot imagine the scale of the slaughter that took place. That which you will see is a vast area of row after row after row of the graves of the slain. If you pause awhile to read the inscriptions you feel as if your heart will break. The majority were no more than lads. The flower of youth blown away, an entire generation gone.

The War Graves Commission first came into existence a few years after the Great War. They carry on giving a heartfelt service to mankind. All of the tombstones are identical, except of course for the engravings thereon giving details of the deceased soldiers. Private and general alike are buried side by side. No rank was 'pulled' in death. Some families would have preferred to have their loved ones brought home and buried close by, perhaps in a local graveyard, but it was not allowed.

The Commission decreed that they fought and died together and that they would stay together. That must have been a decision in contention at the time. I can imagine the heated debate and argument and the disappointment of many when it was finally settled. It was a brave arrangement that could not have been capped for equality, honesty and in befitting those who died. Even after all the years, since 1923, those cemeteries are looked after and kept in immaculate condition.

I heard of a mother who checked a war memorial for the name of her RAF son who, she thought, was lost at sea, and had not therefore been buried. In fact it was the one at Runnymede which bears the name of my cousin, already mentioned. Her son's name was not there. She contacted the Commission and reported it. They told her that if the name was missing then her son did indeed have an individual grave.

War cemetery in France.
They lay as they died – side by side

Very quickly she was informed where that was, and on the anniversary of his birth, she went to that 'foreign field' to stand by it, to mourn her loss, and have closure.

Whilst there, in that location, I spent a few days in a Saharan oasis. It had no connection to the war but because it was such an unusual experience, I feel the urge to mention it. It really was a 'one off'. My sleeping quarters were so different to the mundane hotel rooms where I usually bed down when I'm on my hols. It was fun and I rate it high on my 'lark scaleometer'!

Chapter 14
My German Travels

I Never Wanted to Go, but I Did

When I was in my eighties, I went to Germany with Rupert Morrison, a special friend. He was born and reared in Berlin until his parents, soon after the Kristallnacht atrocity and ominous warnings of what was to follow, put him on a train bound for Hamburg where, alone, aged 14 and never having travelled by himself before, he boarded a ship for England. His mother, who had married someone from mainland Europe, was English, and Rupert was going to live with his relations here in England. That was in 1938, one year before the exit gate would be closed. The only way out after that was by way of the cattle trucks transporting the Jewish citizens of Berlin to their short-lived futures; where they would be separated by gender and age, husbands from wives and children from their parents. Young and fit-looking adults taken for slave labour and the rest degraded, gassed and their bodies burnt in crematoria. After the war, like so many others, (especially if you were Jewish), I vowed never to go to that country, like my ex-bomber RAF navigator Uncle Monty, who never again flew in German air space.

But now it was different. I did go. I thought it right to go to pay homage to all those who had perished at the hands of Hitler and his evil adherents. And I went because Rupert and I were an 'item' of long standing. He wanted me to see where he had grown up. I felt very strange and uncomfortable on the streets of that city. But Rupert was thoughtful and understood.

He showed me the building where he had lived with his parents and their live-in help. She was a middle-aged lady who had been with them for years and Rupert often spoke of her. He called her, as far as his Teutonic humour would allow, 'the factotum'. I think that he had two 'Muttis', as you call your mum in German. We even climbed the stairs and stood outside the front door of the apartment. We didn't have the nerve to push the bell buzzer and to ask if we could have a 'look see'. Perhaps it was best for him that we did not.

* * *

Rupert's History

Rupert's father was a wholesaler in the tobacco trade – it was a time when smoking was the 'in thing'. He carried out his business from a shop premises. In spite of the aerial bombardment on Berlin during the war, I was surprised that all the buildings that Rupert knew and remembered from his youth were still there for me to see. And I saw the shop where his dad had worked.

After the awful events of Kristallnacht in September 1938, as previously described, Rupert's family lost their livelihood. German SA Paramilitary, (German Storm Detachment or Sturmabteilung), brown-shirted thugs, smashed the windows, damaged the property and looted the stock. Rupert said he remembered that night. I believe that his father was not in particularly good health, and after this incident he gradually spiralled into a decline from which he never recovered.

Of course Rupert spoke his mother tongue. His late wife was Dutch. When the Germans invaded Holland and began to round up the Jewish population, seventeen year-old Hilda, for that was her name, and her parents and her twelve year-old sister Dorothy were taken in and hidden by non-Jewish friends. Today we call those people 'Righteous Gentiles'. Well at least three of them were. Not so with the family who sheltered Hilda's sister. She was betrayed: taken, transported alone without parents and murdered in Auschwitz.

So it was reasonable that Hilda forbade the use of the German language when she had her own home. I spoke a kind of pidgin German. I had three years of tuition in the subject before I finished my schooling, but I had retained much of what I had been taught. It pleased me when Rupert often remarked that my German was quite good – for a novice! I practised sometimes when we were together, and I remember we once did a trip down the Rhine and I startled people on board that boat when I burst into song: *"Ich weiss nicht, das soll es bedeuten, dass Ich so traurig bin"*.

I remembered the famous German folk song about the mermaid in that river, who lured sailors to their death: 'Die Lorelei'. I must have had an excellent teacher but he had taught us that language with a Dutch accent. I discovered that by accident at a later date, but that is another story.

* * *

Touring in Berlin and an S&S Lunch

Rupert took me to the school from which he had been expelled, as were all the Jewish boys when Hitler came to power. Incidentally, it's a Jewish school now. We went to the building where he had his Bar Mitzvah, and to the wonderful museum which was once a synagogue where his parents had been married. Almost like a 'ya-hoo' to Hitler, that building, with its high-domed, golden-coloured roof, shines out like a beacon across Berlin. "We're still here Adolph, where are you?" There is a lovely tale about that edifice. How it was saved and not demolished as were so many others of its ilk; not degraded or blown up by the regime. But that is also another story.

Of course we also saw other places in Berlin. We progressed to 'Platform 14' where the trains had left with their Jewish 'cargo', and took stock of what we know and what we saw. It is now a memorial, almost a shrine. Marked along the long platform, the destinations and dates and how many wretched deportees there were are recorded on a day-by-day basis. We lit our memorial candles and Rupert intoned the prayer for the dead. How could it all have happened? We visited the site where the 'Burning of the Books' had taken place, and admired the imaginative way in which it has been immortalized.

We lunched at a famous eatery and ate German sausage and sauerkraut, with Rupert eating the authentic dish. Not adhering to the German tradition, I sated my hunger on veggie sausages, but it was a satisfying meal.

* * *

Old Stones and the New

En-route to further scenarios I found myself in Cologne. It was an interesting 'first'. I had not been there previously and I am always excited at the prospect of treading untrodden paths. When in Cologne one will always visit the towering edifice of the Cathedral. I was duly impressed by its size and grandeur as I am when exploring large and famous architectural structures, including sites of worship in so many parts of the world. I have visited churches, temples, mosques, synagogues and of course, cathedrals.

So Cologne was no exception. Here I discovered one particular aspect which intrigued me. I should have expected it. I saw the spectacular memorial to their 'Glorious Dead'.

Like we in Britain, as in so many other countries around the world, Germany too has so many to mourn for.

In Cologne, that once war-torn city, I thought of another place that was also subjected to aerial bombardment, but not as lucky as this one. Here the cathedral stands as it has for hundreds of years. The one I was thinking of was destroyed. A city much nearer home, Coventry, victim of Goering's vendetta.

It has to be remembered that I have travelled to many lands, in some instances decades after the war. Bombed and affected sites have been cleared, rebuilt, refashioned and modernised; unrecognizable if a comparison were to be made with pre-war photographs, so it should not be surprising if one is unable to visualize the extent of the devastation. Only from memory can I recall how it was when I witnessed newly-flattened and ruined buildings, later to become derelict, and depressing to look at and live with. I ran that gamut of emotions, as a Londoner, living through our Blitz.

And I recall how it was when I went to Coventry, to look at the rebuilt cathedral. It is a masterpiece of uniquely talented planners and builders. The ruined, ancient stone, incorporated into the new. What a magnificent outcome. The brilliance of those who brought it to fruition are to be applauded and I literally bow to their imagination and foresight. But my musings on the subject are not complete. There is another with a similar history. It too was a revered church, or it might have been a cathedral, like in Coventry; and I discovered it when I wandered around the streets of Berlin. Here the old and the new also cling together. The history is writ. The eye now cannot now see it. But the proof is laid bare. Those two monuments in Coventry and Berlin, dedicated to 'Remembrance' should serve as a reminder.

* * *

I Didn't Feel Much like Waltzing

I have been to Vienna many times. It is a very beautiful city. I have always been impressed with the music and the art that has emanated from its sons; the music of Mozart, and from the paintbrush of the artist, Klimt. But Vienna has had a difficult past. It was the capital of the Austro-Hungarian Empire, where the match that lit the fuse exploded into the First World War.

Austria was annexed by Hitler in 1938. He proclaimed that he had the right to do so. Austrians spoke the same mother tongue as he. Whatever, Austria was now Germany.

They fought as one, the German way of life was copied and the Jewish people were the first to be affected. Many of the Jewish children were sent away by means of the 'Kindertransport'.

I have used my foreign and British excursions as a back-drop to give greater depth to my wartime memories and also to my post-war knowledge. The beauty of Vienna's architecture and present way of life is attractive, but there was nothing there to add to that of which I was already aware.

I knew some of the children, now grown men and women, who had left everything behind while barely out of their playpens. They arrived here in Britain, homeless, parentless, unhappy and lost. How would I have felt as a child in such a situation, saying "Goodbye" to my Mum and Dad? What would have been my reaction, as a mother, bidding goodbye to my children? In Vienna I saw the ghosts and I was not comfortable.

Chapter 15
Onwards to Holland

A Square or Two of Edam

I have meandered around the squares and streets of many European towns and cities. I am a curious and inquisitive traveller. I had a respite of four days from work just before I sat for my nurses' State Registration exam. I was 48 years old. I was a very late starter! Alf Russell at home encouraged me to take a break and he and the big girls minded the younger ones. My youngest Simone, was 7. Her brother, Adam, was two years older. I applied to the passport office for a passport and I had an argy bargy because they would not believe that I had never had one before.

With my third daughter Marian, we did a budget-cost trip across the North Sea to Holland. The Dutch are my favourite Europeans.

We arrived in The Hague and stayed there overnight. We were Youth Hostel customers. Whilst waiting for a bus early next morning, we began to chat to an elderly couple at the bus stop. We spoke no Dutch but they had good English, so the conversation waxed unceasingly. I cautiously introduced the subject of the war and they were more than willing to relate their recollections. They started to tell us how it was to live under occupation. Obviously they had been acceptable of the Hitlerite ideology and had survived.

The story they told us was one of a life of extreme hardship; of years of a constantly present fear; of shortages with barely enough to eat; of the loss of their Jewish friends. What had happened to them? They said that they had been worried about the education of their young children, receiving their lessons in a new language. Well having a second language is useful but not to the detriment of one's own. The indoctrination was not so welcome either. We were told that sometimes in regular nightmares they experienced even now, years afterwards, they could hear the jackbooted soldiers marching down the road and the loud banging on the front doors of neighbours. They shivered: "will we be next?" – for whatever the reason.

They told us of the time when Hitler's columns marched into Holland in that May 1940, six days after the Rotterdam Blitz. The air raid lasted ten minutes.

The town and its docks were flattened and nearly a thousand people were killed. An ultimatum was issued: "Surrender or we will bomb other towns until you do". The meagre Dutch military were no match against the aggressors and Holland complied.

Our bus arrived and we made our farewells. I was in luck, they had spoken our language. I left with the feeling that I had borne witness to a life almost too terrible to bear. I felt that I had listened to a fictitious horror story. But it was not fiction.

* * *

A Dutch Heroine

We made our way to Amsterdam. The centre of my interest in that city of canals was the house that had been the home of the fourteen year-old Dutch heroine, Anne Frank. Everything was in place, exactly as it had been in her time, in its original state. If one has the ability, it is not difficult to imagine what had happened on those premises. We made our way to the building in which thousands of the city's Jewish population were herded awaiting deportation to the death camps. It was a welcome relief to slowly 'barge travel' the canals and to deeply breathe in the fresh air.

Marian and I had a good four days' worth. Our hitch-hiking ploy was a bit crafty. Marian, a presentable 18 year old, stood by the roadside hoping to wave down a car, and me, not such an inducement, stood back in the shadows. It worked. We found ourselves in Rotterdam. I needed to be there and to imagine how it had been thirty three years earlier.

Before we left for our return, we toured the market in Delft and helped ourselves to the cheese samples on show; our lunch for that day. We lived on snacks and on coffee from our flask. I have a sweet little blue and white Delft clog in my treasure cabinet and I am often reminded of that adventure. It was a lark when she and I bunked up in the youth hostel. I recall that we both had top bunk accommodation adjacent to each other, and we played cards just for the fun of it. I also recall the incident when Marian and I hired bikes and took to the streets, on the wrong side of the road. We were in danger on two counts; injury or even death from the oncoming traffic coming towards us, and pierced ear drums from the noise of the horn-blowing motorists. We re-crossed the North Sea overnight on deck, it was cheaper that way. Refreshed and with my batteries recharged I did my final bit of swotting and guess what?

I passed the exam first go. I was truly chuffed. Staff Nurse Russell at the ready!

Myrtle aged 59, 1984.
In her clinical teacher uniform

Chapter 16
Trouble in the Baltic

By Royal Assent

On another trip, I ventured further north to Copenhagen, Denmark. The Danish too have much to remember living under Hitler's regime, and a museum in which to reminisce and reflect.

I was told an interesting tale of Royal interference. The Danish King Christian X secretly heard that a mass deportation of the Jewish population was to take place on a particular date. He surreptitiously arranged for a number of boats to gather in the dead of night to take on board those fleeing. They were undetected and all safely arrived in neighbouring Sweden where they sought refuge. Just a few of their co-religionists were left behind and sad to say, their untimely fate was sealed. But eight thousand were saved.

* * *

An Attempt to Finish the Finns!

Whilst travelling around Baltic lands I arrived in Finland. I found myself in Helsinki. I enjoyed my stay there, it is a lovely city. I had two contrasting thoughts churning around my brain. I thought about the Finnish wars and I realized that there were only two war stories coming out of the Baltic States where the Jewish population had survived. One was Denmark, which I have already wrapped up, and the other was in Finland.

Russia and Germany signed their pally-pally pact in 1939, until two years later when Hitler got a bit annoyed with his mate Stalin, and stuck a knife in his back. A secret stipulation in that agreement was the Soviet right to take Finland. Whilst in that lovely country I became aware of some of the finer points with reference to that time, if one can comment on any aspect of any war as having 'finer points'. However, there is a story to be told.

On the 30th November 1939, just twelve weeks after the German march into Poland, and our declaration of war with Germany, the Soviets invaded Finland.

The Winter War, as it was called, had begun. By the 13th March 1940, in only three and a half months, and in spite of the amazing Finnish tenacity both by the military and the civilians, the Russians had fulfilled their objective. The defenders were overcome by the vast numbers and well-serviced Red Army. The Winter War was over. A treaty was signed and the Soviet Union had gained more territory than it had previously demanded. The period of peace was widely regarded by the Finns as a temporary interlude. In spite of the so called armistice the Soviets maintained an intense pressure on the population and help was sought from the United Kingdom and Sweden, but none was forthcoming. Britain had her own commitments and Sweden pleaded its neutrality. Finland turned to Nazi Germany and German troops arrived in answer to their plea for help, and took up positions in Lapland, Finland's most northerly region, from where they would ultimately invade Russia. The Finnish military actually took part in the planning of that invasion, code named Operation Barbarossa, which entered into the history books on the 22nd June 1941. German troops were not yet active against the Soviets but were now conveniently in a position to do so, on Finnish soil, when the opportunity presented itself.

The war with the Soviets was not over. They launched massive air raids against Finnish cities and Finland declared war against them, unlike the Soviets who had violated them without even a declaration of intent or warning. The Finns acted at least conforming to the rules laid down. The second phase of hostilities drifted into what was to be known as the Continuation War.

* * *

A Toxic Mix

During the summer and autumn of 1941 the Finnish Army was able to retake land lost to the Soviets in the previous Winter War, and even made further advances towards Leningrad. This upset the British and they declared war on Finland. On the 31st July 1941 the UK bombed several Finnish towns to show support to their Russian Allies. Everybody needed to get into the act. In March 1944 President Roosevelt called for Finland to disassociate itself from Nazi Germany. On the 9th June 1944 the Red Army set into motion a major strategic offensive against Finland with vast numerical superiority, and surprising the Finnish army, who by now had exhausted its resources and was nearly at the end of its tether. But with a delivery of weapons from Germany, and with German military aid, the Soviet advance was halted.

A total of 204 Finnish Jews fought in the Finnish Army during the Winter War when Finland was engrossed in their struggle against the Soviets. In the continuation war the Finnish Jews fought the Soviets with German forces as co-belligerents. Three hundred Jewish refugees from German occupied territories joined the Finnish forces. Some were fluent German speakers and saw service in the Finnish and German military intelligence. The Finns established a field synagogue, a house of Jewish worship, in the presence of Nazi troops. Can you believe it? Jewish soldiers were granted leave on Saturdays to celebrate the Sabbath, and on Jewish Festivals. It was a bizarre reversion of events; Jews taking sides with the Germans; can one even envisage such a scenario?

A young Jewish singer, Sissy Wein, dubbed the 'Soldiers Sweetheart', a counter-part of our own Vera Lynn, (known during the war as 'The Forces Sweetheart'), entertained the Finnish lads but she refused to perform for the Germans.

By now the campaign in Finland had become a side-show for The Russian leadership. They needed to race towards Berlin before the British and Americans got there first, and they had suffered heavy losses at the hands of their Finnish foe. A ceasefire was agreed and the Moscow armistice was signed on the 19th September 1944 ending the Continuation War but a final Treaty was not under-written and validated until 1947 in Paris.

It was all-change time. The third act took the stage.

* * *

Who was Fighting Who?

The Lapland War was fought between Finland and Germany. The main interest of the Germans was the nickel mines situated in that area. Initially they confronted each other with caution, but by the end of 1944 the fighting had intensified. They agreed to enter into a formal agreement, brokered by the British, tabling a schedule for a German withdrawal from Finland to German-occupied Norway.

The show of agreement and 'buddy' relationship did not suit the Soviets and they pressurized the Finns to be more aggressive and active in getting the Germans out, and fighting flared up again.. The Germans did go, but not before they carried out a 'scorched earth' policy. They proceeded to lay waste the entire northern half of the country as they went.

Finland's Raw Deal

The Paris Peace Treaty of 1947 classified Finland as a German ally, and so that country was also held responsible for the war. Large reparations were levied on Finland and it was stipulated that that the lease of an area near Helsinki, the capital, should be a military base for fifty years. The reparation order was cleared by 1952 and the leased land was returned to Finland in 1956.

Finland, had no option during the war except to depend on Germany for food and armament shipments, however, it still retained an independent democratic government. It was the only European country in a similar situation to do so. It kept its army under its own command and not within that of the Wehrmacht structure despite German insistence that it should.

One hundred thousand of the Finnish population were left homeless, adding to the burden of post-war reconstruction. One thousand of their soldiers were dead. German losses accounted for double that number. The Finnish Army expelled the last of the foreign troops from their soil in April 1945. Those three combined wars, forced onto that blameless nation, had taken six years to settle.

During World War Two Finland was in many ways a unique case. It was the only European country bordering the Soviet Union in 1939 which was still unoccupied in 1945. Of all the countries of the European land mass embattled in that conflagration, the only three capital cities which were never occupied were Moscow, London and Helsinki.

In my layman's opinion I feel that Finland had a raw deal. To repeat, I am no expert on historical events, and certainly have no military knowledge, and I am not clever enough to see behind the corridors of power where 'great' and wise men make their decisions. All I can offer, I hope, is a fair-minded assessment of what I know, garnered from the books I have read and from the people I have spoken to, and those with whom I discussed and argued a point or two, and from various other sources. And from my own evaluation of what I think is fair and just.

I have always considered that country, Finland, to be less prominent in international affairs than, for instance, Norway or Sweden. Yet it was, through no fault of its own, embroiled in a massive upheaval for six years. Even at the end of it the country was condemned by the terms of the final peace treaty; how could it dared to be classified as an ally of Germany? It requested German aid out of necessity.

It was either that or to be taken over by the Soviets and suffer in bondage to them. Finland was never an Axis partner. It was abhorrent that it should be considered so. It was a diabolical decision that foisted a reparation upon it as a financial burden. The boot should have been on the other foot. The Soviet Union was responsible; it was an act of criminality to be judged otherwise; the pay-out should have fallen on their shoulders.

As I have said before, perfection does not exist. But consider the record of the two countries Finland and the Soviet Union since those war years. Of course no comparison can be made regarding size or population or the places they occupy in the political arena in relation to worldly matters. We do not hear a great deal of the day-to-day agenda of things that take place coming out of Helsinki, but we are educated in the stuff that emanates from the Kremlin, and a lot if it ain't much good. Well, perhaps I am biased. I prefer the little and unpretentious rather that the great and arrogant.

In November 1942, eight Jewish Soviet refugees in Finland, along with other deportees, were transported to Germany when the Chief of Police betrayed them. Seven of them were immediately murdered. The media reported the incident and it became a national scandal. Ministers resigned in protest. Lutheran ministers, the Finnish Archbishop, and the Social Democratic Party registered their protests; the deportations of Jewish refugees ceased.

In 2000 the Prime Minister of Finland, Paavo Lipponen, issued an official apology referring to this matter. Approximately 500 Jewish refugees had arrived in Finland from other countries during the war, although 350 moved to other places, including 160 who were welcomed in Sweden to save their lives on the direct orders of Marshall Carl Gustave Emil Mannerheim, Commander of the Finnish Army. About 40 of the remaining group were sent to do compulsory labour service in Lapland in March 1942.

Later in the war the German ambassador reported to Hitler that the Finns would not endanger their citizens of Jewish origin in any situation, which according to some was realistically accepted. Well, why shouldn't it have been? They did fight with his lot!

Three Finnish Jews were offered the Iron Cross, a high ranking German award for wartime service. One, a Major Leo Skurnik, district medical officer in the Finnish Army, organized an evacuation of a German field hospital when it came under Soviet shelling. More than 600 patients including SS personnel were moved to a safe and secure place. Captain Solomon Class, also of the Finnish Army, who had, incidentally, lost an eye in the Winter War, led a Finnish unit in the rescue of a German Company that had been surrounded by Soviets. Dina Poljakoff, a member of the Finnish women's auxiliary nursing service, was a nursing assistant who helped to tend German wounded, and came to be greatly admired and respected by her patients. All three refused the award. No thank you, Herr Hitler.

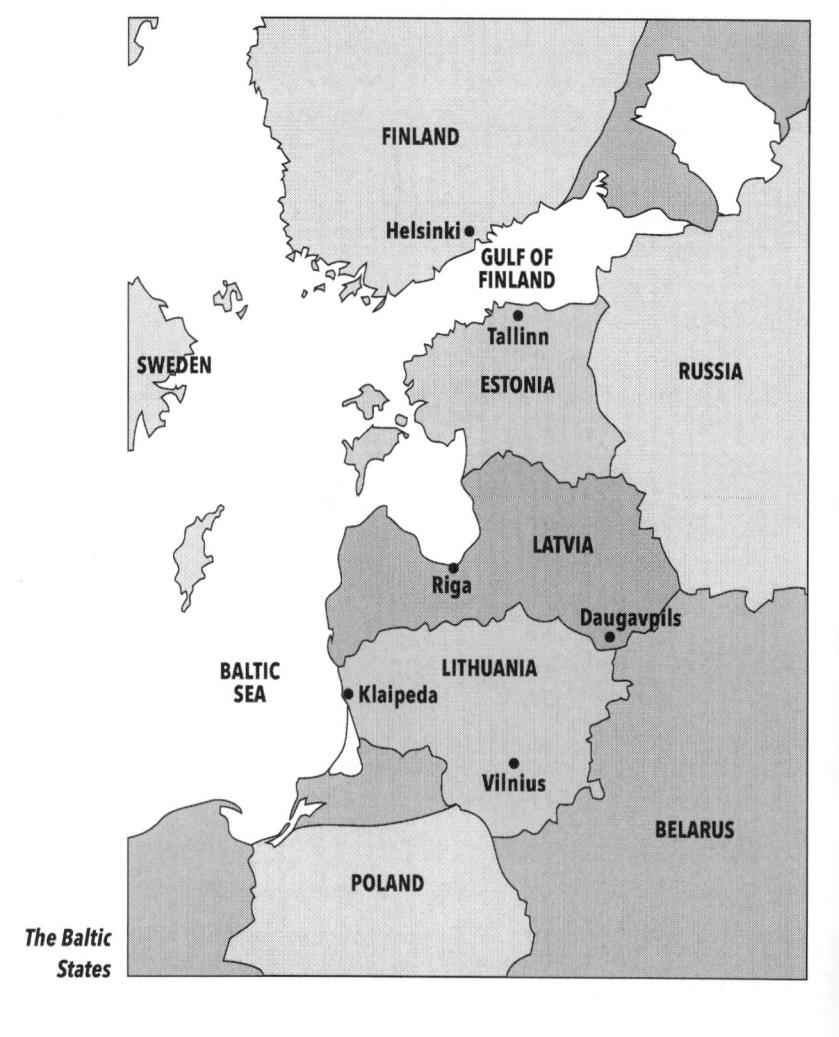

The Baltic States

Chapter 17

More Trouble in the Baltic

The Devil's Advocates

The Molotov-Ribbentrop 1939 Pact was the bogeyman that was the root cause and the curse which beset the Baltic States: Lithuanian, Latvia, and Estonia, also Finland and of course, Poland. In 1939, when Hitler and Stalin moved everything in that region, it shook, and that which those lands were and stood for, moved too. An earthquake without disruption of the earth's crust affected those territories.

Those two signatories were the channels through which their respected masters dispatched their infantry and armoured divisions throughout the region, and carved it up like using an electric knife through a joint of meat. Germany and the Soviet Union made agreements and treaties with the leaders of those blighted countries almost on a daily basis – promising, threatening, demanding; they did 'deals' which were not reciprocal agreements. They used the negotiations as excuses to take what they wanted. It was all a sham, and the end result was always the same. They destroyed the very essence of those lands and stole whatever they pleased. Finland was the only state that said "no" and was rewarded with six years of conflict. It was an overall disaster for all of those locations and for the people who lived in them. Even between themselves, the Germans and Soviets cheated and acted without honour towards each other, taking what the other had had assigned to it in that hollow and ruinous pact. Sorry, 'honour' was incorrect; that word had been deleted from their vocabularies. There was no right-mindedness or justice in what they did. That pair of wicked men cared not the moves they made to gain their own ends. The avaricious motives and the outcomes were always beneficial to them and disadvantages to those they fooled. The people and their leaders were hood-winked and they suffered under the yoke of those fiends. When Hitler was busy with the battle in France, Stalin advantaged himself and took what the Germans had already squeezed from somebody else. It all boiled down to: "I want it, and come what may, by hook or crook, I mean to have it".

* * *

Stage One: The Soviets

The Lithuanians with the Soviets in occupation were pressurized to conform and the occupiers had free rein to do as they pleased. They set up bogus elections and being declared 'the winner', used that as propaganda to claim that the people had voluntarily joined the Soviet Union. I'll wager that the voting slips were destroyed and never counted! They bamboozled their way into the setting up of five military bases housing 20,000 of their troops, and then falsely accusing the Lithuanians of kidnapping some of them. Despite the attempts the accused made to negotiate and resolve the issue, the Soviets responded with ultimatums. The Lithuanians had no choice but to accept them. The Soviet military took control of major sites that they had not yet helped themselves to. Sovietization policies were implemented. All political, cultural and religious organizations were shut down, except for the Communist Party and its youth branches. All the banks and other private enterprise organisations were nationalized. Land holdings were taken over and large farms reduced in size, and distributed to small farmers. This disruption caused a sharp drop in food production. The enormous influx of soldiers eager to spend their newly-acquired roubles resulted in a massive shortage of general goods. The local currency, the Lithuanian litas, was drastically devalued and eventually withdrawn from circulation. The Soviets arrested 2,000 of the most prominent political activists which paralysed any attempt to create anti-Soviets groups. An estimated 12,000 were imprisoned as 'enemies of the people'. When farmers were unable to meet new exorbitant taxes they were put on trial. In June 1941, one week before the German invasion, some 17,000 Lithuanians were deported to Siberia and the Gulag camps, where they perished owing to the inhumane conditions therein.

* * *

Stage Two: The German Turn

On 22nd June 1941, simultaneously with the onslaught on Russia, Lithuania was invaded by the co-signatories of the bedevilled Molotov-Ribbentrop Pact. The Germans were in. The preliminary air raids against the cities caused the loss of 4,000 of its citizens. They advanced rapidly on land and were faced with a weak resistance, and aided by Lithuanians who hoped that the Germans would re-establish their independence. They viewed them as liberators. They took up arms in an anti-Soviet and pro-independence revolt. They took control of railways, bridges, communication equipment and food warehouses. The majority of anti-Nazi resistance in Lithuania came from the Polish and Soviet partisans.

The Battle of Raseiniai began on the 23rd June 1941 as Soviets attempted to mount a counter-attack but were defeated. Some 16,000 to 30,000 civilians took part in the uprising and 600 died. The Germans entered Vilnius, the capital city, unopposed, and within a week they controlled the entire country. During the early days the German military was mostly concerned with security and tolerated Lithuanian attempts to set up their own administrations, and left them to look after their own issues and to undo the damage of the one year of Soviet domination. They formed a provisional government which, in its six weeks of existence, issued dozens of laws and decrees, which everyone ignored. Its policies were both anti-Soviet and anti-Semitic. Within a short time, the German army set up commands to deal with mass executions of the Lithuanian Jewish population.

* * *

The Jewish Population under Siege

The Lithuanian port city of Klaipeda, (Memel in German), had historically been a member of the Hanseatic League and had belonged to Germany and East Prussia prior to 1918. The city was semi-autonomous during the period of Lithuanian independence and under League of Nations supervision. Approximately 8,000 Jewish people lived in Memel when it was absorbed into the Reich on March 15th 1939, six months prior to Hitler's invasion of Poland. Its Jewish residents were expelled and they fled into Lithuania proper. In 1941 the German killing squads, the Einsatzgruppen, followed the advance of the German army and immediately began organizing the murder of the Jews. The first recorded action of the group took place on the 22nd June 1941, the very day Hitler invaded Russia. The border town of Gargzdai, which was one of the oldest Jewish settlements in the country and only eleven miles from Germany, annexed Memel. Approximately 800 Jews were shot. That day is known as the Garsden Massacre. About 100 non-Jews suffered the same fate, many for trying to save their Jewish friends.

The treatment of Lithuanian Jews was unlike the schedule in other German occupied countries, where the Holocaust was first evidenced by the liquidation of the civil rights of the Jewish population; followed by concentrating them into the bounded areas of ghettos; transporting them to the death camps, or in some cases force-marching them to secluded areas such as forests and gunning them down as they stood by the hand-dug graves which the German murderers had forced them to dig, ready to receive their bullet-holed bodies. In Lithuania executions started within a few days of the German arrival. The system was well planned in advance. A command arrived one day before the main onslaught, specifically to organize and encourage what they called 'self-cleansing'.

Before the Holocaust, Lithuania had been one of the greatest centres of Jewish theology, philosophy and learning, and an estimated 230,000 Jews lived there. The Lithuanian Holocaust can be viewed as an event divided by three mass executions which took place from June to December 1941. The killings provided justification for rounding up Jews and putting them in ghettos, as the Germans announced, to 'protect them'. The ghetto period was from 1942 to March 1943; and the final extermination, April 1943 to July 1944. Executions in Lithuania started on the first days of war. They wasted no time in setting up units of pro-German partisans for Jewish harassment and localised and widespread murder sprees. It was a number one priority. Many synagogues were set on fire and each day another batch of Jews was killed. The ultimate aim of the German savage and heinous programme was the extermination of the innocent.

The majority of Jews in Lithuania were not required to live in the ghettos, nor were they sent to the Nazi concentration camps, which at that time, were just in the preliminary stage of operation. Instead they were shot in pits near their places of residence, with the most infamous mass murders happening on a site, the Ninth Fort near Kaunas, a large town in central Lithuania. In the Ponary Forest near Vilnius, the most notorious Lithuanian unit collaborated with the German SS and killed thousands of Jews and Poles in the Ponary Massacare.

* * *

The Reasons and the Results

A unit of insurgents, encouraged by the Germans, started a series of anti-Jewish pogroms on the night of 25–26th June 1941. More than one thousand Jews perished over the next few days; it was the first of its kind in Nazi occupied Lithuania. Many units of that type sprang up. German commanders filed reports purporting that the zeal of the Lithuanian police battalions surpassed their own. Many of those involved were members of the Lithuanian Labour Guard and from the Lithuanian fascist 'Iron Wolf' organization.

Overall the nationalistic Lithuanian administrations were interested in the liquidation of the Jews as a perceived enemy and potential rival to ethnic Lithuanians. Not only did they support the Nazi Holocaust policy, they adopted it as their own.

It is thought that partisan Lithuanians were put in place to carry out further pogroms. They murdered, and they burnt the synagogues. They repeatedly used brutal and pitiless strikes of mass butchery. They dispatched the victims in mass graves or as perhaps the Germans might have done, into a flowing river. In the town of Kaunas in December 1941, only 15,000 survived: 22,000 had been executed.

The Nazi collaborators administered, directed and supported the original killing of the Lithuanian Jews. Local Lithuanian auxiliaries of the Nazi occupation regime carried out the logistics for the preparation and execution of the murders under Nazi direction. One SS Brigadefuhrer Franz Walter Stahlecker arrived in Kaunas three days after the initial takeover and gave agitation speeches in the city to incite the murder of Jews. In a report, Stahlecker wrote that they had succeeded in covering up their vanguard unit actions, and it was made to look like it was their own initiative; the local population felt that it was all their idea.

The surviving Jews were concentrated in inhumane ghettos and forced to work for the benefit of the German military industry. On the 21st June 1943, Heinrich Himmler, the German high-ranking aficionado of death, issued a liquidation order for all ghettos and the transfer of the residue of the Jewish people to concentration camps. The genocidal rate of the Jews in Lithuania, 96%, was one of the highest in Europe.

A combination of reasons serve as an explanation for the participation of some of the Lithuanians in genocide against the Jews. They include the national and traditional values of the incumbent population which they held as their birth-right; and an inherent anti-Semitism, common throughout contemporary Europe in those years; a specific desire for a 'pure' Lithuanian state which they believed was not possible alongside the Jewish co-habitants. There was some element of jealousy and resentment when, in some instances, Jewish property was seen as superior to those of some of the poorer Lithuanian people, when severe economic problems arose. When Jewish homes were left vacant, goods and chattels left behind were quickly looted.

The Jews were also seen as having supported the Soviet regime in that country during 1941–2. The Germans were just continuing their policy of mass murder incorporating it into their 'Final Solution' which they brought with them from Germany, so it was expected that they would encourage those in their control to do likewise. Up to the time of that invasion, the Jews were blamed by some for virtually every misfortune that had befallen Lithuania.

I divert from my thoughts of that country, and I wonder if, in 2016, the rise of the malevolent spectre of anti-Semitism can be mirrored, world-wide, for the same reasons as it was in Lithuania in the days of World War 2?

My Baltic travels included Vilnius. I stood by the Holocaust memorial in Subaciaus Street. Words failed me then when I thought of what had happened there, and they fail me now as I write of it.

* * *

Prologue to Latvia

A staged and bloodless coup d'état on the 15th May 1934 established a nationalistic dictatorship in Latvia that existed until 1940. Most of the Baltic Germans left. On 5th October 1939 Latvia was forced to accept a 'mutual assistance' pact with the Soviet Union granting them rights to station 25,000 troops on Latvian soil. On June 17th 1940 the Red Army occupied the country. Rigged elections were held and a puppet government was installed leading Latvia into the USSR. The coming months would be known as the 'Year of Horror'. Mass arrests, disappearances, and deportations culminated on the night of the 14th June 1941. In less than a year more than 27,500 persons were arrested; most were deported, almost 1,000 were shot.

Resistance in Latvia is a complicated story and it's confusing. There were those resisting the Soviets, happy to work with the Germans, and Soviet supporters resisting the Germans. There were nationalists resisting everyone who was in occupation, or trying to be. To add to the farrago, there were those who changed their support when the Soviets started the deportations or when the Germans did the same. Some 'crossed the house' when the Soviets returned in the summer of 1944. And finally there were those who felt persecuted and who resisted anyone trying to kill them, be it German or Russian, or anti-Semitic Latvians.

Public displays of resistance resulted in arrests of young nationals, and when in early 1943, partisan activity increased, after an operation undertaken by the Germans, who, in revenge destroyed 99 villages in eastern Latvia, 600 villagers were deported for forced labour and 3,600 shot. Soviet-supporting partisans, who were actually soviet soldiers working behind the lines, sent back to Moscow wild exaggerations of their successes, which those back home used for propaganda purposes. Resistance continued at an ever-increasing rate when the Red Army returned. An estimated 40,000 Latvians were involved, with 10,000 active at any given time.

During the war in Latvia, more than 200,000 Latvians served in either the German army or with the Soviets: 100,000 were killed on the battlefield.

* * *

The Set-up to Murder

The German army crossed the Soviet frontier early in the morning on 22nd June 1941, on a broad front from the Baltic Sea to Hungary. The German army moved forward rapidly through Lithuania and other strategic points in Latvia. The Nazi police state included an organization called the 'Security Service', generally referred to as the 'SD', with its headquarters in Berlin. The SD was made up of four Special Assignment Units known by their German name – Einsatzgruppen. Whatever they were called, their purpose was to kill large numbers of people who were regarded as 'undesirable'. The Einsatzgruppen followed closely behind the German invasion forces and so it was that they were in Latvia within days, if not sooner, ready to work. They could be identified by the 'Death's Head' symbol on their caps.

The SD was allotted Latvia as its pitch and it was they who were tasked to carry out the work of the Einsatzgruppen. They were the ones in residence. The eastern region of Latvia, including Daugavpils and the Latgale area, were assigned to Einsatzkommandos 1b (EK 1b) and comprised 50 to 60 men commanded by one, Erich Ehrlinger. They set to work on the night of 23rd–24th June 1941, and in the cemetery in the town of Grobina they murdered six local Jews. Thirty five were their next victims the following day in other towns.

That was the opening of the floodgates. Riga, Latvia's capital was subjected to pogroms under one Viktors Arajs, a 31 year-old member of a student fraternity, who was appointed executor of the programme. He had worked in the Latvian police and was noted for his aspirations to power and extreme mode of thought and action. To enlarge on the description of this man is to add that he was an idle external student supported by his 41 year-old wife. He was well set up, well dressed, well fed and wore his hat at an arrogant angle. He formed an armed unit of men. Three hundred had applied to join him, mainly from student fraternities.

On the night of the 3rd July, the group started their work; there were beatings and robbing and the Riga Jews were arrested. The next day they began to burn the synagogues and many of the worshippers died: dead at the hands of these savage devotees of evil. In carts and in blue buses these murderers went from place to place killing thousands of Jews as they went. Their actions served as an example for other anti-Semitic supporters of the Nazi hoards; officers of the SS and the SD supervised the activity. Later in that month the mass killing of 4,000 of Riga's Jewish community took place in the Bikernieku Forest. As stated by a Latvian historian, one Andrievs Ezergailis, this was the beginning of "the greatest criminal act in the history of Latvia".

From that month the Jews of Latvia were humiliated and degraded, and deprived of the rights enjoyed by others. They were strictly forbidden to leave their homes in the evening, at night, and in the morning. They were allotted lower food rations and could only shop in some special shops set aside for them, and they had to wear the mark of recognition, the yellow Star of David. They were forbidden to attend public events; cinemas, parks, sport areas. They were barred from travel by train and trams, to go to bath houses, use pavements, public libraries, museums or to go to school. Their bicycles were confiscated together with their radios. Jewish doctors were only allowed to treat Jews, and they were forbidden to run pharmacies. Furniture, clothes and linen were subject to forfeiture, for the needs of the German Reich. Jewellery, securities, gold and silver coins had to be surrendered on demand. The system became a source of enrichment for Nazi officials and their collaborators. The extermination of the Jews was a convenience; there would be no one alive to demand the return of the stolen goods.

* * *

The Killing Squads in Action

In Liepaja the first mass killing took place early in July 1941. Four hundred were shot dead: a repeat of that atrocity was executed a week later when three hundred were killed. A German group of the SD did the shooting and Latvians conveyed the victims to the killing site. The synagogue in that town was destroyed; its scripture rolls were put on the ground of the town's main square, and the Jews were forced to march on the sacred texts while onlookers laughed at what they considered to be an amusing scene.

The killing squads moved on to Ventspils. On July 16th–18th 300 were massacred in the Kazinu forest. In July and in August the remaining 700 of that town were done to death by gunfire while other Jews in that region followed their brethren in the autumn. That episode was carried out and overseen by Latvian, Estonian, and of course German SD operators. Soon a poster appeared on the main highway; it said: "Ventspils Judenfrei" (free of Jews).

In Daugavpils the extermination of Jewish citizens was initially commanded by the afore-named Erich Ehrlinger, chief of SD1b. By the 11th July, they had killed 1,150 people. And his running mate added to the total a further 9,012 in that city and in southern Lingala. The chief of the local auxiliary police had rendered active assistance by ensuring the removal of any remaining Jews to the Griva ghetto and transporting them to the killing site.

In Rezekne, the killings were the work of a German SD group. An estimated 2,500 lost their lives by gunfire. By October, in the spate of three months, 35,000 of the old and revered religion were gone.

* * *

The Rigan Ghetto

The Germans, in their offices, argued about the future of the Jews. One opinion was for the extermination of those still living, and others made the point that they should be used as a source of cheap labour, paying the lowest of wages or supplying them with any food that was left after supplying the indigenous Aryan population. To settle the question, a ghetto was set up in Riga. An area was selected. It was one of the poorest, already inhabited by Jews, Russians and some from Belarus. About 7,000 non-Jews were moved out and an estimated 23,000 Jews from other areas of Riga were ordered in. With those already there, the total of inmates now registered about 29,000. A Jewish council was organized which was assigned the task of regulating life generally; also a Jewish police force for maintaining law and order. It was enclosed by a barbed-wire fence. Latvian police guarded the entrances, where wooden log barriers had been installed. Jews were allowed to leave only in work columns, accompanied by guards. Individual Jewish specialists could come and go by displaying a yellow ID. Leaving independently was severally punished.

Ghetto space was 3–4 square metres per person. It was extremely crowded, and acute poverty persisted. Food rations were distributed only to those who worked which accounted for half of the ghetto population. Over 5,650 children and 8,300 elderly and disabled people had to be maintained by the others. The place had a pharmacy, a laundry and a hospital headed by a professor Vladimir Mintz, a surgeon. The historian Margers Vestermanis writes: "The members of the Jewish Council, including three eminent Jewish lawyers and their volunteer assistants did all they could to somehow relieve general suffering". Jewish policemen too, tried to somehow protect their fellowmen. Those people strived to preserve themselves; there was an illusion of survival.

* * *

A Plan for Mass Murder

The Rumbula massacre was a collective term for incidents on two non-consecutive days in November 30th and 8th December 1941, in which about 25,000 Jews were killed in or on the way to the Rumbula forest near Riga. It is estimated that 24,000 of the victims were Latvian Jews taken from the Riga ghetto, and approximately 1,000 were German Jews transported to the forest by train in cattle trucks.

The massacre was carried out by the Nazi Einsatzgruppen A with the help of local collaborators and with support from other Latvian auxiliaries. In overall charge was SS Police Leader, Friedrich Jeckeln, who had previously overseen similar massacres. It was he who organized the killing of 30,000 Jews in The Babi Yar massacre in the Ukraine. It was Himmler's motive to eliminate the Latvian Jews in Riga so that Jews from Germany and Austria could be deported to the Riga ghetto. Similarly motivated mass-murders of Jews were confined to ghettos in Kovno, Finland, where 10,000 were killed, and at Minsk where 13,000 were shot on 7th November 1941, with an additional 7,000 on the 20th of that month.

Jeckeln was Himmler's man. To carry out Himmler's order, Jeckeln estimated that to clear the Riga site he would need to kill 12,000 people per day. At that time of year, there were only about eight hours of daylight until twilight, so the last column of victims would have to leave Riga for the killing sites no later than noon. Guards would be posted on both sides of the column along the entire route.

The whole process required about 1,700 personnel to carry it out. Jeckeln consulted a construction specialist, who later claimed he was shocked when he learned in advance of the number to be killed; nevertheless he made no objection at the time and proceeded to supervise the digging of six murder pits, sufficient to bury 25,000 people.

The excavation of the pits needed 200–300 Russian prisoners of war. The pits themselves were purpose-designed: they were excavated in levels, like an inverted pyramid, with the broader levels towards the top, and a ramp down to the different levels to allow the victims to be literally marched into their own graves. The work took three days.

* * *

The Jeckeln System

It was called 'The Jeckeln System'. During the many killings he had already organized, he called it 'sardine packing' as a means of avoiding the extra work associated with having to push the bodies into the grave. It was claimed that even some of the experienced Einsatzgruppen killers were horrified by this cruelty. Extermination by shooting had its problems when it came to women and children. One commander, Otto Ohlendorf, himself a prolific killer, objected to Jeckeln's techniques, according to his testimony at his post-war trial for crimes against humanity. Jeckeln had staff which specialized in each separate part of the process, including 'neck-shot marksmen'. There were nine components to this assembly line:

1. The Security police roused the people out of their beds in the ghetto.

2. They were organized into columns of 1,000 and escorted to the killing grounds.

3. The German order police led the column to Rumbula.

4. The digging of the pits was now completed.

5. The victims were stripped of their clothing and any valuables.

6. They were run through a double cordon of guards on the way to the pits.

7. To save the trouble of tossing dead bodies into the pits, the killers would force the living victims into the trench on top of others who had already been shot.

8. Finnish submachine guns or semi-automatic pistols were used rather than German arms, because although the magazines held fifty rounds, the weapon could be set to fire one round at the time.

9. People were not bullet-sprayed. To save ammunition, each person was shot just once in the back of the head. Anyone not dead outright was simply buried alive when the pit was covered in.

Their Last Vision - the Trees of Rumbula

Rumbula was a small railroad station 12 kilometres (7.5miles) south of Riga, which was connected with Daugavpils, the second largest city in Latvia, by the railway line along the north side of the Daugavpils River. Located on a hill about 250 metres (820 feet) from the station, it was said the massacre sight, "was a rather open and accessible place". The view was blocked by vegetation, but the sound of gunfire would have been audible from the station grounds. Rumbula was part of a forest and swamp area known in English as Crow Forest. The soil was sandy and it was convenient to dig for graves. Jeckeln, when selecting the site, estimated the water level; that was the reason why the high ground of the hill was essential. While the surrounding pines were sparse, there was a heavily forested area in the centre which became the execution site. The railway line and the highway were well placed to move the victims in from Riga. It was within walking distance of the Riga ghetto on the southeast side of the city. The murderers and their arms were transported using the eleven cars and seventeen motor cycles that Jeckeln had at his disposal. He needed more and heavier transport for the sick, disabled or other intended victims unable to march the distance. He also anticipated there would be a significant number murdered along the way, and he would need about twenty five trucks to pick up the bodies. He ordered his men to scrounge around Riga to locate suitable vehicles.

* * *

The Gypsy Holocaust

Jeckeln was found guilty in the post-war trials and publicly hanged in Riga on the 3rd February 1946.

Less is known about the Holocaust in connection with the Romani people (Gypsies) than about other groups. Most of the available information regarding their persecution in Nazi occupied Eastern Europe comes from Latvia. According to the country's 1935 census, 3,839 Gypsies lived in Lithuania, the largest population of any of the Baltic States. Many of them did not travel about the country but lived settled lives. In December 1941, a decree was issued. It stated that Gypsies who wandered about the countryside represented a two-fold danger. Firstly, as carriers of disease, especially typhus. Secondly as unreliable elements who neither obeyed the regulations issues by the German authorities, nor were willing to do useful work. There existed a suspicion that they provided intelligence to the enemy, and thus damaged the German cause.

Therefore an order was issued that they were to be treated as Jews. Gypsies were forbidden to live along the coast. A historian believes that this restriction may have been the reason for the first large killing of Gypsies in Latvia. On 5th December 1941, the Latvian police in Liepaja arrested 103 Gypsies. Of these, 100 were put into the custody of the German police for 'follow up' – a Nazi euphemism for murder. On the same day that became a reality. As with the Jews the killing of the Gypsies proceeded throughout the small towns with the aid of the Latvians. One such episode occurred in April 1942, when fifty women and young children were assembled in a jail, then taken out and shot. It is not known exactly how many were killed by the Germans and their Latvian collaborators in total. It is estimated to be one third of the Gypsy population, but a finite number may never be known.

* * *

The Aftermath

After the Second World War, the Soviet Union once again occupied Latvia, this time from 1944 to 1990. It did not suit Soviet purposes to memorialize the Rumbula site or to acknowledge that the victims were Jewish. Until 1960 nothing was done to preserve the killing grounds. In 1961 young Jews from Riga searched for the site and found bones and other evidence of the murders. In 1962 the Soviets staged an officially-sanctioned memorial service at Bikernieki (another site), which made no mention of the Jews but spoke only of the 'Nazi victims'. In 1963 groups of young Jews from Riga went out to Rumbula on a weekly basis and cleaned up and restored the site using shovels, wheelbarrows and other hand tools. The site has been marked by a series of makeshift memorials over the years. Throughout the Soviet domination of Latvia, the Soviets refused to allow any memorial which would specifically identify the victims as Jews.

The Soviet Union suppressed research into the memorials of the Holocaust in Latvia until 1991, when its rule over Latvia came to an end. In one particular incident a memorial that was placed there which the authorities did not approve of, was simply hauled away in the middle of the night, with no explanation. Occasional references were made in Holocaust literature during the Soviet era. A folkloric figure called 'zidu savejs' (Jew shooter) turned up in stories occasionally. The poet Ojars Vacietis referred to the Holocaust in his work, including in particular his well-regarded poem 'Rumbula', written in the early 1960s. One notable survivor of the Latvian Holocaust was Michael Genchik, who escaped form Latvia and joined the Red Army, where he served for 30 years.

His family perished at Rumbula. Many years later he recalled: "In later years the officials held memorial services every year in November or December. There were speeches reminding of the atrocities of the Nazis. But saying Kaddish (the Jewish prayer for the dead) was forbidden. Once, after the official part of the meeting, some Jews attempted to say Kaddish and speak a little about the ghetto, but the police didn't permit them to do so. Until 1972, when I retired from the army, I did my best to keep the place neat."

In Latvia, Holocaust education would only be resumed once the Soviets had left. Much of the post-war 1991 work was devoted to identification of the victims. This was complicated by the passage of time and loss of records, and the concealment of others by agencies of the Soviet secret police. On November the 29th 2002, sixty-one years after the murders, the highest officials of the Republic of Latvia, together with representatives of the Latvian Jewish community, foreign ambassadors, and others attended a memorial dedication at the Rumbula site. The President and prime minister of the Republic walked to the forest from where the Riga ghetto had once been. On arrival President Vaira Vike-Freiberga addressed the gathering:

"The Holocaust, in its many forms, has painfully struck Latvia. Here in Rumbula where the earthly remains of Latvia's Jews rest, we have come to honour and remember them. I wish, therefore to extend a special greeting to the representatives of Latvia's Jewish community for whom this is a special day of mourning, all the more so since here lie their loved ones, relatives and members of their Faith. This is an atrocious act of violence, an atrocious massacre. And it is our duty, the duty of those of us who have survived, to pass on the commemoration of these innocent victims to future generations, to remember, with compassion, sorrow and reverence. Our duty is to teach our children and children's children about it. Our duty is to seek out the survivors and record their recollections, but, above all, our duty is to see that this will never happen again".

To write about the war in Latvia was not difficult; it did have a story to tell. What I found a formidable and exacting challenge was the narrative I could use to portray the time and drama of the Holocaust in that country. It was not easy to write and I am certain that it will not be easy to read. But it happened; it could not be omitted or ignored. It was no problem when I recorded the Finnish story and I did find the Holocaust account in Lithuania harrowing enough, but when I considered the murder and mayhem in Latvia I was reluctant to begin. As I have said in other instances,

"It is true and it happened" and I repeat that now. I realize that my account of it is quite like a collections of numbers and dates. That too was important to highlight. A collective figure and one inclusive date would not have been good enough. Like so many other heart-rending events during the war years it had to be brought to the surface.

* * *

Here We Go Again - and It's Really Not Funny

The Republic of Estonia declared its neutrality in the war. But the pattern of wartime activities in Lithuania and Latvia was 'same old, same as', here in the fourth Baltic state to be invaded, fought over, and decimated by the two never satisfied aggressors, the demonic Adolph Hitler, and the vulpine Joseph Stalin. Before the outbreak of the war, Germany and the Soviet Union signed a non-aggression pact, (joke). It was a plan for the dismembering of all of the Eastern European Republican countries. And Estonia was one of them. It was occupied by the Soviets on the 16th June 1940, and – 'here we go again'; mass political arrests, deportations and executions, punitive punishments and looting: 'if you don't like us, we don't like you', system.

In July 1941 their 'non-aggression' soul mates, Hitler's lot, thought it might be a lark to give the Soviets a kick up the backside. And they did. Stalin's gangs were not overjoyed and a good old scrap ensued. The Estonians were pleased as punch. Well we got rid of that lot and things will be much better now. Sorry to disillusion you, they were not. Life in that country was just as bad, maybe even a tad worse. All the naughty and not nice things that those Slavs did, the Teutonics replicated. Estonians were in a pickle. "Who should we help? Which side are we on?" They made their decisions, all except the ones that nobody liked and they were duly despatched in their tens of thousands without as much as a nod to basic humanity.

With the Germans on the receiving end of a few wallops from the Soviets in Russia, they had another shock when the round-about deposited Red Army callers on Estonian soil in 1943, and the high-jinks between them carried on anew, and the nasties they perpetrated, went on unabated.

There was always a good turn-out for a series of events such as a 'do' at Pikk Hermann. Pikk Hermann, is a tower in the Toompea Castle, on a hill in Tallin, the capital of Estonia. It is situated next to the Estonian Parliament building, and on top of the tower at 95 metres above sea level, is a symbol of the government in command, the National flag.

It is raised and lowered every day. As the flag descends, the anthem, 'My Fatherland is My Love' is sung with gusto and deep emotion by the Estonians. I have been there and I have heard them.

At one time, the flag of 'Nasty', (sorry), Nazi Germany blew in the breeze from the flagpole. When the Estonian independents were victorious it was replaced by the National flag of the Estonian Republic. On 22nd September 1944, the flag with the Hammer and Sickle of the Soviets replaced it. By now I reckon that those in charge were rather anxious about the strength of the up-and-down supporting ropes and the mechanism of the working pulley, because, guess what, the Soviet flag was brought down and the Independence flag went up, and finally that was the end of that little episode. Now the Estonian flag is proudly displayed over its citizens. And so it should. Long live the Republic!

My rambling around the Baltic had come to an end. When I went to Riga, in Latvia, I had a general idea of what had happened in that country and I arrived there in a calm and congenial frame of mind. There I learnt the finer details of life under occupation and I was not so cock-a-hoop and euphoric when I left. I went to Tallinn, previously having some general knowledge of events in that country, and having visited Lithuania too I knew more or less what to expect, and I was not disappointed, but I was totally shattered and depressed as I travelled home. I reminded myself how lucky I was to live in the United Kingdom and that there was Mr C to take us through the war. And I blessed my ancestors, long since gone. They left eastern lands and crossed the English Channel to safety.

Chapter 18
Poland and Russia

Dairy People Times Two

I thought it would make a nice change to travel by a different mode of transportation when I planned my next vacation. That was the reason I decided to travel by train from Waterloo Station, London. That was the departure point for Eurostar then, now it would be St. Pancras Station. I travelled to Poland via Germany. It was a very interesting trip.

Trains were frequent, fast and reasonably comfortable, as I sped across Europe. It changed when I reached the Polish border. Most of the tracks were single lines, so there were frequent delays as we waited until a train travelling in the opposite direction passed us. There were no 'through' carriages, so you were a nuisance when you needed to go for a 'comfort break', and it was a bother when you had to move when somebody else needed to do likewise.

At one point in the journey the train dropped its speed, which could not have more than 20mph at any one time, which I reckoned was considered normal for that railway authority. So the train was now crawling, I would say at about 5mph, and I could not believe it when looking out of the window I espied a railway official walking in front of the train with a RED FLAG. Where had progress disappeared to? Or maybe he was a paid-up member of the Communist party! Well I did say it was an interesting trip!

I reached Warsaw. I was pleasantly surprised to see its delightful continental-style houses and shops. It reminded me of the central square in Brussels. Warsaw had been destroyed by the German bombardment when it was being fought over. It was rebuilt as a carbon copy of the original. I acknowledge the efforts of the planners and builders. The result was a pleasure to behold.

Apart from the fact that I travelled to see new places, I decided to go to Poland in general, and to Warsaw in particular, for two reasons. Firstly my paternal grandparents lived and emigrated from there in the late 19th century. By virtue of their name I am certain that they were dairy people. Our family name is Peterman.

In Poland it was probably Bitterman or Butterman (dairy worker – probably a milkman). The name-change possibly happened during the registration process when they were newly arrived here in England. If they had any English at all it was undoubtedly poor, and a registering clerk not quite getting the gist of it thought it sounded like Peterman and there you go! Families such as theirs left the land of their birth when life became difficult, as it does when anti-Semitism rears its ugly head. I hope they left behind a suitable replacement milk delivery service.

The second reason for my presence in Warsaw is obvious; I wanted to be able to trace the events that took place there during the war. Hitler invaded Poland on the 1st September 1939. He advanced with speed and had overrun the entire country within one month with his superior forces, and he entered Warsaw soon afterwards. It is a fact that Russia, purportedly our friend, was also involved with the invasion of Poland. Stalin's legions swarmed over the frontier on 17th September 1939 and advanced eastwards, where they met and shook hands with the Germans.

* * *

A Polish Carve-up

Finland had been invaded by Russia, in what we now know as 'The Winter War'. The League of Nations expelled the Soviet Union for what they recognized as an illegality. Stalin's troops annexed Estonia, Latvia, Lithuania and parts of Rumania. The Ribbentrop-Molotov Pact of 23rd August 1939 was violated when Germany considered that Russia had bitten off a bit more than it was entitled to. The existence of the pact was denied by the Soviet leadership until 1989, when it was acknowledged and denounced. Well, after the Russian war against Germany 1941–45, and remembering its suffering in Hitler's name, it would be, wouldn't it?

They very quickly changed their tune when it was their turn to be invaded!

* * *

The Ghetto and a Little Light Music

Hitler, without delay, organized Warsaw and its population and, as always, he vented his spleen on the unfortunate Jews. There were 350,000 Jews living in Warsaw pre-war: 30% of the population. It was their heartland. Hitler planned and put into practice the ghetto. They herded tens of thousands of these innocent people into a small area of the city. Guilty on no other charge other than they prayed wearing their skull caps!

The people of the ghetto, living in squalor and starving, had reached breaking point. In upmost secrecy, the men organized an uprising which held out for four weeks. Its official dates are recorded as being from 19th April to the 16th May 1940. The valiant attempt had no chance of success against armed soldiers and soon the ghetto population was dissolved and deported. I toured the site of that locality. I was a tourist there years after it had happened, and yet I felt a cold wind blowing. It was the atmosphere of 1939 permeating through my body. When the war was finally over, a memorial was erected to the ghetto in Warsaw. It is impressive and one is moved to tears to see it. The then post-war German Chancellor, Konrad Adenauer, paid tribute on a visit and got to his knees in an act of contrition.

I have just read over this piece and in doing so, I suddenly remembered a lovely little incident that happened whilst I was in that city, which I feel would be a pity not to relate. Wherever I am, I make it a habit to visit the local synagogue. I just locate the building caretaker and I am allowed entry. That day happened to be a weekday so a service was not in progress. It is a beautiful building and I was so pleased to have discovered it. On leaving, I noticed that a theatre was nearby. And what do you know? They had on stage that night 'Fiddler on the Roof'. Wow, I thought, that story could have happened right here in real life. And, what's more, Tevya, the main character, was a milkman, wasn't he? I bought my ticket and I did enjoy that performance, even though I was not able to understand a bloomin' word! Well I didn't need to. I almost know the dialogue off by heart.

* * *

Krakow - A Place not for Pleasure

The museum and tourist centre in Krakow were interesting. I noticed that many of their artefacts related to the war, in particular the newspaper copies in circulation during the Nazi occupation. I was not able to read them fluently, but could understand a smattering of their contents. It reinforced my opinion that life under German rule at that time was hazardous and extremely dangerous, which did not surprise me. Why should it be different here?

As was the routine, the Jewish population was rounded up as soon as possible after the Germans entered the town, and were deported without delay. I have some data which might tell the story better than I. Pre-war, the Jewish count was sixty thousand in Krakow – that is 25% of the population. Today they number but a handful.

German newspaper 1943 – in the Museum of Krakow

In Polish towns and cities pre-war life was vibrant and busy. The Jewish population was not a wealthy one. Mostly they eked out a living tailoring or cap-making in small concerns, but they were extremely rich in their culture and the care they gave to others and to their own.

Now I was close by the concentration camp named Auschwitz, I felt more than duty bound to go there. We are all aware of its history. I do not need to enlighten you further. I went there to pay homage and my respect to those who suffered and died in that place. I arrived thinking that 'I knew all about it'. I had watched the news of its liberation on a cinema screen on the 27th January 1945. I had friends who were survivors of Auschwitz and I knew families whose relatives were murdered there, or in similar 'hell holes'. Because Rupert came to Britain as a refugee, I was involved with him and the Association of Jewish Refugees. Oh yes, with my cavalier attitude there was nothing new for me to learn. How wrong I was!

Going off at a tangent, just for a few sentences, I can relate another little anecdote. Two years ago, 2014, we celebrated the 100th anniversary of the outbreak of the Great War. I went to France to visit the sites of the battlefields and other places appertaining to that event. I went thinking: "Well it will be interesting, yes, but I know all about it, so what's new?" I had read the history of it. I had seen numerous films with it as a backdrop. I had been engrossed in the TV documentaries from well-known historians. But I knew nothing. Being there brought the conflict into focus and I felt myself part of it. It had completely changed my perspective.

And that is what happened when I went to Auschwitz. I went stony-faced. When I took sight of the pile of discarded suitcases each labelled with the name of a country from where they had come, I saw one labelled 'Holland' from where Rupert's sister-in-law Dorothy was taken, and I sobbed until I was empty of tears and I weep now as I write of it.

The Russian Nightmare

I travelled to Russia. I toured that country via its rivers. I was enthralled when I was 'look seeing' many sights so different and unfamiliar. My dreams were of onions! The first sight of St. Basil's Cathedral in Moscow stopped me in my tracks. I compared the grandeur of the city's underground railway stations with the rather drab confines of London's tube stations. I met the locals on small river islands and was sometimes lucky enough to arrive on a festival day, and as I was more mobile then, I was able to join in the dancing and larking about.

But I did none of that when I went to St. Petersburg. I stayed in that city for days mesmerized by its palaces, but there was one site I deliberately left to see before I departed that wondrous place. During the war, St. Petersburg was Leningrad and it was besieged by the Germans for 872 days. That is, two years, four months, two weeks and five days. It was the longest and most destructive siege, encapsulating the largest loss of life in modern history.

It suffered attacks from the skies and from long-range artillery bombardment. The population starved. In the winter of 1941–42 the daily food allowance was 126 grams of bread, made from 50% sawdust mixed with other inedible ingredients. Winter temperatures registered -30°C (-22°F). At times during the siege, people died at the rate of 100,000 per month. The total count of civilian dead was 642,000, and to add to the catastrophe, one and a half million soldiers lost their lives. Civilians died in the streets, and those still breathing became accustomed to the horror of witnessing it all.

Cannibalism was a long hidden secret. In 2004, a report was published proving that it had taken place. A story emerged of a mother smothering her eighteen month-old to feed her other three children; of a man killing his wife to nourish his sons. I went to a cemetery there in St. Petersburg, where half a million of its citizens are buried. And I stood in misery before the truly magnificent memorial.

During the war, the city of Stalingrad, as it was known, underwent a similar nightmare. It was here that the Germans laid siege which was upheld for five hellish months, from the 23rd August 1942 to the 2nd February 1943. People suffered like no other. They ate rats to appease their hunger. They died starving. They froze in the winter. They had nothing to sustain life. They perished in their tens of thousands.

That city is now called Volgograd, and as I always do, I made my way to its memorial to stand and think of its men and women, and of the children who had lived there through that time; of the 40,000 ordinary helpless innocents who had died there in those horrific circumstances. I gave to thinking about my own existence through the Second World War years. It felt to me that I had been on holiday. I was ashamed.

* * *

Four Men in Long Coats and Three Around a Table

I sailed down The River Danube, boarding a river boat at Passau in Germany, heading for the Black Sea. I arrived in Kiev in the Ukraine where heavy fighting had taken place during WW2. There was no visual damage to be seen and it was difficult to converse because I have no Russian and they had no English. I stood and gazed at the multitude of memorial sites in bronze and in clay, and so I am sure that the population had not forgotten.

The memory that made its mark left me with a different impression and an unusual train of thought. Some of my fellow passengers on that boat were very tall men wearing very long military-style coats and trilby hats worn low down on the brow. They looked sinister and I could not understand why. I later saw them in the streets of Kiev and instantly I understood. They were German and they sauntered around with an arrogance which suggested their thoughts were: "This is where we should be now. By right this should be part of the Third Reich". I flatter myself that I have the ability to perceive people's thoughts, and that is what I strongly felt each time I espied this quartet. If it had transpired that war had ended with an alternative outcome, I would not have been there gazing at compelling and beautifully carved war memorials.

Our next disembarkation point was Yalta. We had reached the Black Sea. Yalta is a modern coastal resort which I estimated to be a very affluent area for the wealthy to live in or a resort to spend a vacation. The ladies were extremely smart and I felt somewhat shabby in my jeans and trainers.

The 'Big 3' (Churchill, Eisenhower and Stalin) met here to discuss the future of Europe in general, and Germany in particular. The Yalta Conference held in February 1945, three months before the end of hostilities on 8th May, devised plans, at Stalin's insistence, for the carve-up of Europe after the war. And it came to pass. Russia was 'rewarded' with large chunks of Poland and other areas in Eastern Europe, which was the ominous forerunner of the 'take-over' by Russia of other areas which led to the 'Cold War'.

It was also here that post-war Germany was discussed which resulted in that country's future; leading to the partitioning into zones. It was the presage which culminated in the building of The Berlin Wall which was constructed by the German Democratic Republic. That was the name of the area which was occupied by the Russians in East Berlin. That wall, regarded with ignominy, was the site of the death of so many East Berliners who attempted to escape to the West of that city, occupied by the British and Americans. They were shot by the Russian-inspired border guards from their watch towers. That Wall stood for twenty eight years: 1961 to 1989.

The room where the conference took place was open to visitors and of course it was not to be missed. I stood there by the table around which they had sat together with their aides. Mr Churchill wore naval uniform; Stalin in the style of clothing in which he was always portrayed – the garb of a Cossack peasant. The American President looked tired and frail. In fact he died soon afterwards. It was a woeful pity he did not live to see the end of the conflict. I saw them in replica. The wax figures looked as if they had come alive.

* * *

A Role Model to Follow

We had come all the way down the Danube waterway and were now in the Crimea. If any of my readers are interested in history in the slightest degree, the name 'Crimea' will ring a bell. Here we fought the Russians on the 25th October 1854. The battle of Balaclava gave rise to the famous incident of the Charge of the Light Brigade, enacted on the very field where I was standing. It was history brought to life. I shut my eyes and could hear the sound of the horses' hooves and the clash of sabres and the call of Lord Cardigan urging his men on.

Our guide pointed to a position of special interest to me. He indicated where a military establishment had been sited. It was here where that illustrious person, Florence Nightingale, had maintained the hospital for her lads, wounded, sick with fever, and dying: 'The Lady with the Lamp'; a role model for me, and others like me, following the nursing profession.

I do not intend to elaborate on the finer details of this conflagration. It has nothing at all to do with the theme of this project. But how could I resist the prospect of engaging with that time and place?

The Legacy of Hitler and Stalin

I was one of ten who went to Minsk. It was a dedicated journey to seek out wartime history. Minsk is the capital city of Belarus, occupied by the Germans during the war; now a post-war part of the Soviet Union and an independent State. Whilst there we met no-one who could talk to us on the subject; perhaps they could, but I am of the opinion they were not going to. Belarus came under the jurisdiction of Stalin in its Soviet days. No one said so, but I felt that he still held sway and these people were nervous who they spoke to and what they said. The town itself seemed to reflect this perception. It seemed to be under-populated. Stalin showed his dominance by building wide, six-lane roads. There were not too many people using them.

The buildings are of a particular style, all identical, in a square utilitarian shape. That is, the official buildings, for example the university and municipal sites. Living quarters for the population of the class of people that we met, and were invited to partake of Vodka and meagre refreshments with, transmitted the message that they were living in poverty. Their rundown apartment in the dilapidated building indicated the habitats for the working people.

We later discovered the truth of that impression. There was employment, but wages were barely enough to exist on. Pensions were not distributed. Public professionals were earning the equivalent of fifty dollars per month. The ten of us pooled some of our pocket money as a gift to this family. It was exceedingly welcome. We took a bunch of flowers for the 'babushka', (grandmother). She wept with joy. She had never before had a bouquet presented to her with the effusiveness that we offered.

We sauntered around the streets of Minsk and we did manage to find a young lady who probably earned less than a living wage as a teacher. We were delighted. And so was she when we remunerated her for her service. Most of her discourse, and it was in English, related to incidents of the intense brutality which the Germans dealt out. Those that were not deemed 'fit', were taken 'en-masse' into the streets and shot where they stood. Doctors and nurses from the hospital; orphans from the orphanage. It was shocking and it affected us deeply. We were standing on blood-soaked ground. No memorial here to stand and gaze at. Oh no! This was actuality.

We came to Minsk to 'find out'. And we certainly did. After leaving this lady, we trudged back to our very basic hotel which I understood to be a '5 Star', with a little old lady 'watcher' sitting in her chair, one on every floor, keeping her eye on visitors.

We all sat together on our leader's bed and someone uncorked the vodka and we all drowned our depression. I, who had never tasted it before, rather took to it. I helped to empty the bottles. It was not of any great consequence because we could easily restock. One could buy it in the 'supermarket' next door for a pittance. It was a store with hardly anything on its shelves. The only thing that was 'super' was the price of that vodka. Very early every morning, a queue would form outside this emporium, hours before it opened. Each customer, carrying empty jars or bottles, hoped he would get a refund of a kopek or two.

* * *

From the Sublime to the Ridiculous

Overall the trip to Minsk was no laughing matter, but laugh we did in between the tears that we shed, like showers in April. We lit our candles in the streets where it happened. We had enjoyed being together. We had made merry but basically we were traumatized to know that there were persecutors who could execute such acts of evil.

The day before we were due to depart, a gentleman of our group announced that he had bought seats for us to visit the Minsk Opera that evening. Wow! What a surprise. Dressed in our smartest, we ten toddled off to the opera. The performance that night was Carmen. The seats allotted to us were the very best in the house. We were in for big surprise, or shock! Naturally enough we had the mental image of the Covent Garden Opera House in London or even some lesser venue. The performance was passable, that is, what you could hear of it. I think the audience had mistaken the opera for the market place. They chatted; they opened their food bags and partook of their supper. They left their seats to wander around to meet their like-minded friends and family members. Everyone was having a jolly good time. Later that night our benefactor told us that the price of those ten tickets was the equivalent of £2.50, in roubles!

We all had another round of Vodka and slept soundly in our beds.

Chapter 19
Malaya, Singapore and India

Geography of Malaya

It is not possible if one endeavours to tell the story of World War Two involvement of Malaya if one has no understanding of the geographical set up in the South China Sea. In 1963, Malaya was united with North Borneo, Sarawak and Singapore to form the Malaysia Peninsular.

Malaya is two islands almost adjacent to each other lying from north to south. The western branch shares a land border with Thailand, whilst to the south its immediate neighbour is the island of Sumatra. Singapore is situated at the southern tip of this branch of Malaya, and Kuala Lumpur (the capital) is half way down.

The northern half of the eastern branch of Malaya is connected by a land border to Borneo. Their nearest neighbours, to its east, are the islands of The Philippines. In 1941, Borneo was a country of divisions. The western zone was part of the Dutch East Indies, the Kingdom of Sarawak; North Borneo and Brunei were crown countries; and the rest was held as a British Mandate.

This description is hardly one that would gain the approval of an academic geographer. He or she would in all probability suffer an epileptic fit, but what other means have I to inform my readers of the problems of this region if one has little or no idea where it is that I am talking about? Hang on for a minute. I have a brainwave. I am forgetting that my eldest daughter Sheila is well able to produce one-line maps or if she cannot, diagrams of these land masses. She is, after all, her father Raymond's daughter, and like a few others of my clan, has inherited his great artistic talent. Me, their Mum, I am not able to draw an apple. I just talk a lot! In the final countdown the maps were produced by Cristina, the well and able graphic designer who has done so much in the emergence of this book. Right, to continue with the war.

In November 1941, Britain became aware of a large-scale build-up of Japanese troops in the islands of French Indo China, (now Vietnam), Laos and Cambodia. Thailand, (then Siam), and Malaya were considered to be under Japanese threat.

Thailand was subsequently subjected to a Japanese invasion and became a partner in the Axis regime. That year the Japanese were in occupation in French Indo China which offered them a number of advantages. As was their wont, they were not too shy at using these people, disrespectful of all other considerations. Firstly, it was a convenient spring-board for approaching and attacking North Borneo across the China Sea, and secondly, it was a useful diversion to ongoing troublesome affairs in China. And it gave their lads an opportunity to relax and focus on the sweet lasses therein.

The capture of Borneo was part and parcel of a complete take-over of the Pacific and all other places in between. And if these were not sufficient enough reasons, just think awhile of all the goodies that awaited their coming across that stretch of water. Its rich oil fields and unlimited guzzling of the same. It was the gateway to the main sea routes between the neighbouring islands, which was a priority in the far-sighted view in the thinking of the 'Top Brass' back in Tokyo. They all had the urge to travel. The Missus back home would appreciate a good holiday in pastures new. Furthermore, the Japanese were aware that the Allied defences in Borneo were poor and inadequate. The signs were in their favour for an easy-peasy victory.

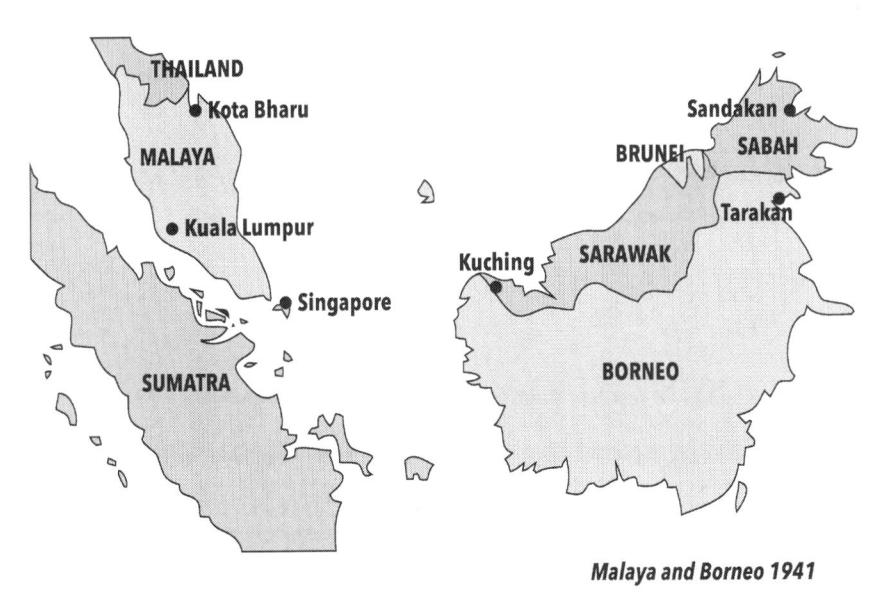

Malaya and Borneo 1941

* * *

A Strike from the East

So they forgot the reasons why; they just did it. On the 16th December 1941, the Japanese made their move. They landed on the north east coast of Borneo. The first objectives were the areas of Sarawak and Brunei. They worked with speed and precision. Three days later they took a town, Sandakan, on the east coast, thereby securing the seat of British Government in that country. Their next move was westward to the Dutch-held Kuching, and its strategically placed airfield. That small Dutch possession took their fancy and they were very happy to score.

That airfield was mighty useful. On the 31st December, Brunei had fallen. In the spate of one month the eastern flank of Malaya was overrun and occupied. The defensive Punjab Regiment retreated into the jungle, followed by the British and the Dutch. After a ten-week existence in the jungle-covered mountains, the Allied contingent was surrendered on the 14th April.

Many years ago, when I was still a 'Miss', even before I left school, I listened to dance band music on the wireless. The leader of that band was a gentleman by the name of Harry Roy. He was married to a princess whose habitat before becoming Mrs Roy was Sarawak. I had no idea at that time who or where that name originated. For all I was knew, it could have been fictitious. Harry Roy's signature tune, which started and ended his programme, was a song called Sarawaki. He probably wrote it in her honour. I still remember the words and the tune of it. If this paper had the quality to absorb sound, I would whistle it for your pleasure; (or perhaps not – I am not very good at puckering up).

* * *

Japan on the March

The Japanese landed at the site of Kota Bharu on the north-east coast of Malaya's western flank, and took that vital airfield. Defending forces included Indian infantry, British artillery, and the RAF, but the Japanese successes continued. They linked up with other landing forces and proceeded southwards. Four weeks later, the entire northern region of this Malayan limb was lost to the Japanese hoards. Further south they entered and captured the capital city of Kuala Lumpur, continuing their advance by the day, and adding to it the conquest of the most southern state of Johore, a stone's throw from their ultimate target, Singapore. The road was open and clear.

Singapore, a vital outpost of the then British Empire from the 1920s, underwent a seismic shift largely due to the foresight of politicians and planners, who with an eye on Japan's characteristically aggressive history, had no difficulty in imagining Japan's "where next?".

This entailed the British constructing a major naval base, with particular emphasis on a defensive strategy from which a large fleet could respond to a troublesome 'barney' from that eastern quarter. To this end early in WW2, a high proportion of Australian forces in Asia was concentrated in Malaya. Some of their units were associated in early unsuccessful attempts to restrict the Japanese onslaught. Their commander, Major General Gordon Bennett, held in his charge an army division – four aircraft squadrons and eight warships under the umbrella of the Australian military. It was a heavy responsibility. It was a force based in Singapore, but hardly large enough, or formidable enough, to face a highly-trained enemy, well-practised in the art of an aggressive warfare, which the Japanese would be capable of offering.

* * *

The Tragedy of Singapore

The Japanese rapidly gained ground. They were able to outflank the defenders due to the misemployment of the troops under General Bennett's orders. He sent weak units to where weak units existed, and strong ones where strength was already in evidence.

Gordon Bennett – I had no idea that such a personage bearing that name was real-time. I was always under the impression that it was a title conjured up by comedians to express surprise. 'Gordon Bennett' – how I had laboured under such an illusion. Gordon Bennett – he presided over the 'grand-daddy' of a shocking muck up. As a minor aside to my narrative, Gordon Bennet was later charged in an Australian court of law for cowardice. It appears that in the heat of a losing battle, he handed over to a second-in-command, scurried away from the scene, found himself a small boat and sailed away home.

Commonwealth units did achieve a small measure of success against the foe in Malaya. The new year of 1942 heralded a series of episodes scrapping with the enemy, but they did little more than to slow the Japanese advance, in the process of which we had heavy losses. When I record a phase of this nature, I always need to pause to think about how a loss affects so many people other than the actual casualty.

A mum, worrying about her boy at the front; or a young mother, knowing that her small child will never meet or learn to love his or her daddy. How will she cope? Who has she got to support her in her grief, and maybe in her worry about how she will manage financially to maintain her little family, with no man besides her?

General Lieutenant Percival was the Commander of the forces stationed in the fortress at Singapore. He conceived the notion that the Japanese would eventually land in certain areas of that island, but they did not. Unfortunately he did a ditto following Gordon Bennett's example, and sent men where they were not needed and none where they were. He was misguided in his reckoning on both counts.

The Australians were stymied. By the morning of the 15th February, the enemy had broken through the last line of defence. The Allies were depleted of food and ammunition. They were in no position to continue a defence, and Percival surrendered to the Japanese under their terms. All the military were ordered to surrender unconditionally.

Mr Churchill was devastated when the news reached him. In his estimation the retention of Singapore was of paramount importance. Its fall represented the most extensive and humiliating surrender of British-led military personnel. In his anguish he said that the fall of Singapore to the Japanese was "the worst disaster" and "largest capitulation" in British military history.

During the entire seventy-day campaign in Malaya and Singapore, nine thousand Allied troops were killed or wounded. One hundred and thirty thousand were taken into captivity. The Japanese had advanced 650 miles through both the east and west land masses that now comprised a conquered state.

The Battle of Singapore, also known as the 'Fall of Singapore', was a tragedy of immense loss from different angles. Firstly the human count; in death, injury, and forfeiture of freedom. Singapore was the major British military base in South East Asia, and the keystone of British Imperialism. Its fall was a huge demoralizing factor to everyone; to the British government, to the British military, to our Allies, the Commonwealth, and of course to the British people. And to a youngsters like me. I was seventeen when it happened, and I well remember replacing the Union Jack flag pinned on Singapore on my war map with the Rising Sun, weeping as I did so. Naturally it had the opposite effect on the enemy. Can you think of the uplift in morale, self-confidence and esprit de corps of all concerned in Japanese circles?

Their great achievement in the capture of Singapore had taken but eight days. And having completed their mission, they sought and enacted a full programme of vengeance on the defeated protagonists and on the indigenous population and other groups living in that beaten city.

* * *

Revenge

I take the Alexandra Hospital Massacre as a point of reference. The day prior to the surrender, when it was obvious that a British defeat was about to happen, the Japanese moved towards the Alexandra Barracks Hospital. A British Officer approached with a white flag of surrender. He was bayoneted to death. The barbaric villains entered the hospital; the fifty patients, including those in surgery in the process of being operated on, were killed in similar acts. The medical staff, doctors and nurses of both sexes, shared the same horrific fate. Two hundred male staff, still alive, were assembled and bound, and force-marched to a specific place. Those who fell by the wayside were bayoneted. The remainder were left in small unventilated rooms in stifling heat, held overnight with no water. Most of these pitiful recipients of this unleashed brutality died in the night. Those who had survived till morning were used for target practice for the bayonet wielding thugs. You probably realize by now that I am no acolyte of warmongers. Can you but wonder why?

Thinking retrospectively, this was not the first of its kind. It was a repeat performance of the final act when the curtain came down in the battle of Hong Kong. The residents of Singapore under Japanese tyranny would endure diabolical hardship in the three-and-a-half years of their tenancy. Many British and Commonwealth prisoners remained in Singapore's notorious prisons and many died there. Thousands were deported by prison transports, known as 'hell ships', to other sites in Asia. The story of the building of the Siam-Burma Railway by prisoner of war slave-labour is the legend of those who lived a life of going to hell and back again.

After the war, the Japanese Commander Yamashita was tried by a United States Military Commission for war crimes. He was convicted and hanged in 1946. He should have been bayoneted to a violent death like so many who suffered at the hands of his underlings. How can one balance one life for the many deaths attributed to him? The quick manner of his demise would have been a welcome relief to the many who died in his name.

British military bosses had the intention to undertake a liberation campaign at some later stage, but the end of the war forestalled that plan. Singapore was re-occupied by British, Australian and Indian personnel in September 1945, following the Japanese surrender one month earlier.

* * *

Warriors' Day

To give this report a little light relief, if one can describe it as such, I can recall a visit to Kuala Lumpur, breaking my journey home from my last visit to Australia in 2000. To satisfy my indefatigable curiosity, I sought out sites in that city which would perhaps give me an insight to its connection during the conflict. And so it was that I located the glorious commemorative monument, sited not too far from their seat of government. At that time it was the world's tallest bronze free-standing grouping. It might be transcended now, but by anybody's standard it is magnificent. As I wandered around that locality, I was puzzled as to why there seemed to be much more activity than one might expect on an ordinary day. I was very pleased to discover that it was, in fact, no hum-drum every day of the week. It was a very important day – the 31st July, and every year that day is marked as special. It is delegated as 'Warriors' Day'. On that anniversary the Prime Minister leads a deputation to the memorial, and flowered garlands are laid. I was particularly impressed by the inscription in archaic Malayan. Translated, we would surmise it to read: "To Our Glorious Dead". In actual fact in authentic English it reads: "To Remember the Service of Warriors Who Have Fallen". It is of no consequence where or when or who; it is at moments like that, that one stands there and the heart strings tug, and one is in mourning.

* * *

The Brave Sons of India

When my family had grown and I was retired, I compensated for the difficult times I had known and I became an intrepid traveller. The frustrations betook me each time I unpacked my suitcase at the conclusion of a recent trip, and I began to think, "Where next?" On one such occasion, I went to India. I flew there. I stood at a dockside and tried to imagine the battalions of Indian troops leaving their homeland and embarking on the troopships on their way to the UK or anywhere else they were to serve. They were good and brave sons from the Commonwealth. Their long voyage was fraught with danger. My journey lasted twelve hours and I was guaranteed complete safety.

When the calamity of the Second World War started, the count of the military in India was 200,000. In 1945 when it finally ended, that number had risen to 2.5 million. It was the greatest volunteer army in history. It included men from areas now known as Pakistan, Bangladesh and of course from Nepal, which was always Nepal. It fought in Europe, North Africa and Asia. It engaged with the Germans and Italians in the Middle East, but the bulk of the Indian Army was committed to fighting the Japanese in the devastating Allied fight in Malaya and repeated in Burma. The heavy loss of life during the retreats amounted to 36,000 killed, 34,000 wounded and 67,000 taken prisoner. They were awarded 4,000 decorations including 38 Victoria or George Crosses earned by their extreme valour in the field. They gave true allegiance to their King Emperor.

The British Field Marshall Auchinleck said: "We couldn't have come through both World Wars if we hadn't had the Indian Army". Mr Churchill paid tribute when he described them thus: "The unsurpassed bravery of Indian soldiers and officers". In my opinion it comes with the job that all the great men praise the underlings but there was no exaggeration here. They were indeed the bravest of the brave. No messing when they were around.

The Indian army was, as is customary, made up of numerous divisions. To write about them all would necessitate four volumes which I am not prepared to undertake and I am sure that you would not take the time to read. I have always been drawn towards the division of the Chindits, and I feel that I owe them a few sentences. They were the brainchild of Brigadier Orde George Wingate, who assessed that long-range penetration raids behind enemy lines should become the main front against the Japanese in Burma. The Chindits were just ordinary down-to-earth infantry who were arbitrarily selected for a mission on the basis of availability. They undertook daring and dangerous targets. Our Prime Minister was particularly impressed with the brilliance of Orde Wingate. In true 'Churchillian' style, he commended him for his audacious and forthright attitude to the task. I have an idea that 'the Governor' was looking in his mirror! When Wingate was killed in 1945, the Chindits were disbanded. They were reformed and merged into the British army's Airborne Division.

* * *

One Country, Four Divisions

One special engagement area involving the Indian Army was in the Anglo-Iraqi war in 1941, to safeguard the overland supply route to the Soviet Union. In April of that year they landed at Basra, and marched onto Baghdad securing Iraq for the Allied cause from the pro-German top dog. Operation Barbarossa, the German invasion of Russia in June 1941, placed the Persian oil fields in danger of being captured by the advancing German army. In August, two Indian Divisions invaded southern Persia to secure those oil installations.

The strategic location of India with its southern tip meeting the Indian Ocean, the vast numbers of its volunteers, and the massive production of armaments as their war effort for the Allied forces, gave the Indian civilian population and its military, the right to be a factor towards the ultimate outcome of World War Two. The effects of the war in that land were life-changing. Vast political upheavals were afoot, which had consequences in the post-war era that changed the lives of its people forever.

There existed in the sub-continent four ruling or organizational authorities of substance. Firstly the British Raj held sway under its Viceroy, sustained by more than 500 of the princely autonomous states providing the man-power, and bases for the Americans, necessary for the United States support for the Chinese with their struggle in Burma and India, and in China itself.

Secondly, the Indian National Party with Mahatma Gandhi as the leader of its Congress Party, advocated independence for India, and its mammoth exertions to bring that to fruition led to clashes with the government in London and to the imprisonment of its leaders for the duration of the war. And so it was to be expected that the Party was not prepared to be overtly hostile, but unwilling and determined to abstain from allying itself to the British side of the warring nations.

Thirdly, the Muslim League was inclined to favour the Indian British Matter, and I honestly cannot report definitely on one side or the other. They were probably non-hostile, and not active either.

Last, but not least, under the leadership of one Subhas Chandra Bose and several other dissidents who were also seeking independence from the British, the Indian National Army (INA) was formed in direct opposition to the Allied cause and aligned itself to the Imperial Japanese Armed Forces. The Japanese released Indian prisoners of war who readily joined this newly set up INA. They fought with them in battle when Japan opened an offensive in Arakan in 1942–1943, when one battalion reached Mowdon and Chittagong, on the very edge of India's western border, almost on the eastern border of Burma on the coast of the Bay of Bengal. Other units were directed to Imphal and Kohima in Burma when battle raged for those twin towns. In 1945, at the time of the liberation of Rangoon, the renegade army fell apart.

It was thought at the time that no population in any country engaged in the 1939 to 1945 dissonance, was more affectedly protected from the horrors of war than the people of India, and it fell to the British to exercise it. There was no actual military activity to despoil that land. The Indian fighting forces fought away from home. Japanese aggression was played out in Burma. They did display aggrandizement on some of the smaller islands in the Bay of Bengal, for instance, Andaman and Nicobar Islands, which were of Indian possession, and they did attack and take positions close to the Indian-Burmese border, but never on the mainland of India itself. India had its problems and its own war, after this one had ended.

* * *

What Happened to the Mules and What Happened to Me

Probably the most unusual postings of any unit of the Indian Army was in 1940 when four mule companies of the Indian Service Corps joined the British Expeditionary Force in France. They were evacuated from Dunkirk and were stationed in England for a further two years.

I never did encounter any mules gallivanting around on the dance floor in London, but I did met some very handsome turbaned Sikhs and jolly nice guys they were too. They were polite and respectful to us ladies and I have retained a soft spot for those Indian gentlemen. At the end of the war, many of the Sikh ex-warriors settled in the Home Counties.

I was first widowed was I was 32. Having two school-aged children and a baby just ten months old, I was not prepared to leave my young ones in the care of a stranger whilst I undertook to work in a daytime job. Having a helpful neighbour willing to babysit unsociable hours, I took part time, evening and week end work at the local pub. It wasn't really my forte but in the pre-benefit era you managed the best way you could. A turbaned gentleman and I struck up an over-the-bar acquaintance and a platonic friendship developed.

I valued that in no small measure. I had mourned for two years and was very restricted socially with my young brood in tow. He was a kind and articulate person and helped me to resettle into the norm. When I say these gentlemen from India were polite and respectful, I speak from first-hand experience.

* * *

Jack Jacobs

Staying in a hotel in Chennai, I became engrossed in conversation with an elderly gentleman sharing a meal-time table. I thought that he had the air of a veteran, ex-soldier type. This is the story he told me:

"Lieutenant General Jack Jacobs, born in India, rose from the ranks to become one of that country's greatest military leaders. Disturbed by the news of the war in Europe, particularly of Nazi unbridled brutality, he enlisted into the British-controlled Indian Army. After taking a commission he was sent to Iraq." (I wondered if he had the opportunity to listen to Alf Russell, and to enjoy the music issuing forth from the music man's trumpet.)

He continued: "In 1943 he was posted to North Africa, where the Germans suffered a defeat at El Alamein, after which he served in Burma fighting the Japanese".

My companion at dinner continued the biography of the General's life. He went on to tell me of an era much later in the timescale, and not really pertinent to my war story, except for the opportunity of winding up this miniature biography of an eminent Indian gentleman.

He commanded an infantry division rising to the exalted rank of Brigadier in the Indian war with Pakistan in 1965; and to Major General in 1967 – two years later, as Chief of Staff. His career climaxed in 1971 when he campaigned in the ongoing Indian-Pakistani troubles. The new State of Bangladesh was born due in part to his ability in the planning of its creation. He retired in 1978 after 37 years of army service.

I was given the impression that the gentleman who espoused this interesting 'tit-bit' had been a close acquaintance of his subject. He spoke of him as if he had known him on an intimate level. He did not admit it, but I intuitively felt that he too had served in the Indian Army and had fought for Britain. He intimated that he had fond memories of that time in the Service. Perhaps he had served in one of the General's commands.

I thanked my informant and we said "goodbye". He left with a twinkle in his eye. I do believe that he personally knew 'J.J.'

I recently discovered that Jack Jacobs had died this year in 2016. After his death, the Indian Prime Minister Narendra Modi declared: "I will always remain grateful to him for his impeccable service to the nation at the most critical moments".

As well as General Jacobs there is another high-ranking Indian Army officer who I have already mentioned, and I think that he too warrants a few sentences.

* * *

A Personality to Admire

I have an interest in the life and times of the British General Orde George Wingate. I felt admiration for this warrior when I heard and read of his exploits at the time when they happened, that is, during the war. I have gazed at the memorial to him and to the Chindits which stands on the north-east side of the Victoria Embankment, in London. I have wandered around 'Orde Wingate Square' in Jerusalem. I decided that he fits in well with my story of the Indian Army: I am taking the liberty of a 'double whammy'.

He was born in India in 1903, the scion of a military family. They were committed Plymouth Brethren. He completed his English education at eighteen and was accepted into the Royal Military Academy receiving a Commission two years later. Even in these early days, he displayed a tendency to do things differently. He was what one might recognize today, as a 'bit of a lad', a 'tearaway'. He was all of that in his later professional career: an unconventional man who did things his way. The seeds were sown even when he was still at school. He was often in trouble, especially with his peers, but even as a youngster he never said 'no' and he stood up for himself. I must admit the character of the man appeals to me.

His relatives had held important civic offices, and one of them had occupied the post of Governor General of the Sudan. Orde was influenced by this, and became interested in the affairs swirling around the Middle East. He took a course in Arabic, and an army secondment in 1928, at the age of 25, to the Sudan which gave him access to an East Arab corps serving on the borders of Ethiopia. Within another two years, in 1930, he was in command of a company and saw action in the bush, tracking illegal traders and poachers and the like. Please take note that all of the information I have so far relayed occurred in peace-time, and I have deliberately reminded you of this by compiling this timeline.

He mounted several expeditions and was supported by the Royal Geographical Society of Britain. In 1933, he was back in the United Kingdom and was occupied in army retraining programmes for the lower ranks. In 1936 he was posted to Palestine and became caught up in that country's Zionist cause. He and his family were devout and practicing Christians but he believed in, and voiced his opinions loud and clear, advocating favourably for a Jewish homeland. The outbreak of war in 1939 found Wingate back in England, and he was soon off again to Ethiopia forming a guerrilla force fighting against the Italians. He was much loved and admired by the Emperor of the then Abyssinia.

Burma saw his final posting. It is here that he reached the pinnacle of his fame. Indeed it was his final setting. On the 24th March 1944, whilst on a sortie to access the situation of the Chindit Burma bases, the United States Air Force plane, in which he was travelling, crashed into the jungle-covered hills, where he died alongside a nine member crew. He was 41 years old. They were originally buried in a common grave close to the crash site. In 1950 their bodies were exhumed and they received full military honours at a re-interment ceremony in Arlington National Cemetery in America.

Chapter 20
Ceylon and Burma

They Did More Than Grow Tea

Britain had occupied the coastal area of Ceylon, (now Sri Lanka), since 1796. The pre-held military garrison was de-established after 1917. A Ceylon Defence Force and a Ceylon Naval Reserve already in place was expanded at the outbreak of the war. The RAF had set up an aerodrome at a site, China Bay, in the area of Trincomalee, and the Royal Navy had maintained installations at that town long before 1939.

The fall of Singapore and Hong Kong changed the entire configuration of the British military establishments. Whereas they had been based at those important and strategic sites, now they could not. As a consequence, in 1941 the RAF secondment in Ceylon was broadened. Airstrips were instituted across the country and several squadrons of personnel were posted there from the UK.

In keeping with the policy of the other British Colonies, conscription was not mandatory, but the population were encouraged to volunteer their services. Many of them did. They enlisted into the Ceylon Defence Force (CDF) which was transformed from a reserve unit to a mobilized force of ten battalions. For the first time Ceylonese were deployed away from home. That is, until the Cocos Islands Mutiny, after which service abroad ceased, with a few exceptions.

The Ceylonese continued to swell the volunteer numbers. They joined the British army, the RAF and the Royal Navy which were supplemented by CDF personnel who requested transfer to the main British Forces. They saw service in Burma and later in Malaya; they fought as Royal Engineers in Italy and with the Royal Army Service Corps in the Middle East and in North Africa. A battalion of the Ceylon Corps of Military Police operated in Malaya until 1949. Several of those who gave service during the war went on to do likewise in the Sri Lankan Armed Forces after Ceylon gained independence in 1948. The Ceylon Navy Voluntary Reserve was taken over by the Royal Navy. They manned trawlers and Artic whalers converted into minesweepers fitted with guns, submarine detection equipment and anti-submarine weaponry.

Ceylon Goes to War

The sinking of the battleship HMS Prince of Wales and the battle cruiser HMS Repulse, and the subsequent loss of Singapore, punctured forever the British myth of their invincibility. Against this backdrop and the agitation of a Trotskyist inspired Lanka Sama Samaja Party (LSSP), soldiers of the Ceylon artillery garrison at Cocos Island mutinied on the night of 8th May 1942 with the intention of handing the island over to the Japanese. The uprising was suppressed within an hour and three of the mutineers were later executed, the only British Commonwealth troops to be tried, found guilty and punished in this manner for that crime in the Second World War. The outcome was the discontinuation of Ceylonese troops in combat but a number of supply and transport units were used in rear areas in the Middle East. The defences of Ceylon were reinforced with the arrival of an Australian division and elements of an African division. Defence of the island was essential owing to its strategically important and vulnerable siting in the Indian Ocean. With the Japanese acquisition of the rubber plantations in the Pacific, Ceylon resources of that commodity were now essential to the British Empire. We needed Ceylon: as a gesture, and in an effort to prevent the dissatisfaction of its people, the implemented food ration was greater there than that of their Indian neighbours!

The Japanese attacked Ceylon. The Easter Sunday air raid on 5th April 1942 over Colombo was followed a few days later with a repeat performance on the harbour of Trincomalee. The raids coincided with Japanese harassment of the British fleet in the Indian Ocean. Two cruisers and an aircraft carrier were lost. The effect on the Ceylonese populace was far greater as it had knowledge of the Nanjing Massacres, and they learned about the brutality of the Japanese as captors in occupied states. The civilian population began a panicked flight from Colombo by boat to India. The massacres of Nanjing relate to the turn of events in that Chinese town, once known as Nanking, and one time capital of the Republic of China. It was a case of mass murder and mass rape against its residents over a six-week period, from the 13th December 1937. Men of the Japanese army murdered disarmed combatants and Chinese civilians. Historians argue about numbers since the military files were kept secret and then destroyed, but it is estimated that up to 300,000 died.

* * *

Political Disharmony

There had sprung up a resistance to the British, encouraged by the indoctrinated Trotskyite party which supported the movement for independence and took the lead for anti-war sympathizers to follow. The LSSP made it clear that they were not supporters of either the Axis or the Allies. They considered that the war was an external conflict. The Communist Party of Ceylon, although in political terms akin to the LSSP and also with an anti-war agenda, saw it as the war of imperialists, but in 1941 when Germany attacked Russia, they changed their minds and joined the war advocates. They then supported the British and changed the title: The 'Imperialists' War' was now 'The Peoples' War'. In my understanding, the three nominated headings were all correct. But whatever the called it, everyone suffered.

The opposition to the war generally came from the working class and the nationalists. Many of them hoped for a German victory; the general public dreaded a victorious Japanese. The Buddhist fraternity were disgusted that their monks of German origin were interned as enemy aliens and Italian Roman Catholic priests were not. Two young members of the governing party had discussions with the Japanese seeking collaboration to oust the British. They did not follow through since a much older government principal, (later to become Prime Minister Senanayake), intervened. (I remember the gentleman. The name intrigued me and hearing about him at that time, I thought what a good and wise man he was.) The independence agitation turned to opposition and altered ministerial support for the British war effort. Public discontent with British rule continued to flourish. There was trouble amongst the unions of the colonial tea planters taking sides, for and against. There were colour-bar problems practised by the leading elite clubs. One such Civil Defence Minister was called 'a black bastard', by the Commander of Ceylon, one Admiral Layton. Sri Lankans in Malaya and, before its fall, in Singapore, formed the Lanka Regiment of the Indian National Army, in league with the Japanese and directly under the leader of the LLSP, one Netaji Subhas Chandra Bose. A plan was devised to transport them to Singapore and India secretly by submarine, but it was aborted. The leaders were able to escape with the help of one of their guards. Several of them did flee to the Sub Continent where they co-joined in their common aim, underscoring what had been established there before the war, and they worked together in a common cause.

My, there was troubles aplenty on that island pushing its nose out into the ocean.

I am not sure who was the greater enemy, Japan or themselves; but at least they did not kill each other and I never heard of violence emanating from that situation. But I guess everyone was happy when the war ended, and as with India, they did achieve their independence.

* * *

My Dear Little Sri Lankan Student

In my working life I graduated from being a ward sister in the old Edgware General Hospital here in Greater London, which used to be Middlesex when I worked there. I advanced into being a Clinical Teacher and I taught student nurses on their first training module in medical matters. In fact it was my responsibility to guide and cosset them when they were newly-arrived, some having left home for the first time and many from places a long, long way from Edgware General. I distinctly remember one such eighteen year-old miss from the island which I have just been 'scribbling' about. She was a sweet young lady, full of charm and respect. She was shy – a refreshing change from some of the 'pushy' ones. She had obviously had had a good upbringing. At the end of my eight week slot with a group I would photograph them en-masse, and individually. I remember when I handed her the pictures she said: "I will send it to my family and it will stand on our cabinet, and, Mrs Russell, I will always think of you". Well, I will always remember her.

* * *

On the Road to Mandalay – In memory of Rudyard Kipling

Japanese raids on Rangoon, Burma, began before the end of December 1941. Defending forces were weak. The British contribution was one squadron of fighter aircraft and one from an American voluntary group, originally formed pre-war to support the Chinese in their struggles with the Japanese. Even so those two squadrons inflicted heavy losses on the raiders. Japanese air-raids achieved limited damage to the targeted military installations, but the bombing caused havoc and many casualties on a multitude of the population.

The Japanese advance from their allied nation Siam into neighbouring Burma had begun in earnest by the end of February 1942. In that month, the Japanese claimed victory at the River Sittang, (now Sittaung), a swift flowing river, 500 yards wide and spanned by just one old iron railway bridge. The British General Sir John Smythe was in charge.

The British and Indian forces engaged there were trapped, and the general was called upon to make a difficult decision: it was a situation where he could get his men safely over the other side and to a safe retreat, or to destroy the bridge, thus impeding the enemy advance. He decided on the latter. The bridge was blown. From the river bank the Allied force found itself faced with liquidation. Even so 3,300 men contrived to cross – they swam. All be it with a loss of most of their warfare hardware, and many without their boots. In a military context the Battle of Sittang River was a major disaster and seemed to forecast the fate of that country.

* * *

Churchill v Curtin

Amid the stresses and strains of the bitter fighting in Burma, and at that time of the remorseless tide of defeat and ruin which dominated our fortunes, the Australian government and military pundits could feel little confidence in the British conduct of the war, or in our judgement back at home. It was time to give all the strength they could muster to face a likely life or death peril which menaced their shores, their cities and their people. We had been subjected to that same hazard in 1940. We had been exposed to that similar awful danger in a much closer and much more likely scenario, but we did not lose our sense of proportion or hesitate to add to our own risk for the sake of others who needed us. It was in the Churchillian psyche that others would act accordingly for us. Mr Churchill thought of a previous prime minister of Australia, Mr Menzies, who volunteered four army divisions to fight side-by-side with us in North Africa.

Churchill and the Australian government were engulfed in a painful episode in their relationship. An Australian troop transportation convoy was in the Indian Ocean, currently sailing south off Colombo (Ceylon), not too far from the arena of conflict. Our PM requested the Australian government under its then serving PM, Mr Curtin, for permission to change the homeward-bound convoy to give succour to those in combat with the Japanese. The Australians replied with a 'no can do'. In retrospect they did have a viable reason. They feared a Japanese assault on their continent. And they were not prepared to spare those military divisions away from home to fight abroad. In their estimation, also in ours, Burma was just one feature of a world at war. The Japanese advances in the Indian oceanic region gave no rise to worry that they might invade the British Isles, but the prospect facing Australia was a different kettle of fish entirely.

Mr Churchill appealed again and again, and was never-endingly answered with a negative response. He sought President Roosevelt's assurances that he would support the anxious Australians with a promise of vast numbers of American troop reinforcements, but Curtin was not convinced. Mr Churchill further compounded his argument. He enlightened Mr Curtin that there were no other alternatives to fill the gap, and that this was a vital state of war emergency that could not be ignored. The response from Canberra was unchanged. To settle the matter our Winston took the matter into his own hands, and in spite of the contradictions of those 'down under', he assumed a "yes, you can do and I will see to it" attitude. The convoy anchored at Rangoon, but not for too long. It did leave, turned about and sailed on home.

* * *

Churchill Faces His Nemesis

Based on his experience of war time tactics, Mr Churchill reckoned that the Japanese had much more to gain by concentrating on the capture of the Dutch East Indies with its rich prize of resources, rather than despatching an army across the equator 4,000 miles southward to instigate a mammoth struggle in Australia and to face the ANZAC (Australia and New Zealand Corps) forces, who had proven themselves worthy and reputable opponents. He faced yet another dilemma; one of his own making and in hindsight, guilt was its residue. It appears that his decision to prioritise, all be it in vain, the deployment of defence battalions to Singapore when perhaps it might have been wiser to deflect some of those hoards to Burma, (which he did not), was wrong. With the fall of that bastion, it was Rangoon who was first in line for reinforcements which were not forthcoming, and with Mr Curtin's obstinate attitude it was not going to happen. Churchill had no choice but to override the authority of the Australian top man. The reaction of Mr Churchill's unsolicited decision was not well-received. A message was passed from Mr Curtin informing the Governor of Burma that no help would be forthcoming from the Australians and that Rangoon must continue the fight regardless. It did, but victory was too much to expect. It was an uneven match, and who knows it could have been avoided.

Churchill sent our British General Alexander to that war zone. It was a perilous journey, flying over enemy-held territory. On the 5th March 1942, he took over command with instructions to withdraw to upper Burma, keeping contact with the Chinese on his eastern flank if Rangoon fell, which it ultimately and not unexpectedly did. The Japanese attacked in an attempt to cut the road from Rangoon to Prome, (now

Pyay), in upper Burma, thus barring the last land exit route from that city. The entire defeated Allied forces were to use that as an escape route. Their first attempt was repulsed. A fierce battle endured for twenty four hours.

* * *

The Burmese Retreat

A long and shattering struggle was required to finally extricate the remnants of the army from that war scene in Burma. There was no possibility that General Alexander's forces would be reinforced from any quarter. Aircraft from neighbouring India managed to drop stores and medical supplies and to evacuate 8,600 persons including the wounded, but for the remainder of the troops and the civilians there was no way out except for a 600 mile march through jungle and mountains.

On the 24th March, Japan resumed their offensive by attacking the Chinese at a site, Toungoo, north of Prome. It was captured after a seven day savagely fought confrontation. Four days later they advanced on both sides of the Irrawaddy River. Come the end of April and they stood before Mandalay. The optimistic assumption that the Allies would be in a position to maintain contact with the Chinese would remain feasible was an impossibility, and the hope of keeping the Burma Road open, the life-line to China, had faded. Part of the Chinese forces fighting with the Allies withdrew back to their homeland, and the rest followed the American General Stillwell; he was a good and trusted friend to the Chinese and he spoke their language. From the Irrawaddy River they struck across the mountain ranges to India.

General Alexander with the British marched north-west to Kalewa. Only here could they guard the eastern frontier of India, which was already threatened by a Japanese column moving up to the River Chindwin. The routes were little more than jungle paths.

In the meantime, President Roosevelt had kept his promise to reinforce the military in Australia with almost a million of his troops, and he vouched to extend the commitment to defend Australia by offering the assistance of the United States Battle Fleet. It was in his interest too that Burma did not fall to our common foe. The US needed China's assistance and there would have been unremitting consequences if China were to be cut off from the connecting link with Burma. That would surely happen if Rangoon fell. The route to China was via that country and Rangoon was the lynch-pin. The loss of Burma affected the United States as well as the rest of the warring nations.

A Song on the Brain - Not Cake in the Tum

I could have headed this story of the war in Burma 'In memory of Rudyard Kipling'. Why, you might wonder? I have an idea that Kipling is a brand-name for a bakery turning out cakes and the like for super-market shelves. Nothing to do with it, and I don't eat cake anyway. Fattening!

Joseph Rudyard Kipling was an English journalist; he wrote short stories for children and for adult readers and he wrote poetry. He was born in Bombay in 1865 and returned to India after an English education. He was offered a knighthood, but he refused the honour. He did accept a Nobel Prize for Literature, and was the first Englishman to have an accolade in that subject.

I am sure that many of my readers will be well-acquainted with much of his work. He wrote 'Jungle Book', 'Kim', 'Just So Stories' and 'The Man Who Would Be King'. If you have not read these titles, I dare say that you have seen the screen versions. And he penned the poem 'Gunga Din' and my favourite, 'Mandalay', which was put to music, and was once a well-loved and popular song rendered by male baritones. The title of it was 'On The Road to Mandalay'. I learnt the words of that song as a 'young-un', and sometimes I sing it to myself even now. Whilst doing my rendering of the military battles in Burma, and telling of the political goings on in 'Oz', (depressing enough to be sure), but that song has been running around my brain, even bursting forth in sound, and it was a relief.

Rudyard Kipling died in 1936 and is buried in Westminster Abbey. I go to that revered building, and to stand by the memorials to the great and the good is one of my special treats.

* * *

The Battle of Kohima

In 1944 the Japanese were in trouble. They were being ousted in the Pacific and were anxious that the Allies were preparing offensive action elsewhere. Japan had plans and aspirations of its own. They looked forward to a takeover of the entire sub-continent of India and the overthrow of the British Raj. They code named it 'U Go', and for starters to this plan they intended to capture the town of Imphal, capital of the State of Manipur in north-east India. This affair was a precursor to the Siege of Kohima. This historic event is world famous not only for its story but of the legacy that it bequeathed.

Imphal was linked to a large base by a road that wound for a hundred miles through steep and forested hills. It was in fact in a valley. Other areas round the capital were garrisoned by divisions of the British and Indian armies and the Gurkhas, and the Japanese hoped to destroy and isolate these forward areas resulting in a very favourable position to begin the onslaught on Imphal itself. It seems to me to have been a sensible and workable scheme especially as the road involved was a direct route to Burma already in Japanese hands. When the two British commanders leading the campaign received some intelligence appertaining to it, they misjudged the timing, and Imphal was faced with an exceedingly vulnerable dilemma and attacked.

The Battle of Kohima was directly linked to the Imaphal troubles in more ways than one. Firstly, the fight for its survival was simultaneous with spats between the Japanese and the Allies in some of the outlying areas, and secondly, it was linked by a road in a very strategic placement. Its site was atop a steep ridge which dominated a pass through the hills. It was in fact a hill station with the entire basic infrastructure that one might expect to serve a small local community and the military stationed there.

That road offered the Japanese the best route into the heart of India, in addition to being the main supply link to Imphal, without which that town would be deprived of all the main ingredients with which a battle is fought. So it is understandable that those men from the East were itching for a dust-up to take that valuable prize. It was a 'do or die' turning point in their 'U Go' caper. It was a fierce and horrendous experience for any of those British and Commonwealth defenders who fought there, and many did not live to tell the story of it.

The siege began on the 6th April 1944, and the garrison was continually shelled and mortared and was very soon driven into a small perimeter on the hill. Fighting confined to a small area was devastating, and sometimes soldiers resorted to hand-to-hand combat. It is said that the zone could be compared to that of a French battlefield in The Great War; smashed trees, ruined buildings and the ground covered with craters. The monsoon had broken by this time and the steep slopes were covered in mud, and were treacherous to even the slightest movement. The Japanese occupied deeply dug-in bunkers, well supported and concealed, dotted about the hillside.

It was a ferocious fight with a 'ding dong' effect. Each side counter-attacking in a constant battle. And it thus continued until the 11th May, after five weeks of fighting and existing in a living hell. It ended after a barrage of smoke shells blinded the

Japanese machine gunners and it allowed the British and their Commonwealth counterparts to secure the hill and to dig in.

* * *

Defeat on an Empty Stomach

The Japanese surrender was decisive mainly because their food supply was exhausted. Once the official rations were used, they existed on meagre amounts which they had foraged from increasingly hostile villagers. Shortly before the siege, they had captured a huge warehouse containing enough rice, it was said, to fortify a division for three years, but it was immediately bombed and the stock was destroyed. At the time of their collapse those soldiers were starving; when they initially arrived to fight they brought with them good stocks of ammunition, not food.

But they did not concede entirely. They abandoned the ridge but continued to block the Kohima to Imphal road. From the 16th May to the 22nd June 1944, the British and Indian and Nepalese troops were in pursuit of the retreating enemy and the road was finally opened. The Japanese retreat from Kohima was reduced in many instances to that of a rabble, abandoning artillery and transport, and many soldiers too badly wounded or too sick to walk. The prize-winning blokes from both relieved sites of warfare met up at a place called Milestone 109. It must have been a time of good will and celebration and plenty of swigs from the beer cans.

The Battle of Kohima is often referred to as 'The Stalingrad of the East', and in 2013 the British National Army Museum voted the combined pair, Imphal and Kohima, Britain's greatest battles, which qualified as the largest defeats in the history of Japan. After the siege, the terrain had been reduced to a fly and rat-infested wilderness with half-buried human remains everywhere.

By mid-1944, Allied air forces enjoyed undisputed air supremacy over Burma. The monsoon in no way diminished their capabilities. The contribution they made to the victorious outcome of the twin operations was of immense value. The British and Americans could, and did, fly men, equipment and supplies into Imphal airstrips, so that the town cut off by land, was not without a life-line. By the end of the conflagration, those air forces had transported 19,000 tons of essentials; 12,000 men into the two participating towns; and taken out 13,000 casualties. They carried into the stricken areas over one million gallons of fuel, one thousand bags of mail and 40 million cigarettes.

Several thousand mules were used to supply outlying districts, so animal fodder was added to the shopping list. They parachuted in ammunition and other articles of war and essential supplies of drinking water.

For other data on dates, the war in Imphal was from the 8th March to the 3rd July and in Kohima, 4th April to the 22nd June 1944. Allied losses amounted to 4,000: almost all died entirely as a result of the battle. Japanese dead counted as 6,000, mostly of disease and starvation, and they lost almost every one of 12,000 pack-horses and mules and 30,000 head of cattle that were used as beasts of burden. There is an end-piece to this story.

* * *

We Are Mindful Every Year in November

The Kohima War Cemetery lies on the slope of a hill. The epitaph carved into the stone has worldwide renown and is recited every year at memorial monuments during Remembrance Day parades. It reads: "When you go home tell them of us and say: for your tomorrow we gave our today." It brings a lump to my throat as I write of it and hear it intoned. The verse was attributed to John Maxwell Edmonds, and is thought to have been inspired by an epitaph written by one Simonides to honour the Greek Spartans who fell in battle in 480 BC.

In York there is a Battle of Kohima Museum. If you are interested, and happen to be in that city, go and visit. I did. I bet you can guess that it was a must for me.

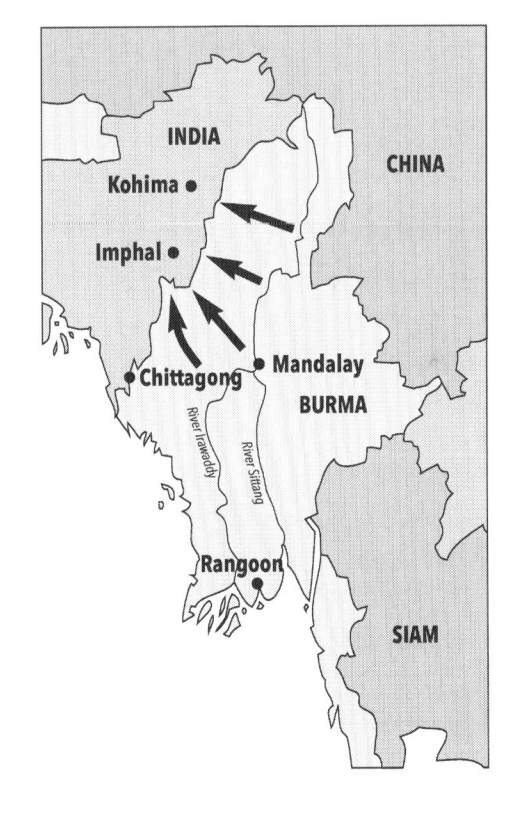

Map showing the Japanese advance in Burma, 1944

Chapter 21
War in the Pacific

The Dutch East Indies

To co-ordinate the forces in the defence of the Dutch East Indies, now known as Indonesia, the Allies formed an assemblage for that purpose. The acronym ABDA, representing America, Britain, the Dutch and Australia, started action on the 15th January 1942. However, like all good friends, their priorities differed. For Britain it was the defence of Singapore, (before its fall), the eastern entrances to the Indian Ocean and the route to British India and British Ceylon, (now Sri Lanka). America and Australia were not happy to see a total penetration of South West Asia which would deprive them of bases necessary for future counter attacks; and the Dutch deemed that Java and Sumatra, their second homes where they had lived and had been trading for three centuries, to be the most important countries to defend.

It came to pass that even the unified forces were unable to stop or even to slow the Japanese advance across the conglomeration of Pacific islands. They were overwhelmed by the sheer numbers of the enemy, namely the attacking Japanese naval fleet. They captured the airfields at Tarakan in north east Borneo on the 17th January 1942, and Balikpapan, further south, one week later. By the end of the month the Imperial Japanese Army had control of the island of Celebes and the entire Dutch possessions of Borneo. In February Sumatra lay in bondage. The Allies were crushed in the naval battles of the Java Sea and Sunda Strait, and again in the second battle of the Java Sea.

They fared no better on land. Allied forces were out-fought and quickly diminished. Within two months of the initial Japanese offensive, the ABDA was dissolved, just two months after its inception. Its members surrendered to the Japanese at Bandung, in Java, on the 12th May 1942. It was a shameful and disastrous outcome. The team just could not cope with the volume of attacking marauders. Japan conscripted many of its men-at-arms from its holdings in Korea and Formosa (now Taiwan).

The Allied forces did not attempt to retake the islands of Java, Sumatra, Timor or Bali during the war although American General MacArthur was eager to do so, on orders from President Roosevelt he was forbidden, and the Japanese remained in situ until the final Japanese surrender in 1945. In all, the offensive in the taking of the Dutch East Indies encompassed thirteen battles. Together with the capture of New Guinea at a later stage, the Dutch East Indies faded from history, except of course the story of its demise.

Most of the population of Indonesia, (as it is now known), were overjoyed in welcoming the Japanese as liberators from their previous Dutch masters. The sentiment changed as they were subjected to greater hardships and tribulations. By the end of the war, however, the changes had become so numerous and extraordinary that a subsequent Indonesian National Revolution was possible in a manner not feasible three years earlier. Unlike the Dutch, the Japanese facilitated politicisation, and gave the national leaders a political voice. The Japanese occupation created the conditions for Indonesian independence within days of the eventual Japanese surrender.

*　*　*

Introduction to the War in the Pacific

If a Martian landed here from outer space and was a rabid cinema addict he would be imbued with the notion that America had won the war in the Pacific Zone of conflict single handed. Australians were active as United States allies, and I have never yet watched a film of that genre that gives any indication that anyone else was involved other than American, Japanese, and sometimes the local inhabitants, wherever the two main protagonists happened to be.

I can present evidence of some of the narrow-minded ignorance of the facts of World War Two, which might easily have been picked up, inadvertently from a movie. I can recall being in the company of a group of people from the North American Continent. I was asked by an erudite gentleman, a high-ranking individual from an important organization: "What was it like living in Britain, under occupation?" I put it to you rhetorically: "Can you believe it?" I once mentioned that I came from Wales, (when I still lived there), and the retort, from a similar type of individual was: "Do you live near the sea, are you with the fish?" It was a serious question and not meant as a pun.

The nitty gritty of the Pacific War operation is that it was a dastardly and devastating affair. It was a contest to the death between ferocious, 'never say die', and 'Hari Kari' (suicide), rather than surrender, Japanese; and the determined and tenacious, but perhaps less-conditioned, Americans. The contrast to the war that was fought on the

Normandy beaches throws up a completely different projection. Not to say, that is, that the efforts on both sides was less dramatic or the resolve to win, diluted. The difference was the nature and characteristics of the enemy.

* * *

The Who and the Where

The overall confrontation, sometimes called the Asia-Pacific War, was fought in the Pacific Region and in Eastern Asia over a vast area that included the Pacific Ocean and its islands, and South-East Asia and China. It was witness to the Allied Powers herculean struggle against the Empire of Japan. The premier defender to sustaining the free lifestyle of the Islands was the United States, aided and abetted by Britain, and especially with the Commonwealth support from Australia. The Indians, New Zealanders and Canadians were also there. Fijians, Samoans, and Philippine Islanders were able to aid in the defence of their islands when the call came. The Dutch from their holding in the Dutch East Indies were on hand to play their part. Mexicans, and the Free French as back up, were available. The Soviet Union fought two minor border incidents against Japan in 1938 to 1939; but declared itself as non-committed in the Pacific conflict when fighting the German might from 1941 in defence of its own land. They re-joined the Allied involvement in August 1945 to liberate the Japanese conquests of Manchukuo and of areas of today's Korea.

The war in the Pacific was geared into action before the Allies realized it had happened. It took off on or around the 7th–8th December 1941, when in collusion with the Thai people, it was undertaken to appease the Empire of Japan's long-suppressed hunger for the expansion into widespread Asia. The British outposts of Hong Kong and Borneo and Singapore were unlawfully targeted. The Japanese attacked the United States bases in Hawaii. Wake Island, Guam and the Philippines, Okinawa and Saipan and Iwo Jima all fell foul to the aggressor. There was no compunction of law before an actual declaration of war. They just carried out their aggression regardless; the affected lands were illegally violated.

The collapse of the British possessions in the Pacific heartland led Australia to reorient its position on foreign policy to the United States, loosening its ties from the Allies. Large numbers of American military personnel had been based in Australia since 1942. Almost one million had passed through it since the outbreak of war. They were needed, and on hand, when Japan struck.

The Japanese were kept pretty busy and fully employed. I wonder if they were remunerated with overtime rates for week-end work! Joking aside, it was not a time for humour when one considers the apocalyptic loss of sacred human life in the course of those years, and of the indignity that lowers the concept of the spirit and the senses.

* * *

Defeat and Victory

In the early days, defeat followed defeat for the Americans. The Philippines, hitherto in the control of the United States, were assaulted, taken and occupied by new masters for the next three years. The American General, Douglas MacArthur, Commander of the South West Pacific Area (SWPA) was ordered by his president to withdraw his person to Australia when the situation was reduced to an abyss of disaster after the fall of the island of Bataan in March 1942. His famous leaving speech: "I will be back" foretold the future, but echoing around the world, loud and clear, one could hear the Japanese word 'sensho' (victory). He did indeed return in 1944 to oversee 'take back time'. When the Philippine islands were retaken, the Japanese humiliation must have been of maximum proportion. 'Sensho', once announced so loud and clear, but not now around the Pacific.

Apart from some of the smaller islands which had been by-passed by the liberating Forces, the conflict which was enacted in that vast zone was concluded and the Philippines set free. The abandoned Japanese personnel were simply left as they were. Ignored by the Japanese high, and now not so mighty, at home, and certainly by the victorious Americans and their Allies, who considered that to fight for the release of those small outposts was not worth the time or trouble, they were left alone for years, living off the land. Occasionally a few old Japanese soldiers would surface and become a TV news item.

* * *

My Education of the Affair

My personal experience as far as the Pacific region was concerned is limited. I have never visited that location. The little I do know was acquired second-hand. I have been sufficiently inquisitive enough to watch TV programmes on the subject and to hear the views and opinions of the specialist historians, and I read a lot, (past and present tense).

I read the story of the Bataan Death March. In 1942, with the Japanese in their zenith, they rounded up the defeated troops and orchestrated a forced march to POW camps. Abuse was rife. Six hundred and fifty Americans and ten thousand Filipinos died on the way. During their captivity it was estimated that up to 80,000 of them were either starved or beaten to death.

I watched scenes of Japans success and Allied defeats transmitted in episodes on the television and from my seat in a cinema; in particular the loss of the island of Leyte. It was upsetting and it dimmed the sense of right and wrong; so much to absorb, and to fathom out why? The carnage, and the destruction, and uppermost of all, the tragic loss of life, and repression of the human psyche. I was in possession of a season ticket to our local picture house, the Troxy, in the Commercial Road, Stepney, close to where I lived. I always went on a weekend afternoon whilst my brother was at sport or visiting his friends. My Mum and Dad made sure we went out so that they could have some free time together. The four of us shared one bedroom until I was ten, when I was transferred to a narrow wooden pull-out armchair in the 'front room', which was usually reserved for guests. I had to fold up the bed linen, revert the chair to normal and leave it tidy every morning before I left for school. Well, we were 'brung up' in the proper way.

I remember the sequences in those depictions of the war. The glamourous leading lady in her low-cut gown with the equally handsome opposite number in his spotlessly white tropical uniform. Without a doubt they all had a 'happy-ever-after' finale. Of course those members of the Filipino army who had carried out a guerrilla war against the Japanese all through those years and fought side-by-side with their American counterparts, were forgotten. In any case, how could they be screened in their third-rate army gear, doled out by the US general issue, wearing their rubber army footwear worn through in two weeks? There were shortages of every type – blankets, mosquito nets, gas masks and helmets. They operated with so little US training that some of them did not know how to fire a gun. I don't think that they even had a mention in the credits. Film buffs amongst my readers will perhaps remember an American-made movie based on the theme of this time in history.

I cannot imagine a portrayal of the labouring units of the hard-working Australian army construction detachments, who so quickly and efficiently relieved the dearth of aeroplane take-off and landing facilities for the American flyers. I am certain that they were much appreciated and so they should have been, but not on film.

I wonder if there was a certain element of not being as 'good as we are?' Maybe a whiff of snobbery, with a touch of arrogance.

Several films were rolled out depicting specific issues. The development and cinematic presentations of these were obviously post-war. By reason of the time lapse, some basic facts might have been omitted in the script, or perhaps not noticed, or forgotten by an audience, which I can rectify. The Battle of Bataan, in real life, was enacted from January to April 1942. The Battle of Leyte was fought in October to December 1944; and the authentic Battle of Leyte Gulf occupied the military in the same year. In all, twenty six battles and skirmishes were the final count. Jolly good job that only a few were transferred to the 'Silver Screen'. I suppose though, that utilizing the full quota of the list would have been a mega economic boom to Hollywood and the moguls.

* * *

The End of the Story and It's Quiz Time

The casualty lists were astronomical. Four million young men died in the Pacific territory during those few years for the right for us to live without fetters in a free world. Twenty six million civilians were killed in their own countries to rid themselves of the evil occupiers. When I read the figures in numerical form, I repeatedly count the noughts. I thought it must be five, but no it was six and I was stunned.

I realize that the facts of the war in the Pacific can be somewhat depressing. I have decided to 'lighten the load'. It's Quiz Time. The conundrum is based on an old adage: "One man's meat is another man's poison." So who benefited from the 'meat' and who lost out by the 'poison'? I expect you to be able to answer; if not, it will be proof that my story is a flop.

Have you an answer to my question? Are there any 'clever-clogs' out there? The film companies had the meat and all that lovely 'lolly', and the Japanese had the bitter taste of defeat. If there had been any cyanide around they would have found a use for it. Award yourself a 'Brownie' point. Perhaps 'take two'?

* * *

Japan's Come-uppance

During the course of the war, Allied air forces attacked the home islands of Japan.

They used aircraft carriers as airfields. The shortfall of regular take-off and landing sites presented no other option. But sorties from ships were limited, and gave restriction to travel time. Basically, short-range targets were possible and long range sorties were not. It was a set-back for the United States Air Force.

A few minor air raids materialized over Japan early in the war, but in 1944 and with Allied successes in the Pacific, heavy and concentrated stuff was the order of the day. The liberation of the Philippines gave the Americans a window to ease the problem. They now had the advantage of using airfields on previously-held occupied territory, enabling them to engage in long-range tactical bombing which allowed them a much closer range to Japan itself. Japan, having a taste of its own medicine! The raids were intensified in mid-1944, and during the ebbing months of hostilities the culmination of the unleashing of atomic warfare, in the shape of the bombs that obliterated two towns, Hiroshima and Nagasaki, was the prelude to the Japanese surrender.

Led by General MacArthur, in his role as Supreme Commander for the Allied Powers, a deputation set foot on the soil of Imperial Japan. It was the first time in its history that a foreign power arrived as an occupier. That state of affairs stood until April 1951 when a Peace Treaty was signed in San Francisco. It transformed Japan into a parliamentary democracy.

Chapter 22
Southern Africa

Southern Rhodesia then, Zimbabwe now

Southern Rhodesia, as it was at the time of World War Two, was a self-governing colony of the United Kingdom. It entered the war as did Britain when Germany invaded Poland. During the war over 26,000 mixed races, black and white, served in the armed forces. There were 8,000 in overseas operations in Europe, the Mediterranean, Middle East, East Africa, and Burma and elsewhere wherever they were required to participate. They made a huge contribution by operating an air training scheme under which 8,000 Commonwealth and Allied airmen received their training in Southern Rhodesian flight schools.

Since that country's reconstitution as Zimbabwe in 1980, the modern government has removed references to both World Wars, such as memorial monuments and plaques from public view, regarding them as unwelcome vestiges of white minority rule and colonialism. The dead of Southern Rhodesia's war heroes have no official commemoration, certainly not in Zimbabwe or overseas. They are never mentioned in any commemoration here in Britain. Maybe they should be.

I have no connection, in any shape or form to that country. But I remember Ian Smith, the last Prime Minister. I had a girlish crush on him. At the time of the country's independence he was prominent in the news and I would literately drool at his image on the TV. I even had a newspaper cut-out picture of him in my bedroom. Heck! I was middle-aged. Did I say a 'girlish' crush? Such are the wiles of silly females!

***

Herzog v Smuts

The 1931 Statute of Westminster awarded the Union of South Africa Commonwealth status, with the British monarch as its head. In September 1939 the South African Prime Minister J.B.M. Herzog, leader of a pro-Afrikaner and anti-British National Party, was in partnership with a pro-British gentleman, Jan Smuts. The National Party was born and developed.

In accordance with the Polish-British pact of 1939, terms were agreed whereby mutual aid would be available in troubled times, if an attack by a third party was instigated. At the outbreak of World War Two, South Africa was obligated to support Great Britain versus Germany and the Axis powers.

A furious rumpus arose in the South African Parliament pitting the pro-British members, who were in favour of entering the conflict, with the anti-British members who sought to keep their country neutral, if not downright pro-Axis. On the 4th September Herzog was deposed and the incoming Prime Minister Smuts declared war on Germany, following Britain by one day.

Smuts immediately set about fortifying the country against a German sea invasion; bearing in mind its global position and strategic importance controlling the long sea route around the Cape of Good Hope. I need to remind my readers of the fragile vulnerability of the Suez Canal, and that it was vital to keep this alternative sea route around the Cape open, absolutely a priority so that the route was always and readily available. One of my relatives who was shipped off to Burma rather enjoyed the weeks at sea, except that he mortgaged his army pay for months, losing to his fellow card-playing mates. Well, he was young and a novice, so I hope he learnt his lesson.

* * *

A Fan Club Membership of Two

Field Marshall, (formerly 'Mr') Smuts, was the only non-European general whose advice and friendship Mr Churchill adhered to and appreciated. He called him "my old and valued friend", and asked him for his good counsel; but Jan Smuts had lost the popularity of the Afrikaners at home, which led to his later eventual downfall.

I took quite a fancy to this not very young gentleman. He sported a light grey beard and whenever I saw his image in the newspaper or on screen, I was reminded of my grandfather. They could have been cloned. And I was very fond of my grandpa.

At the time of the declaration of war, the South African army numbered 5,353 regular soldiers, and 14,000 men from a force which had offered peace-time training to volunteers; quite like the Territorials here in Britain, but the exercise and equipment was geared up to bush warfare. One of the problems which faced South Africa was a manpower shortage of suitable applicants aged between 20 and 40. Racial differences added to the dilemma; only white men were entitled to carry arms.

Conscription was unpopular and recruitment depended on volunteers. A number of corps formed to provide drivers, and pioneers were drawn from the Cape Coloured and the Indian population. They were not allowed to be in combat against Europeans. Ultimately 334,000 volunteers served in the army comprising 211,000 white, 77,000 black and 46,000 Cape Coloured and Indian people.

* * *

They Did Good

General Smuts and his forces served the Allies well. In the North African Campaign they supplied troops, airmen and supplies. Many flew with the RAF. They accommodated the ships that docked at crucial ports situated on the coastlines of both the Atlantic and Indian Oceans. They defeated the Italians in 1940–41 in the melee in East Africa, in Abyssinia and Kenya, and pulled their weight to liberate the island then known as Malagasy, now Madagascar, on the 4th May 1942. That land mass, an easterly neighbour, was invaded by the South Africans directly from home. Previously Madagascar had been the domain of the French, now transferred to Vichy. It was in danger of being seized by the Japanese, and it seemed sensible to safeguard it in Allied hands.

South African troops helped out in the Battle of El Alamein. An armoured division fought in Italy in 1944–45. The South African Air Force flew their craft in both the East and North African scenes of wartime activity, as well as being involved in cover commitment in Sicily, Italy, the Balkans, and as far east as the Rumanian oil fields. They were included in a mission of support in Poland, involving the uprising in Warsaw.

In the war effort against Japan the South Africans supplied men and ships in naval engagements. It was a veritable catalogue of duty and service well done. The War Graves Commission possess records of 11,000 men, known to be South Africans, who died. It is an amazing fact that far-away colonies with tiny populations can provide such a varied and wide-spread source of help and commitment. It was not all doom and gloom in those long ago dark and uncertain times.

Chapter 23
Australia - Part One

Initiation to Oz

My second daughter, Diane, with her husband and young family emigrated to Australia in 1982. I retired three years later and the first item on my agenda was to visit them. I had never travelled that far. I returned to London three months later. That holiday took place thirty-one years ago and it is as fresh in my mind as if it were a vacation break last year.

I was on the lookout for an adventure and I was party to one before I even arrived. A member of the flight crew announced: "We will be landing in Melbourne in three hours". Wow I thought we must be approaching land coming in from the Indian Ocean via the west coast, maybe over Broome or Derby. Geography was always my strong point in school. It was night-time dark and most of my fellow travellers were asleep. I left my seat to find an accessible window to catch this moment of transition from water to land.

The aircraft captain happened to be passing through the cabin and questioned me as to the reason for my nocturnal activities, and I explained why. "Mrs", he said, "We have been flying over Australia for hours". Well, did I feel a ninny. "Mrs", he said again, "Would you like to come into the cockpit and have a look?" "Wow" I said to myself. I was dumb-struck, and believe me that is something different to my normal garrulous characteristic. Who thought that one day cockpit doors would be locked and barred? I took up the kind, and certainly unexpected, offer, and I will never forget the moment. I was lost for words (again an unnatural state), to be surrounded by cockpit controls and to look down and see that blessed land of kangaroos and wallabies bringing me closer to my loved ones.

* * *

Australia Attacked

I have a deep bond and affiliation with Australia. I have spent very happy holidays there, enjoying the life-style of its people, the sense of space that it affords and the beautiful and wondrous locations that I have travelled to. I dare say that I have a certain bias.

My children and grandchildren and great-grandchildren live there. But to present a travelogue is not the purpose of this chronicle. Neither is it a genealogy of my wonderful family. I intend to pinpoint sites of interest which are connected as a backdrop for war.

For the first time in its colonial history, the continent of Australia was attacked by a foreign power; from the sea and from the air. War was raging in New Guinea and the Dutch East Indies, a stone's-throw from Australia's northern coast. The Japanese efforts to secure this territory included a prolonged submarine offensive against Allied lines of communication between Australian and the United States, close allies in the war of the Pacific.

Japanese submarines operated offshore in Western Australia and along the eastern coast, disrupting merchant shipping and supply convoys. Off the state of Queensland they torpedoed a hospital ship and 263 lives were lost. A German submarine cruising off the Australian and New Zealand shorelines destroyed Allied ships in those areas. On the night of the 13th May 1942 a midget sub raided Sydney Harbour. Considerable Allied resources were devoted to the protection of shipping and ports. The Royal Australian Navy escorted more than 1,100 coastal convoys.

The Imperial Japanese Air Force and its sibling the Imperial Japanese Army Air Service violated Australian air space a hundred times in the spate of the time-frame February 1942 to November 1943. It achieved this undertaking by bombing and strafing runs using fighter aircraft. The heaviest of the raids fell on Darwin, so called 'Top End' in Northern Territory, in Queensland, and on Broome and Derby in Western Australia: all coastal towns where the Japanese objective was to destroy harbour facilities, shipping, and to eliminate routes for departing reinforcements to the Pacific areas of combat and for retreating personnel from battlegrounds lost.

* * *

My Backpack at the Ready

It was wonderful to be with my family and I loved being in that country. Both my daughter Diane and my son-in-law, Lenny, were out to work every day and the children were at school. I decided that basking in the sunshine in their tropical fruit-growing garden was not enough to occupy my day. I decided to consult the 'info' offices (information, in Queen's English), with a view to a bit of 'look-seeing'.

For starters, I did afternoon trips in and around Melbourne. I remember one 'must' on the tourist list – a house built before 1930. Heigh ho! I thought of our Tower of London, constructed in 1100! Gaining confidence and knowing that I was up for a bit of adventure, I started to take full day-trips to outlying areas.

It was approaching my birthday and Diane had arranged a birthday party 'barbie' (barbeque, as we say in the UK). No need to be anxious about the weather when Aussies plan one of those outdoor 'dos'. It was February, hot and sunny. But I had previously decided to travel to 'Tassie' (Tasmania) with a back-pack and a Youth Hostel subscription. Ha, I would be in line for an OAP pension on my return home. After swearing on oath that I would be back in time for the celebration I crossed the Bass Strait that night by ferry with a budget ticket which entitled me to a chair on deck. It was amazing; the dark-blue of a Southern Hemisphere sky. And the brilliant stars set in a different sequence to that which I was used to here at home. I did arrive back in Melbourne in time for the party and was able to meet the family friends. They are a well shod-bunch, articulate, and from high places. Diane and Lenny were horrified next day when I produced the Australian 'bible' guide for travellers and an announcement that I intended to travel the continent. They extracted a promise that I would contact them (no mobiles yet available), every Tuesday and Friday. I had already purchased a long-distance bus pass which would give me unlimited mileage, and I was off.

Ten weeks and 15,000 miles later I returned to my daughter's house unannounced and tanned to the colour of mahogany. No thought in those days of sun damage. I had thirty-six rolls of thirty-six exposed films. My Mum in London knew that I had bought an open-ended airline ticket when I left, so she did not fret on a return date, and I did write long letters on a weekly basis. I did what I set out to do. I circumvented Australia. I had had a holiday and the experience of a life time. My first port of call after I left Melbourne was Canberra.

* * *

Canberra

The splendid edifice of the Australian War Memorial in Canberra is a sight to behold. Its white marble rises up like the spirit of those it commemorates. Once seen, this magnificent structure is never forgotten. The sons and daughters of this commonwealth nation fought courageously alongside those of the Mother country. The particular action this memorial evokes is the part played out in an earlier conflict. The combined Australian and New Zealand Armies, the ANZACS, engaged in the Gallipoli Campaign in 1915. That was a disastrous affair, leaving so many laid to rest in Turkey. That defeat has been seared into the intelligence of all of their fellow countrymen, even to the present day. I do not believe that they have whole heartedly forgiven us, who live in Britain, or the instigators of that plan.

With my thoughts hovering on actions in the Dardanelles, a name flitted from my sub-conscience: John Monash. He was the first Jewish General of the British Commonwealth and the Australian Military Commander during the Great War. He commanded a brigade in Gallipoli, continued his service in France and the Western Front, and engaged in activity in Amiens which expedited the end of the war itself, as a result of his foresighted planning. He spearheaded the British Forces including those serving from his native-born Australia, and from Canada. It is a name much revered by all, even now, more than one hundred years hence.

Monash is a name familiar to me. My Melbourne-dwelling grandchildren graduated from the Uni (as they say in Oz), bearing the name of that esteemed warrior, also of Melbourne extraction. Furthermore my late brother-in-law bore that name. He was of South Wales extraction. No, not the Australian State with Sydney as its capital: the United Kingdom region where one arrives by train from Paddington railway station, London to Cardiff. I am without a clue as to why such a famous name was bestowed on him. His parents, my in-laws, were of Russian extraction, and emigrated to South Wales in the late nineteenth century. I guess that the name was free-wheeled in the press during the Gallipoli affair in 1915, even though our Monash first saw the light of day at a much later date.

As is to be expected, the names of the fallen in the 1939 to 1945 conflagration are carved into the stone together with those of the previous generation. No matter which, the former or the latter, that structure is there for us to stand before, and offers us the opportunity to direct our meditation from disillusionment to hope that there will never be a reason to add to those inscriptions. In all honesty one cannot dissociate the two World wars, one from the other. The shocking loss of life; the terrible outcome, give rise to the same consequences.

* * *

Historian on Board

I had left Canberra still thinking of its splendid war memorial. Long distance bus journeys are apt to be a tedious pastime, but if one is lucky enough it is quite useful to have the opportunity to chat to fellow passengers.

Long conversations were embarked upon with a gentleman of obvious mature years. He questioned my sombre mood and I explained my recent visit to the capital. He was intrigued by my strong emotional reaction and in my interest in Australia's World War Two history. He began to relate his own war-time experiences and continued to tell me that as a Professor of History, his civilian calling after the war, he had expounded upon that subject in particular, long and often to his students. Viola! I had struck oil!

And so I was relieved of long hours of on-the-road boredom, and as he began talking and telling me of his wartime military service, I scrabbled around in my travel bag for pencil and notebook. The Australian declaration of war matched the day of Mr Chamberlain's announcement here in London. This gentleman, (Mr Samads was his name), enlisted in the Royal Australian Air Force (RAAF). His early posting was to a training establishment in Canada, and as a fully-fledged fighter pilot he arrived in the UK and saw service in the Battle of Britain in 1940.

This ex-RAAF airman even in advanced years presented a homely not unattractive appearance. I surmised that when young he must have been quite a handsome fellow. I wondered how it was that we didn't meet up in my old halcyon WLA days. But I do him a disservice by my inattention to his story. He was a mine of information and could recall and relate explicit details of World War Two history of his country. I scribbled and scribbled by the light of the overhead lamp on the bus, all the while registering amazement at his profound ability to recall such detailed data.

It was, in reality, a war that could be measured in two halves. As far as Australia was concerned it was a bilateral undertaking. They fought the Germans and Italians in Europe and the Japanese in the South West Pacific. The range of combat duties spread world-wide: from home to the UK, and to Europe and the Mediterranean; to the Middle East, North Africa; and in the South West Pacific and South East Asia; to Russia and back again to home. It executed loyal duty to Britain and to its main ally, the United States.

The Royal Australian Army (RAA), the Royal Australian Navy (RAN) and The RAAF were sometimes partners in battle with Britain; sometimes with other Commonwealth Countries; often with the United States and on occasion independently. From the beginning to the end of the war in August 1945 it suffered frequent ups and downs, failures and successes. Early losses and later victories.

* * *

Diary of the Army

During the first years the Australian military was closely aligned to the United Kingdom. In 1940 and 1941 it deployed forces in the Mediterranean and the Middle East. It fought in squadrons in the air, in regiments on land and flotillas on the seas. It served in North Africa. In June 1940 Italy entered the hostilities against us and the RAN, together with a British squadron of the Royal Navy, gave rise to successful battles in the Mediterranean Sea.

In January 1941 a division of the RAA, on the desert sands of North Africa, initiated a decisive new campaign. It attacked the town of Bardia in the coastal area of Libya and a successful result ensued. Three weeks later the division executed a repeat performance in Tobruk. (Now at least I recognized this name and I remember pinpointing its position on the map I had pinned onto the inner door of my bedroom.) From Mr S's commentary so far I was familiar with the names of the Mediterranean and Tobruk. Other place names mentioned were strange until I familiarized myself with them from my map when I returned home some months later.

Back in 1941 the action in North Africa was a regular subject when I listened to the wireless news. That area in Libya was held by the Italians, and with its fall the Allies depleted the defending hoards by 65,000. I wonder how they housed that vast crowd of POWs? Perhaps some were shipped to the UK to be land workers on a farm near Grantham in Lincolnshire! Perhaps I had worked with some of them in the fields.

In the summer of 1942 the British, led by General Montgomery, made a stand west of Alexandria at a railway siding at El Alamein. It halted the Axis advance. In October 1942 Montgomery's 8th Army launched a major offensive with the help of divisions from Australia and New Zealand. During the affray the Australian government requested that their men be withdrawn and sent home as it was no longer possible to provide sufficient reinforcements with which to sustain them.

It happened that there was some discord between the Australian arch planners and Mr Churchill. They often disagreed regarding programme alignment. Well good friends do sometimes, don't they? I disagree with mine sometimes, but that doesn't make us life-long enemies. And us and the Ozzies still love each other. But to order a fighting division to withdraw and come back home mid-battle, is, I think, beyond the pale and a bloomin' cheek. I feel terribly let down always having had a great admiration for that democracy and their rule of decency and fair play. Having had my say on the subject, I hope to goodness I haven't started a family feud with my 'relos' (relations) 'down under'.

The Allied victory in El Alamein ended the Axis threat to the Middle East. It revived the morale of the Allies generally and to the British public in particular. The casualties numbered 14,000, so those loved ones at home did not have much to celebrate. I recall the excitement when the news of the victory broke. Headlined in all the newspapers and first items on the wireless news broadcasts, and thrilling to watch on cinema screens.

Newsreel programmes were the sole feature in some specialised cinemas at that time. There was no other source of visual impact except for the cinema screen and pictures in the newspapers. In the West End of London small venues of a cinema chain were very popular. Naturally enough they were called Newsreel Theatres, and when I had time to spare I would often visit them. The programmes were only an hour in length and I would pay one shilling old money (5p today). Treating myself to a choc-ice in the interval the total cost in modern currency would set me back 6p. My wages from work was the princely sum of ten shillings (50p) per week, so it was all relative, but I did relish those outings.

In North Africa the Battle of El Alamein marked the end of the Australian participation in the region. Their navy remained offshore still supporting Montgomery's big push through Libya and subsequently into Tunisia. Their ships were in evidence in the Mediterranean protecting the invasion forces during later Allied landings on Sicily, and so too were the small and lively corvette vessels escorting convoys. That corvette class of craft, so able and so busy, doing all the odd jobs for the various navies, have rather caught my imagination and I have developed quite a fond emotional tie. They remind me of my little great-grandchildren gallivanting around, active and happy, poking their noses and inquisitive little fingers into all the nooks and crannies where others do not go.

Hope I Have My Pencil Sharpener

My travelling companion James, (for that was his name and I was permitted to call him thus), went rabbiting on, (begging your pardon), continuing unerringly with his history, pausing at times for liquid refreshment – tea or coffee, not whiskey or vodka. He was intriguing to listen to and occasionally I needed to massage my right hand. Pencil fatigue!

And I wonder if this narrative of years gone by is as appealing on paper as it was to me in a verbal presentation? The ultimate answer is not my prerogative to give. But I defend my case. The war story is true and it happened, and it is right that people are aware of its substance. I can imagine that some might, with conviction, think it humdrum and boring. If it is looked at through the prism of a big picture, and not in small bits of information, understanding is apparent. It is not enough to classify it in one sentence or even two or three. The oscillating nature of events must be perceived. A once overall single movement in a battle, or a series of contentions, is simply not a reality and I am recording a story of wartime exploits and not a fictional fairy-tale frolic.

It needs to be acknowledged that the Australian army did its full share in fighting the war. When an overview of victory was examined it was recognized to have been a considerable factor in it. When the secondment in North Africa was completed its divisions were advanced into Europe. They concentrated in Syria and Lebanon to rebuild strength and to prepare for further operations in the Middle East. They shouldered their responsibilities in Normandy. They fought in Greece and Crete. In the battle that was fought in that area, together with the New Zealanders, they mounted a rear-guard action which gave time to other defeated units to escape, seeking the shore for evacuation.

When the Japanese put their plans into action to take the Pacific region the Australian Army made its mark, side by side with the Americans. In March 1942 the American General Douglas MacArthur arrived in Australia. He originally set up shop in Melbourne, later transferring to Brisbane.

* * *

Political Manoeuvres

If one is interested in the course of a war, it is easy to recognize that governments and generals of the various countries involved have no easy chore when planning the enterprise.

I am not only referring to military matters. In the course of this war the Australian government changed five times. That meant that there were five different prime ministers and the political parties changed with them. Some were in power for just a matter of weeks. And with each change, policies changed as well, each government to its own.

Mr Churchill ruling the roost in Westminster not only had a headache, he was wracked, poor man, with a positive on-going, non-relievable migraine. Each time a different Australian parliamentary regime appeared so did the complaints and demands, some revealing a disingenuous mind set, issuing forth from Canberra. Ministers took to 'wheeling and dealing' on all military matters and sometimes a tad more; a climb down from the British had to be a 'done deal'. The poor stricken 'Governor', resting ashen-faced in his office, had no option but to concede, cajole, plead and basically to surrender to their tantrums. I wonder if these 'Ozzie' (bless 'em) ploys were a ruse to upset us 'Poms', or to use the full term, (for the benefit of those that don't understand the lingo), us Pommies. And 'Good-day' to you too mates!

Putting this on paper I am reminded of an incident which happened, if I remember correctly, during my first visit in 1985. Bob Hawke was the name of the Australian Prime Minister. It appears that legislation had been rolled out to change the price of milk. The farmers were in uproar and paraded their livestock: live cows down the middle of the street! I happened to be in the main part of town that day, in the very heart of the city, and I watched it. In short time, pronto, the edict was scratched. It was beyond my London intelligence that such a state of affairs could exist. Could I imagine Mrs Thatcher back home in 1985, in similar circumstances? Never! Maggie was in charge and woe betide any one of her lot who would even dream of a reversion. But times they are a-changing, and even as I write I am aware that government U-turns are almost a daily event. It grates on my equilibrium and upsets me. Why can't they come to a proper, sensible, workable planned decision in the first place and stick to it? I think that it's all 'spin' to tell us that they are listening and are amenable to public demands. In reality they have no intention to put whatever it was on the Statute books in the first place. Who knows, perhaps sometime in the future, if you are not in favour, turn-a-bouts could become a half-daily event!

Australian military numbers were sparse. It was thought they were inadequate to deal with a likely invasion of the Japanese on Australian soil. It was no far-fetched fantasy in the minds of those at the top table to envisage that a Japanese invasion was not impossible. In 1942 United States military units arrived to balance the discrepancy.

* * *

The USA Down-under

The expected assault on Australian soil did not materialize, but the Americans were on hand to oppose the Japanese invasion of New Guinea where they took up the challenge to confront the might of Imperial Japan. From 1944 the Australian military were mainly a subsidiary partner but they were there when needed; when crucial major engagements in the Pacific demanded it necessary, and they continued to do so until the cessation of hostilities in 1945. Many US bases had been constructed in the Northern Territory of Australia and it was a convenient and reliable source of supply.

The Australian Government reluctantly accepted to its shores the presence of African Americans troops. Apart from a non-relationship with the enemy, which one expects, it is strange that that there should exist an embargo on one's ally, fighting alongside you in a shared cause.

I am reminded of a snippet of conversation I once had with a person whilst on my travels. It appears that after the fall of France in 1940, each branch of the Australian forces experienced a surge of volunteer enlistment. Men and women simply desired to fight for Australia and to support Britain. But regulations had been set up by the current prime minister which prohibited placement into the services of people not substantially of 'European' origin. Am I reading the message correctly? Does it imply that the natural-born Australian, the original Aboriginal, was denied the right to do his or her duty for the land of their birth? Seems to me that this attitude, being coupled with the recent reticence to welcome a certain group of Americans fighting for freedom and facing the same risk of dying in battle or suffering life threatening injury, is to be found on the same side of the coin.

When the need for manpower increased, the 'Big Boys' knew who to turn to and the restriction was lifted. I hope they grovelled. Three thousand indigenous Australians eventually enlisted and most were integrated into existing military formations. In the second half of 1941, when the war in the Pacific broke out, most elements of the army returned home to counter a perceived Japanese threat on Australia itself. The question of a Japanese encroachment was a subject often aired by the military and the politicians.

I sometimes think it was scaremongering to keep the locals on their best behaviour. The continent of Australia is the hell of a big whopper to overcome. A 'quid pro quo' arrangement saw the retention of some of their military in the Middle East in return for US troops being deployed in Australia. In addition, the arrangement included support for a British expansion to the RAAF. Well we did our best to help each other, but as I have already intimated, it was a good old merry-go-round. All of the Royal Australian Navy also withdrew from the Mediterranean to the Pacific.

* * *

War in the Skies

My erstwhile friend James was particularly anxious to stress the contribution of his lot, the Royal Australian Airforce (RAAF, in case you had forgotten), and to emphasis its share in the Allied aim to final victory. Of course I thanked him profusely for his interest in my pursuit which was basically to clarify and appease my curiosity in the history and involvement of that country's wartime role. I scratched around with my pencil intending to copy the hardly legible notes into a fair-hand facsimile later on. As I have already briefed you, this exercise was purely to further a hobby. I am recording this experience which happened many years ago, and the idea of my ever writing a book was 'pie in the sky'. I was at that time more interested in the adventure I was looking forward to. Heck! I must have been the oldest backpacker in town!

Mr Samads was a gentleman of what I perceived to be a genuine character and his interest in what I was doing was genuine too. He was a jolly good sort and even politely refused my offers to supply his basic nutritional needs, usually from a 'trading post' in the middle of the night at some desolate spot on a multi-laned, pitch-black unlit highway. Oz is a vast place, and often I would travel days and nights before reaching the next destination. The journey might have been an interminable time of tedium and inactivity, so I had much to be thankful for in the company of this man. If it was his transparent request that the wartime contribution of the RAAF should be highlighted, far be it for me to dishonourably fail to do so.

As dear James began on this particular topic he appeared to wander off at a tangent, almost as if he found himself in a flashback to his wartime days and exploits, and exhilarating they were too. I pocketed my pencil. I was enthralled; it was the stuff of the gossip columns. He had been embroiled in some outrageous and merry frivolities. It is definitely not suitable to write of here. Sorry!

It was a non-stop soliloquy. The input of the RAAF posted to British units made a special contribution to all enterprises and in all areas where aircraft were actively needed. Some of them attached to the RAF played a role in the strategic bombing of Germany and in efforts to safeguard shipping in the Atlantic. They gave evidence of courage at the time when we relied on our airmen to defend us in the Battle of Britain, safeguarding our freedom when the dice could have fallen unfavourably, and a victorious Luftwaffe could have played the opening chords of Hitler's overture on our shores.

* * *

Non-stop Activities of the Royal Australian Airforce

The Mediterranean zone retained several RAAF units. Hundreds of Australian airmen were attached to other Commonwealth forces, and there they served until the war ended. They were active in supporting operations in Sicily and Italy. They provided close cover for Allied armies and attacked German supply lines, and enemy targets in Greece, Crete and the Aegean Sea. One hundred and fifty of their number affiliated themselves with the Balkan Air Force as Special Duties Squadrons when required, dropping men and supplies to guerrilla fighters in Yugoslavia. They attempted to supply the Polish Home Guard during the Warsaw Uprising in 1944. The duties they under took, these Australians in the air, were unflagging.

They were part of a Coastal Command, and in that role were deployed to air bases in Russia to protect supply convoys from Britain and America. As RAF partners in Europe, they were, in part, responsible for the defeat of the enemy having 13,000 Australian airmen operating in dozens of sorties. They displayed valour and ability in their activities with the multi-national crews with whom they sometimes served. They were there on the 6th June 1944 as part of the force assembled for the Normandy landings and their Spitfire Squadrons were to be found deployed at forward airfields in France. When Canadians attacked the southern coast of that country in August 1944, they were there. Accommodating service was ongoing by this ever busy force. When the war ended in 1945 they did not cease to serve. They became involved with the British and Allied Occupation in Germany.

When our bus finally pulled up at some outlandish deserted convenience stop, I uncharacteristically purchased two cans of Aussie beer, which I had never done in my life before or since. Back on the road I opened one can and drank it after offering a toast to the man who was part of this story, and as a token of my thanks and appreciation for allowing me to be part of it too.

"You did good lads, you fellas in blue. Cheers!" I dealt with the second can later.

* * *

"Goodbye Mr S"

I suspect that James was pleased that he had arranged the timing appropriately and that he had almost ended his story of the RAAF before I dropped off into one of my infrequent cat-naps. When I awoke I realized that he had reached his destination and had left. I was upset and disappointed. I did not get to say "goodbye", and "thank you". I think he was aware that I very much appreciated his company and I was assured of it when I read his farewell note. In addition I was flabbergasted to discover that, taking advantage of a previous 'nod-off', he had had the foresight to make sure that I was mindful of the remainder of the Australian war story: his handwritten notes were legible and easy to follow and understand.

I am offering a copy of the information encapsulated within that farewell missive. There are two items, and I hope that like me, you will find them to be interesting and relevant to what has preceded them.

The Royal Australian Air Force was the first of the Services to see action in the Pacific War, when one of its aircraft, which was deployed to shadow a Japanese convoy bound for Malaya, was fired upon. The incident occurred one day before the attack on Pearl Harbour. It might have been that that was their destination and their mission. In October 1944, following a plan to lift the burden of the Philippine population and to set them free of their Japanese jailors under whose jurisdiction they had been subjected to, a flotilla of Australian warships arrived to support the United States Military in the process of landing on the island of Leyte. It was then that the first Kamikaze strike occurred. Some are of the opinion that the suicide pilots deliberately targeted a vessel of the Royal Australian Navy as the first victim of the series.

For the benefit of readers who are perhaps of a more recent generation, the Kamikaze action was the delivery of a calculated crash-landing on sea craft carried out by fanatical Japanese flyers intent on dying, and the destruction of their planes, in the process of which the resulting corollary would be the destruction of the ship and the loss of all who sailed in her. In my opinion it was an act of desperation.

This was not the first time the Japanese had utilized their young men to sacrifice themselves for their country and their god-like devotion to the Emperor. They were known to strap bombs to their person and to toss themselves under oncoming opposing tanks. I am certain that those in authority could foresee that the end was in sight.

I was sorry that James had gone. He was what I consider to be a kind and thoughtful person, and a thorough gentleman. I did however, take advantage of a bit of extra space left by his vacated seat, and within a few hours I myself alighted and onward I went to continue my journey.

* * *

My Australian Adventure

I had the opportunity to chat with many people I met on my travels; young and old, and of all different nationalities. My overnight lodgings at the youth hostel premises wherever I happen to be were mini-adventures, but I think that my fellow travellers thought it a bit odd finding an oldie sharing that particular mode of B&B.

The normal routine of hostelling is that one is expected to undertake a chore in the house-keeping arrangements. A live-in warden would dish out a job for you when you signed in on arrival. It was his/her responsibility to see that the hostel was self-supporting and maintained in an 'elf 'n safety' condition. On meeting the warden I would be received with a quizzical appraisal and informed as to the task I was expected to do. The hostels were always pristinely clean and one was expected to carry out all the necessary tasks to keep it so, even as far as toilet duties or scrubbing the kitchen floor. It was just a bit extra to give in addition to the nominal cost of the 2 dollars (Australian) you paid per night. A real cheapie! So I was met with a puzzled expression whilst the person in charge was in the throes of deciding what my contribution would be. Easy peasy – I would be in charge of the piano dusting, or to make sure that the teacloths were neatly hung on their hooks and very vital duties of that ilk.

I did have some extraordinary experiences; some a great laugh and some a tad scary but all so well remembered. I recall showering in the dead of night, (I arrived at 3am at the hostel on Magnetic Island). It was an outside block of concrete cubicles, and I was nearly scared to fainting when I saw a huge green lizard creeping down the wall. Crikey, I leapt out of that shower as I stood, in the 'all-together' (naked).

I met lots of interesting people and I visited all the sights that only Ozzie land can boast of. It is not permissible now, (but it was then), to climb Ayers Rock, and I recall what a thrill it was atop of that edifice, and at dawn watching the sunrise over it. Frankly, I was having the time of my life!

When I eventually arrived home in London I took up my membership of the 'Oldies' Club, (which I am not now, seeing that I am a recycled teen-ager: I don't work and I'm on drugs). Sorry it just slipped out. The word went round that I had been away – well my skin colour had changed so it was obvious, and I was opted onto the 'speakers' circuit'. I spoke at loads of venues in and around London and I still have a school room wall map and pointer which I used as an aid. I was asked various questions. Sorry not suitable for publication.

This all happened when I was sixty, many moons ago but I can remember that journey as if it was a recent adventure. My agent is on holiday, but I am open to bookings!

* * *

Letter from Australia

Somewhere in my flat I have a mislaid photograph which I have been searching for with no luck. It is particularly pertinent to my story. It is a picture of a Land Army march through Grantham on 'Wings for Victory Week' which I have earlier described. I mourn the loss of this picture. I have also mentioned my 'treasure box', a lifetime of bits and pieces, not of any monetary worth but of great value to me. It is a cache of some of the small items that remind me of the good things that I remember, and keep.

Whilst searching for my missing picture, however, I came across a copy of a letter I wrote in 1985 whilst I was travelling around Australia. I thought perhaps it might fit in very neatly to my Ozzie story. It was written from a youth hostel in Adelaide to a social club I was a member of at that time, when I was living in Cardiff.

* * *

A Letter from Down-Under. 10th Feb 1985

"G'day mates –
I'm having a fair dinkum time here in Oz, but thinking of you all in Cardiff. I'm coping well in the 35C+ heat. But creaming up with 30+ sunblock and sporting my wide brimmed Aussie hat (without corks). When I'm in Melbourne it's great being

there with my family and it's wonderful to establish a rapport with my grandchildren so that they will remember me during the next irrevocable separation. We get on fine, but secretly they think I'm a bit of a queer gran. They probably think that all grans in the UK are slightly barmy.

I've introduced myself to some local social organizations. The members are friendly and welcoming and I have already been invited to join their Sisterhood and a local guild and their Ex-servicemen's association and a new building fund-raising team and anything else that's on offer. If I wanted to stay I could easily settle but of course I will be home sometime in April and will tell you all about my trip, well at least not the naughty bits.

Must go now. The barbie is sizzling and the beer is cold in the fridge. See ya later mates. Love. Myrtle Russell

Chapter 24
Australia – Part Two

The Oz Civilian Story

When a country goes to war everything changes. I remember when and how it affected us here in Britain. It is expected that young men and women leave their homes and their jobs of work to serve King and Country. But life also changes for civilians; for those left to face life at home, the difference was radical as well. Changes occurred for all the countries I have visited and reported on. Being as I am closely connected to Australia, I feel inclined to chart some of lifestyle adjustments that made a difference for those living in that great and wonderful land. Between the two World Wars Australians lived through a severe economic depression, which began in 1929. It was a difficult time for those who lived through it. I think that state of affairs affected most countries between the wars. It did in America, during their Great Depression, and certainly as I remember it here, as a child, growing up in a less than affluent post-code area of London. And so it was in Australia.

When the Second World War was declared by the British Prime Minister, the Prime Minister of Australia, Robert Gordon Menzies did the same spontaneously. He did not wait for the matter to be debated by his parliament as they did in South Africa and in Canada; he made the announcement to his nation and to the free world: "Britain is at war therefore Australia is at war". In any case, his government obviously felt that it was right that it did so. Australian support was primarily on the grounds that it was inextricably linked to Britain. If the war had been lost against us it would have destroyed the system and fabric of imperial defence on which Australia relied for its security against the mighty and ever land-seeking empire of Japan. Their record had preceded them.

Although most Australians lived far from the front line, the home front played a significant role leading to ultimate victory. Mr Menzies set into motion a citizens' militia for home defence. He committed to provide 20,000 men to be conscripted for this purpose.

* * *

New Stuff for the Statute Book

The National Security Act of September 1939 gave the Australian government the necessary powers to introduce new and extensive laws to govern a country at war. Its authority was to direct the war effort using Australian industrial and human resources to support the Allied Armed Forces. It brought in new taxes; it had the right to acquire property and to control businesses. In July 1940 Mr Menzies placed virtually all the newspapers, radio stations, and the film industry under the direct control of a Director General of Information. In January 1941 new directives were issued against speaking disloyally in public or even in private, aimed at 'whisperers' who undermined morale by spreading rumours.

The Security Act introduced industrial conscription. Men and women were directed into essential industries. Aircraft, automobiles, electronics and chemicals had been in production pre-war. These secondary enterprises were integrated into a war economy during 1940-41 and were able to meet most of the army's requirements by 1942. They enjoyed an advanced technology and some notable successes including lightweight radar appliances and optical devices which enabled artillery use in the tropics. Australian scientists and pharmaceutical companies developed important advances into the field of therapy for tropical diseases.

Massive expansion of the military led to critical shortages of male employees; thereby an increase of the female role in the labour force was warranted. Large numbers of ladies had been previously employed mainly in the domestic sphere. Now times were a-changing; their status was elevated and their wages increased. The Australian Women's Land Army was bought to life. They alleviated a serious dearth of farm workers when it was realized that agriculture activity had gradually slowed down. Female branches of the services were inaugurated in 1941 and by 1944 they boasted of having 50,000 women. Food rationing was authorized in 1940 and expanded two years later. Austerity was encouraged and War Bonds went on sale to raise money.

Here at home we had similar schemes. Special weeks were allocated with different themes to collect money for the services or wartime charities. I recall a 'Wings for Victory Week' which benefitted associations connected to the RAF. There was a planned parade to march along the main road in Grantham, and the land girls from the hostel were invited to take part. It was a hoot. An officer from the army camp from across the way came to drill us. We all stood to attention and he commanded us, as he would have done with his men, with a shout of "Chests Out". Well we did 'thrust out' but poor blighter, his face was the colour of beetroot!

* * *

Post-war Australia

In 1945 with the war over, the serving men were rapidly demobilized. Australia had paid a heavy price; 27,000 did not return. They left their homeland and never came back. Their bones are interred in Europe or in Asia and some nowhere at all, except perhaps in an ocean. The financial cost to that country was £3,000,000,000, yes if my zeros are correct, three thousand million pounds, (or 3 billion), converted from Australian dollars; in 1945 financial values!

The war played a major role in changing many of the country's systems and policies. It marked the beginning of a long period of economic growth. It accelerated the process of industrialization, which greatly increased the size and importance of the Australian manufacturing sector and stimulated the development of more technologically advanced industries. The bloody epic of those six years contributed to crucial alterations in the nation's economy, and to its armed forces, which led to the development of a larger peacetime military. Its approach to international affairs was demonstrated in the development of a more independent foreign policy which shifted from Britain to the United States of America. The end of the war fostered the promotion of mass immigration, which gave the country a much more diverse and cosmopolitan society. It offered women the chance to engage themselves and relish becoming involved in higher matters than previously, and it brought a greater maturity to the whole population. In the early thirties, when unemployment was rife and everyone was affected by the fiscal depression here in the UK, my Dad was eager to accept the £10 per family offer to emigrate to Australia. I must have been just a nipper, but I do remember him speaking about it. He was as keen as mustard. To coin a phrase, my Mum was 'the fly in the ointment'. No fear – she was not going. "How can I leave my mother?" she argued. And so we did not go. I often wonder how my life would have unrolled if I had grown up and been reared and made a life in that faraway land.

* * *

Massacre on Bangka Island

I have been a visitor to Australia five times. I have always planned those holidays for February so that I can celebrate my birthday with my family. Until his death in 2000 my son lived in the beautiful city of Adelaide, South Australia. His widow and my two adult grandchildren still do. Whenever I have the opportunity whilst I am staying in that state, I pay homage at the Women's Memorial playing fields on the 16th of that month, or the nearest Sunday to it, to the victims of the Bangka Island massacre in the then Dutch East Indies.

On the 12th February 1942 the Sarawak royal yacht, the SS Vyner Brooke, left Singapore just before its fall to the Japanese. The ship hoped to evacuate many wounded service personnel under the care of nurses of the Australian Army Nursing Service as well as civilian men, women and children. The ship was attacked by a Japanese bomber and it sank. Two nurses were killed instantly. Sixty Australian and British soldiers and crew members of a lifeboat in which they were sailing, survived its destruction. The remainder were scattered amongst rescue boats and were washed up on different parts of that Dutch East Indies Island. Twenty two nurses with wounded men came ashore in one of the rescuing boats. Of the original sixty five nurses, forty one were unaccounted for; they were probably lost at sea after the bombing. Once it was discovered that the Japanese were in occupation in that land an officer of the Vyner Brooke went to surrender the group to the authorities. Whilst he was absent it was suggested that the women and children should leave for Muntok, nestling at the very eastern tip of that land mass, which they did.

The nurses stayed behind to care for the injured in their charge. They set up a shelter marked with a large 'Red Cross' sign. The ship's officer returned with twenty Japanese troops who ordered the ambulant men to walk a short distance around a headland, and a succession of gun shots was heard by the nurses before the Japanese group returned, casually seating themselves in front of the women, and they cleaned their rifles and bayonets.

An officer ordered the nurses to walk into the surf. A machine gun was set up on the beach and when those 'Angels of Healing' were waist deep in the water they were mown down by that machine gun fire. All but one nurse died. The clean clear water changed from blue to red. Wounded soldiers left behind on stretchers were bayoneted and they died where they lay.

When the sound of the soldiers had disappeared, the one surviving nurse crawled into the bush and lay unconscious for several days. She had been shot in the diaphragm. When she recovered from the coma she encountered a British soldier, Private Patrick Kingsley, who had been one of the wounded on the ship.

He had sustained bayonet injuries but he too had survived. She dressed his wounds and her own, and twelve days later they surrendered themselves to the Japanese. Patrick Kingsley died before reaching the prison camp. Sister Lieutenant Vivian Bullwinkle spent the next 3 years of her life in captivity. She lived to give evidence of the massacre at a war crimes trial in Tokyo in 1947. She died in 2000 in Perth, Western Australia, aged 84.

* * *

Soap

In 1900 my great-uncle Aaron emigrated to Australia. His father-in-law was an asthma sufferer and his doctor's advice was to live in a warmer climate than ours. Taking this as a sensible thing to do his entire family, comprising his many grown children with their spouses and their children and his grandchildren, left England bound for Melbourne. Great-uncle Aaron and his wife great-aunt Gertie settled down very nicely amid her dad's coterie. In those early days if you worked hard you reaped the benefits. And they did.

In 1936, three years prior to the outbreak of the war, great-uncle and great-auntie came to visit the family here in London. I vividly remember them. Lovely pair now with an Ozzie 'twang'. But they did have a gripe. They complained that there were no shower facilities in our bathrooms. Well some of us, my immediate family included, did not even have a bathroom; we used the public baths on a weekly basis. Oh dear! It was certainly not what they were used to; in Ozzie land it was absolutely a must. Where we lived, we had an outside toilet. We used neatly cut-up newspaper threaded on a string on a hook as toilet paper. And this convenience was used by eight adults and two children: there was also a family of parents with their four adult sons living in three rooms in the floor above our accommodation. So, according to our visiting 'relos', we were not only barely civilized, we had hardly emerged from the Stone Age. But we said "good-bye" to them in a very loving way and they were off on a posh cruise liner for a vacation in America. During their sojourn here they flew from Croydon Airport to spend weekends in Paris. How's that? They flew to Paris! In 1936! Well they arrived back home and life went on for them in Australia and us in England until everything changed in September 1939.

Lots of people living here under wartime conditions in the UK had 'relos' 'down under'. They received parcels of goodies on a regular basis. Canned foods, dried fruit, confectionary, and at Christmas-time, prezzies for the children. We as a family were also the benefactors of well-sealed boxes. Excitedly we wondered what we could look forward to as a treat. Soap. Never a deviation; the parcel would arrive as regular as clockwork and it was always soap. What do you make of that? I wonder if we really did look as if we all needed a bloomin' good scrub.

Great-uncle Aaron's descendants still abide in Melbourne. When my daughter Diane and her family landed in that city in 1982, they were there to meet them and to help her and my son-in-law Lenny to settle into their new life. When I visit I am most warmly welcomed into their home. And they visit us here and are very welcome in ours.

Great-uncle Aaron (sitting 4th from left) and great-aunt Gertie (standing 2nd from left). Early 20th century.

* * *

New Guinea - Its Rise and Fall

When I thought about the Pacific War I was aware that it was part of a complex history; so many different place names to remember, so many dates and numbers to recollect. It is a history book in its own right, (which this is not); I do not consider myself able to subscribe to that genre of literature. I trust that I have manged that particular story adequately enough to satisfy the interest of most of those willing to read it.

The island now known as Indonesia, formerly in pre-war and during it, was Dutch New Guinea, part of the Dutch East Indies, and is entitled to a whit of notability.

It is synonymous with my story of Australia's wartime by virtue of its proximity. Of sea-flow it is just ninety-one miles from the mainland and twenty-one minutes flying time. My viewpoint is, if one is to fully understand the intrinsic background of a bellicose undertaking, one should have a little understanding of its past. I have attempted to follow that pattern throughout my efforts and I intend to keep on trying. This island by virtue of its different zones of authority has an interesting background.

In 1884 the Germans were keen to trade. They needed coconut-oil and copra. European nations were on the hunt in the colonization game and in 1899 the German Imperial Government took up possession in the north-east of the island, in addition to several small outlying islands. In the following years Britain and the Dutch also staked a claim. The Dutch East Indies was the name given to the western region. In 1905 British New Guinea became the Territory of Papua and 1906 saw Australia administration rights. Come 1914 and the Great War, the German possession was taken by the Australian Commonwealth. Australia was authorized to have a mandate to govern it by the League of Nations in 1920. It remained so until that island was lost to the Japanese in 1942.

The Dutch East Indies government, sensing what was brewing, cannily came to the conclusion that territory-seeking Japan was a possibility. They sent their navy out to sea to their dominion in Malaya, away from the danger of having it at anchor at home, and they mobilized the air force. They declared war in December of that year, five months prior to the Japanese incursion; they were astute enough to take into account previous history. The Japanese reputation had preceded them.

* * *

The War on Australia's Doorstep

The 6th–8th May 1942 saw a new chapter in the art of warfare history. It was brought about during a Japanese attempt to strike, invade, and take as its prize the south-eastern town of Port Moresby situated in the island of New Guinea. The defenders to that assault were the Americans, led by Commander General MacArthur, and the British and the Australians, all with ships from their respective navies. The episode that ensued is designated as The Battle of the Coral Sea. The Japanese did, or at least tried to do, what they had always and most successfully practised before.

They attempted an amphibious landing on the shore of New Guinea. They landed their forces at Buna on the coast of Papua but were thwarted in their hopes to secure it.

The American fleet were on hand and the Japanese experienced the first ever attack to the jugular from a delivery of bombs dropped from an aircraft that had suddenly appeared. From where? There was no airfield or base in sight. An American aircraft carrier had done its job and this was its virgin strike. And a victory for the Allies.

The Japanese, up to that point in time, were not inclined to accept setback or defeat and they had another go using the back door, having no admittance by the front gate. They sought their target, Port Moresby, using a land route which took them across the Owen Stanley Mountain Range. That was the start of their struggle for New Guinea, together with their plan to seize the Solomon Islands and to set off a domino-effect strategy to capture the entire chain of islands in the Pacific. They were already in occupation, holding the small island of Tulagi, and could easily use that location as a launch-pad to construct an air base in the neighbouring island, Guadalcanal. They surmised that having nicely rounded off the control of the latter, and their expected eventual seizure of Port Moresby, they would have a nice little parcel of territory bordering upon the north-east of Australia. And who knows they reckoned, we might even have a chance to envelope that whole continent. In your dreams, mates! They never gave up their wishful ideas. It would be very convenient if, by reaching out to other island groups, they could interfere in sea lanes cutting off communication between the Americans, Australians and New Zealanders. I think that perhaps the high-flying Jap 'bods' sometimes took to planning under the influence of hypnotic narcotics. But if it had materialized, it would not have been a reason for hilarity. They should have had a good look into their crystal ball, seen the Allied victory in the Coral Sea, and realized what a good team we are.

* * *

New Tyres and Loads of Petrol Going Cheap

Sensing the possibility that the country's valuable high-yielding oil installations were in danger of a scorched-earth policy, whereby the Australian government would order their destruction, the Japanese acted without delay. On the 23rd January 1942 they pounced. Their amphibious assault was supported by a large fleet of warships; by wall-to-wall aerial bombardment on cities; and on Allied shipping in the immediate area and those active in the Indian Ocean. Being the Japanese, they did eventually capture New Guinea. To the unsuccessful Allied defence it was a serious setback.

Japan was now able to utilize the rich natural resources that were available.

Pre-war the Dutch East Indies was the fourth largest exporter of oil in the world. The non-existence of its own oil reserve was further aggravated when an oil embargo was exercised by President Roosevelt after the Pearl Harbour strike. Well even the Japanese themselves could not expect otherwise. With the conquest of this Aladdin's cave under their belt they were able to replenish their fuel tanks and use the island's rich harvest of rubber produced from its manifold plantations, not needing now to re-tread their tyres. The Japanese had three-and-a-half years in that location in which to freely help themselves to those vital commodities and there they remained until the end of the war. It was also the final curtain for Dutch Colonial rule in that region.

Despite Australian fears, the Japanese had never intended to invade the Australian mainland. Whilst an invasion was considered by the Japanese Imperial Military in February 1942, it was judged to be beyond reasonable capabilities and no planning or other preparations were undertaken. Instead they shaped a policy to mastermind the occupation of the entire Pacific region and beyond. The threat to the Australian continent no longer prevailed but the government continued to warn the public, until 1943, that an invasion was possible. I wonder if it was a tactic to keep the Ozzies on their best behaviour!

Chapter 25
New Zealand

I Concur with the General

It was at the conclusion of the Allied defeat in Greece in 1941 that a British general wrote: "All New Zealanders are greatly, and justly, incensed, at not being mentioned, adequately, in the BBC and press accounts of the vital and gallant part played by them in the Greek rear-guard action".

Who am I not to endorse that statement? It echoes my own sentiments to the hilt. Since I started to write the story of the war, it has occurred to me that those two media outlets, and everyone else, have lauded, praised and clapped their hands at every turn of events in their descriptions of all and every circumstance and of all who were involved. And yet that statement is true. I have sensed that attitude for many years now. New Zealand is regarded internationally as the poor relation. I think that the problem is geographical. Tucked away, literally 'down under', interest fades with the miles.

I can bear personal witness to that. I have fifteen, fully grown, adult grandchildren. We are a large and close clan and interest and love envelops us all. Some of them live locally whilst others reside in faraway places. It is a natural instinct to tie the bond tighter when one can visit easily and has a convenient route to be more aware of the minutiae of their lives, and them of mine. Of course with the advent of electronic messaging, there is now no problem but there are many elderly who are not able to address themselves to 21st century technology and for them the dilemma exists.

That brings me back to New Zealand. Before the cloud burst of e-mail and Facebook and Twitter and the like, people were not that interested in those two small scantily-populated islands of Maori origin. They were distant and with no world shattering news to publicize, interest dimmed. It is said that "weeds grow on untrodden paths".

* * *

The Second Half of the ANZACs Did as Good as the First

If you read your World War Two history books you will find barely a mention of the New Zealand Armed Forces and yet they have a fine record. Their allegiance to the Crown was proven on the very first day that Britain declared war on Germany on that September day in 1939. They did so simultaneously. They fought in every area of combat, in major battles and in minor skirmishes, generally in a rear-guard capacity thereby giving other units the opportunity to retreat safely when defeat was inevitable.

They manned New Zealand ships of war and were there at the time of the destruction of the German battle cruiser, the Admiral Graf Spee. It was a contest of note and the first major naval battle of the war. It was fought off the Atlantic Ocean at the River Plate Estuary, situated on the Argentine-Ecuador border in December 1939. I distinctly remember when it happened. Even the wireless newsreader momentary lost his customary non-committal, evenly-toned manner of speech which was raised a couple of octaves in excitement, echoing my own.

At the outbreak of war it was thought that as long as the British navy was intact and as long as the fortress of Singapore in Malaya remained stable, no invasion of Australia or New Zealand was ever likely. It seemed improbable that a hostile Japan would dispatch a colonization expedition to those lands and face an indomitable defence from those two sources. Even with that calamitous loss of that so-important city it is not imaginable that an overrun of those countries would be a feasible likelihood.

As one would expect from a meagre population, such as in New Zealand, their forces were few: 140,000 people served. Of these, 11,635 were killed, presenting a ratio of 6,684 dead per one million. It was the highest loss rate within the Commonwealth.

* * *

Lupines and Sheep and a Helicopter Ride

I have been to New Zealand. I did a back-packing gad-about two years after the last bundle in Oz. It was a grand holiday. Two weeks were all one needed and I did both the North and South islands. I climbed a glacier and later viewed it from a helicopter. It was my first such ride. I was so busy with my camera I had no time to be a bit nervous, (or even petrified), and after I had recovered, it was a novel experience to find myself in the unique terrain; glaciers amidst a rain forest.

I sat amongst the sheep, (greater in number than the resident humans), and I thought of that snooty sheepdog in my Land Army days. I ate my sandwiches surrounded by acres of lupines, originally brought in by a couple of English ladies in the early days of settlement, for their garden, and now where the sheep were not, the lupines were.

As I sit here dwelling on my holiday I can recall so many small incidents that culminated into that long-ago adventure well worth remembering. The people I met were welcoming and friendly. It was quiet and peaceful. The land had not been invaded. They suffered a record of loss of such a multitude, and I for one appreciate their stalwart sense of duty and sacrifice, and I salute them.

Myrtle aged 62, 1987. Fox Glacier, New Zealand

Chapter 26
Japan Attacks the USA

A Churchillian Prophesy

Before I tackle the story of the Japanese attack on the United States in Hawaii, I feel compelled to relate a story I once heard which I think slots very nicely into it. Mr Churchill spoke in our House of Commons in Westminster. There was nothing favourable to report to the Members. The war news was depressing. We still needed to credit ourselves with one success, which was as yet, not forthcoming. Coming to the end of his speech he said these words taken from a poem. He recited the last stanza:

> "And not by eastern windows only,
> When daylight comes, comes in the light,
> In front the sun climbs slow, how slowly,
> But westward, look, the land is bright."

This verse comes from the poem Say not the Struggle nought Availeth, and was written by the Victorian poet Arthur Hugh Clough. The members of parliament must have wondered what on earth Mr Churchill was talking about. He must have had a prophetic dream or an inkling that the United States would soon be engaged with us in war against a common enemy.

I have related the years of the war story, and now speak of December 1941. Whilst I am giving rein to the whys and wherefores of my reasoning, it may have come to your notice that the chronological order of my presentation is a bit out of sync. That is deliberate. My plan is to deal with the events that took place during the war in different locations with regard to the geography and not to the time frame. I have tried to tell of incidents concerning specific times and places in an inclusive, but uncluttered fashion. One has no option but to resurrect basic facts which are common knowledge to everyone. I am attempting, however, to add my own opinions about particular dates and events. That is what I hope to do in the case of the Pearl Harbour attack on the 7th of December 1941. I aspired to this idea when I had a shot at unravelling the action in Normandy, and as a background to the war in the Pacific. This chronicle would be incomplete without references to the changing situations of the war which have to be brought to life, and as we all know, the story of Pearl Harbour is such an event.

Considering the possible reasons why the attack took place, apart from the Japanese policy of expansion, is an interesting story in itself. And I present a time-line to suggest the rationale. Goaded by, and jealous of, the Western powers, Japan emerged from its medieval past to become, by the late nineteenth century, a great power to be reckoned with. It shaped its future through land augmentation and carried it out with Japanese efficiency and ambition; and of course, as all conflicts are designed to do, acquire some land from someone else.

* * *

Time-scale to Disaster

In 1894 the Japanese invaded an area of China lying north-west of Korea. This was the First Sino Japanese War. It was primarily to gain control of South East Asia in general and of Korea in particular. In 1895 China sued for peace and a shift evolved which changed Korea as a vassal of China to that of a puppet state of Japan.

In 1904 Japan attacked Czarist Russia. Great battles were fought on land and at sea. Basically the cause of the confrontation was the rivalry between the two nations. Both countries were ambitious for imperial mastery over Manchuria, an area of land in North East Asia, and of Korea. Manchuria, lying at the junction of Chinese, Russian and Japanese spheres became a 'cockpit' of conflict and contention. Japanese aggression escalated into the Russo-Japanese War. Japan fought for, and captured Port Arthur, a Chinese Naval Base and was responsible for the destruction of the Russian fleet. Peace was brokered by Theodore Roosevelt, the American President in 1905.

The disastrous outcome of this incident for Russia, apart from the loss of men and ships, was a devaluation of power and prestige. It was one of the immediate causes of the Russian Revolution of 1905. The Japanese victory enshrined that country as the first non-European and the first non-American imperial country of the modern era.

In 1914 at the outbreak of The Great War, Japan allied itself to Great Britain and her allies, and post-war was a subscriber to the agreement of The League of Nations. From 1929 to 1931 European and American economic troubles were rife and these problems affected Japan. The international trade faded. Countries in a depression were in no mood to import goods. Japan was experiencing a rapid population increase, and suffered a worryingly depletion of raw material. China was now its principal customer and became a ready market for its cotton goods. Japan's hackles rose when it surveyed

China as a source of supply for its much needed coal and iron. It needed to avail itself of some of these benefits; it was a vital requisite to have control of the place where it could procure them. And in its own intransigent way it did so, aggressively. In September 1931, on a pretext of local disorder, Japan attacked the Chinese town of Mukden and parts of the Manchurian Railway. This incursion came to be known as the Mukden Incident.

In January 1932 the Japanese made further demands on China and a noncompliance stance was issued from the Chinese Government. They resisted even with their very limited military capabilities. By the end of February of that year, and after heavy losses, they were unable to pursue their cause and retired from their positions. Japan then proceeded to create the Puppet State of Manchukuo. A year later in 1933, another Chinese province was annexed to it and Japanese forces penetrated further into a defenceless country.

***

Time-scale Part Two

The United States declared the State of Manchukuo to be illegal. America categorically refused to recognize that annexation. It was then that China, an original co-member of The League of Nations, together with Japan, used her right to veto the Japanese claim. At that point Japan withdrew her membership of the agreement and kept control of the unlawfully held territory until 1945. The liberation of those lands came about when the Soviets intervened. It coincided with the time when the Allies were in pursuit of the Japanese in 1944, putting the finishing touches to the war in the Pacific.

The exit of the League of Nations membership was the signal and origin of the cosying up of Japan and Germany. In October 1936 Germany and Japan entered into the Anti-Comintern Pact. It was a show of friendship and the promise of bilateral support against the Japanese archenemy, China. It was mooted as being an anti-Communist proliferation which they hoped would lead to the subordination of Communist China under its leadership of Chiang Kai Shek. Additional clauses included a non-aggression entente between the them and Germany's promise to recognize The State of Manchukuo as a legally acknowledged territory; agreement to never engage in treaties with Communist Russia; and to militarily assist against Russia if either of them were attacked or threatened by the Soviets. In November 1937 Italy became a joint signatory.

In 1940 Italy, Germany and Japan signed the Tripartite Pact which bound them together as partners, the Axis; the common enemy of Britain and her Allies engaged in the developing world war. In 1941 talks were ongoing between Japan and America to settle some outstanding concerns, probably discussing trade matters. One has to be reminded that those conversations were still in progress on the fateful day of the Japanese diabolical attack led by the infamous Admiral Yamamoto. The incident at Pearl Harbour was a vicious barbaric attack in peacetime without a declaration of war or forewarning, unleashed on a sleeping community that fateful Sunday morning.

* * *

Armageddon

One does not need to be a Nobel Prize Winner in logic, or a rocket science academic, or even ordinary common folk such as me to comprehend the erstwhile justification emanating from the Japanese High Command in Government and the military. Japan considered that they had been thwarted and undercut and 'put down' by America for years and the smouldering hate and resentment rose from that country like a rising sun. For decades the animosity between the two nations developed like a cancer in the breasts of men of power.

No soul on earth is perfect or without failings, neither American nor any nationals from any other place. We all act unthinkingly sometimes, and make mistakes, often with serious consequences, but to react in the manner that the Japanese did over past years, culminating on that fateful 7th of December 1941, was beyond decency or legality or perception of rule, or coded law or human regard for any right-minded man or woman.

On Sunday evening of the 7th December Mr Churchill was at home at Chequers in Berkshire, the Prime Minister's official out-of-town residence. Staying as his guest was Mr Averell Harriman, American Ambassador to the Court of St. James. His aide entered the room and informed his boss that there was something interesting coming in over the wireless concerning some bother in America. Mr Churchill telephoned his friend President Roosevelt and listened to a tale of appalling proportions.

Shortly before 8am that morning 360 aircraft had flown in from over the Pacific Ocean dropping the first bomb that changed the course of history. The Japanese had attacked the United States naval base at Pearl Harbour in Hawaii where 94 vessels lay at anchor of which ten were of the American battle fleet. It was an unprovoked strike that was the customary procedure of those fiendish fanatics. At 8.25am the first wave of torpedo and dive bombers loosened their cargo. By 10am the battle was over. The ships of the Imperial Japanese Navy had pulled back, leaving behind a shattered fleet hidden in a pall of smoke and fire; 2,000 dead, 2,000 injured, and only two battle ships still afloat from the original ten, thus provoking the vengeance of the United States nation.

* * *

Britain at war with Japan

Mr Churchill was mortified by this shocking story. He probably retired for the night with two thoughts in his head: one, "At last we are not alone"; two, "Sir Edward Grey was right". Edward Grey was a British Foreign Secretary of a former year and he once said: "The United States is like a gigantic boiler. Once the fire is lit under it there is no limit to the power it can generate". The PM must have fallen asleep in an optimistic mood but by morning I dare say he was not so buoyed up with the bonhomie of the night before. "They are recalling their battleships from Pearl Harbour and we are going to be attacked in Malaya and in the Far East", must surely have been his thoughts, whilst toying with his breakfast. And being 'brain box Winnie', of course his assumptions proved correct, and they did. Within eight hours the Japanese had struck at the British garrison at Hong Kong.

Parliament convened the next day. Under The British Constitution the Crown declares war on the advice of its ministers after parliament is confronted with the facts. Both Houses voted unanimously and from that 8th December 1941 we were at war with Japan.

The American opposition to being involved with the British in Europe vanished. It too declared war on Japan on the 8th December together with Canada and the Netherlands, and on the 9th December the Commonwealth countries, including Australia, did likewise. And Mr Churchill was able to clarify: "At last, we are not alone".

* * *

A Miscalculation - An Unforgiving Population

The Japanese had some expectations as a result of the attack although they knew that it was a gamble. They relied on the fact that the United States, having suffered a sudden and massive onslaught, would agree to a negotiated settlement to allow them free rein in that country. But there was no pay-off to the hoped-for bonus. They had crippled the fleet, destroyed 188 aircraft and the Americans were not so forgiving. American losses were less serious than the Japanese had expected but the US nationals reckoned them to be high enough.

Many ships and planes were out at sea, well away from base. Vital naval infrastructure, fuel and oil tanks, shipping facilities, a power station and signal intelligence were unscathed. Japan was probably relying on a war of attrition forcing the US to come to terms. It was an optimistic prophecy which did not materialize. And I repeat, the Americans did not forget or exonerate. As long as the Japanese were on the horizon the population was hell-bent to get even.

Returning from one of my Australian trips I thought it would be an interesting experience to fly home eastwards from that country instead of west as I had done on four previous occasions. I had pre-planned a stop-over and found myself in Hawaii. I had forgotten that it was an important day in their calendar. It was the 7th December and the anniversary of the Pearl Harbour attack in 1941.

The ships, comprising the American fleet, remained where they had gone down. Their crews with them. The site marks one of the official 'War Graves'. The area was crowded with people. I could hardly believe what I was looking at. A great many of them were Japanese. Why, I wondered, why had they come? Their countrymen were the instigators of that, as Roosevelt called it, "Day of Infamy". Alongside the multitude of American pilgrims, I went out in a boat to the site. Numerous wreaths and flowers were tossed into the sea. From some a single rose – a personal message to a loved one, lost!

* * *

The Doolittle Raid

On the 18th April 1942 the United States Air Force mounted an air-raid over Tokyo. It embodied an entailment of sixteen craft, each with a crew of five men – a total of eighty. Its leader was Lieutenant Colonel 'Jimmy' Doolittle. The squadron took off from an aircraft carrier and its responsibility was to attack military targets, after which their plan was to fly westward and to finally land in friendly China. Their mission completed, all but one of the planes did get to China, and they were forced to crash-land. The remaining one landed in Vladivostok in the Soviet Union. The Soviets confiscated the plane, and its crew were interned for more than a year.

Most of those surviving returned to the United States or directly back to the US-serving forces.

The Japanese Army conducted a massive sweep through the eastern coastal provinces of China searching for the remaining Americans. They captured eight; but later executed three. They inflicted drastic retribution on any Chinese who was thought to have aided them. They energized Operation Sei-Go and proceeded to undertake plans to ensure that these areas would not, in future, have the ability to aid Americans. They carried out a type of 'scorched earth' policy. Within an area of twenty thousand square miles in an area where the American raiders had landed, all existing airfields were destroyed. Germ warfare was used and atrocities were committed. Those discovered with American items were shot. It is estimated that ten thousand Chinese civilians were killed during that campaign.

The raid on Tokyo did little more than scratch the surface. Some municipal buildings were destroyed. The news of the endeavour raised the morale of the people back home. It was only four months after the shock of the diabolical attack on Pearl Harbour, and subsequent Japanese victories. The population badly needed some 'feel good' news. As was to be expected, it did little to do so in Japan. The Japanese press were ordered to describe the raid as indiscriminate bombing against women and children. For years before the Pearl Harbour onslaught mock air-raid drills were organized in every Japanese city as a precaution against raids mounted by the Chinese. In actual fact, the Chinese air force was almost non-existent. The real reason for those Japanese drills was to keep warlike emotions at high-pitch level in the hearts and minds of the populace.

The outcome of the Doolittle Raid was that it gave the Japanese the impetus to attack Midway Island in Central Pacific, in vengeance, but they were defeated by the United States Navy.

* * *

An Atrocity and a Surrender

I have been an intrepid traveller to many countries across this planet. There are a few that I have not had the opportunity of venturing to. I am bereft when I realise that in all probability, I never will. Not for want of enthusiasm to continue my wanderings, but age is a wearisome inhibitor. However, there is one country on this earth that I have no desire to honour with my presence.. It all happened oh so many years ago, and yet I cannot erase it from my mind. The memory of it remains entrenched in my brain. That country is Japan.

The war with Japan outlived the cessation of hostilities with Germany by three months. VJ Day, officially Victory in the Pacific Day, was declared on the 15th August 1945 when Japan surrendered after the aerial attacks on its mainland by the Americans utilizing the newly-developed weapon of mass destruction, the atomic bomb, on two successive days. The 6th and 7th August 1945. The towns of Hiroshima and Nagasaki were singled out. No matter the cause of wars or the rights and wrongs of grievances it is a vicious atrocity to be the instrument of the scale of destruction and the shocking death by radiation of whole cities and their population of hundreds of thousands. I suppose one now has the freedom of hindsight to find oneself in the position to express those views.

The Japanese were one hundred percent committed to their cause and this was reflected in their initial unprecedented attacks on Pearl Harbour, Hong Kong and places in Malaya. In battle they fought the Allies with savage ferocity. Their mindset was the same as a hundred years before the 1940s, when they had stolen lands from China and Russia. But those most recent years are the ones we remember.

They treated captured service personnel and civilians, women and children, with extreme cruelty. They showed no mercy, and were incapable of recognizing the Geneva Convention in respect of the treatment and care of official Prisoners of War. In the annals of the Second World War their history is barbaric and I have not the vocabulary to put into words what I learned, especially with the image of my cousin imprinted in my brain.

So it was no surprise that the Japanese surrender, after those fateful bombings, was applauded by the British, and our Allies and the Australians, who had been rendered vulnerable by the action of the Japanese, and of course, by the Americans. The method by which this was achieved was of no consequence at that time. We were happy and relieved that the war was well and truly over. Memories of that period in history remain with me. I know that it happened a long time ago, but I have a long memory.

The formal surrender was finalized on the 12th September 1945. Lord Louis Mountbatten, the uncle of the Duke of Edinburgh, attended on behalf of the Allies in the City Hall in Singapore. I have been to that important city. I was unable to locate the City Hall. I went to the cricket ground and imagined the British enjoying a match;

playing and watching the national summer sport whenever they have the opportunity. It would be better if nations played cricket instead of going to war. I did stay to ponder a while on the scenes acted out there at the time of the conflict. It does not fit well in my psychological persona to embark on a journey to the land of the 'Rising Sun'.

* * *

An all-American Programme with an Exception

From Hawaii I travelled north-east to mainland America. I had an inclination to visit the Arlington National War Cemetery in Virginia, Washington DC. That too has an interesting history. It was established in the American Civil War era and dates back to 1864. The grounds were originally the home of the wife of the Confederate General, Robert E Lee. But of course to peruse its story was not the reason of my call, although I have discovered that one can soak up a good amount of history from such trips. I consider that one should give respect and to even pay homage to those who paid with their lives, defending their country or for the cause of freedom.

The grave count in Arlington is 400,000. I found it impressive and awe-inspiring. I hoped to find one grave in particular. I have written an account of the British General Orde Wingate of Chindit fame. He happens to be a special hero of mine. He was a man of unusual qualities and I admired his off-the-beaten-track ideas. Mr Churchill had that gut feeling too, and on a sea voyage across the Atlantic to meet up with the US President, he invited Orde and Mrs Wingate to accompany him for the ride. So what you may ask has all this palaver got to do with Arlington? The General died in a plane crash along with an American crew. Their bodies were badly burned and they could not be identified. The Americans were entitled to be interred in Arlington but because of the macabre circumstances of identification, the complete numbers of fatalities were buried in that cemetery together, and I wanted to stand there by that grave as a pilgrim.

Chapter 27
Canada

Canada - It Didn't Have to be, but it Did

Leaving Washington DC I travelled north to Canada. I was aware of the mammoth contribution that country gave to us in wartime. It is no exaggeration to state that without them the possibility existed that Germany would have achieved a victory. I toured the prominent cities and other sites and I had a good holiday. I had no reason to be dissatisfied. The hotels were comfortable and the people affable. The one 'fly in the ointment' which upset me was an encounter I experienced whilst admiring a glorious bronze of a World War Two mariner. There are numerous such edifices in all places and so there should be, to honour the brave men and women who gave their lives for their country and for the right of those who survived to live free under their Maple Leaf flag and not a Swastika. I stayed awhile at this particular statue and watched in disgust as a boy of about twelve started to climb and swing from this memorial, whist a couple, who I surmised were his parents, stood by laughing and encouraging his monkey-like contortions. To use a modern idiom 'I lost my cool'. I confronted the lad directly: "Do you know anything about the figure"? I asked. He looked at me with a vacant stare, but the adults got the message. That incident did not spoil my vacation but it did leave a sour taste in my mouth, until I recovered.

The Second World War was a defining event in the history of Canada, transforming a quiet country on the fringes of the international spectrum into a critical player in the struggle for peace and freedom in the 20th century. It played a vital role in securing an Allied victory and its contribution was well beyond what one might have expected from a population of 11 million. Over one and a half million of its citizens enlisted to serve. It sacrificed 44,000 lives to the conflict in addition to the wounded tally of 54,000.

On the 10th September 1939 it declared war on Germany, likewise against Italy in June 1940. It had no obligation to do either. Previous to 1931 Canada was tied to Britain in a Dominion status and was thus compelled to fight as part of the British Empire in the war 1914–18. Post 1931, Canada, under British Law, was transformed to that of an independent sovereign country. It opted to join the Allied cause with the blessing of its then Prime Minister, Mackenzie King, of its own volition.

He said it was: "Self-evident national duty to back Britain". And the Canadians certainly did just that. After the Fall of France in 1940, Canada was our only ally of sovereign-state standing.

When I ruminated over my intention to write about Canada's wartime history, I realized that there was so much the three armed forces had subscribed to, which encouraged me to emulate my previous arrangement of sectioning my subjects according to the branch of that tripartite. I used this formula in my presentation of the story of wartime events of Australia, and I trust that I managed to overcome a complex matter by using this methodology. The exploits of Canada's 'Big Three' services will not be a combined conglomeration but a separate cameo of each.

* * *

A Fight to the Death in the Atlantic

In 1939 the Royal Canadian Navy and the Canadian Merchant flotillas comprised but tiny fleets. The expansion after that date witnessed the enlistment of 100,000 men and 6,500 women for maritime services. They manned 471 fighting ships. Within six days a convoy left the Canadian port of Halifax bound for the United Kingdom; the larger ships of the navy escorting the smaller cargo carrying craft, the precursor of 25,000 such voyages. The response, to the 'call to arms', after the declaration of war was swift and without delay.

The Battle of the Atlantic, as it was named, was of the utmost importance to Britain and the Allies. The Royal Canadian and Merchant Navies secured the navigable shipping lanes in the Atlantic throughout the longest ongoing deployment in the history of the war. It was not won by the navy in a collective sense. Its victories emanated from the courage, fortitude and determination of those who delivered them.

The Atlantic was alive with rampaging U-Boat 'Wolfpacks', but the Canadian fleets kept those sea-lanes open. Thirty three of those voracious German underwater monstrosities were sunk or captured together with an Axis loss of forty three surface vessels. It was simply a life-or-death struggle. Without the ability to traverse the 3,000 miles of water we in Britain would have starved. Without the troop-carrying transports our military capabilities would have been severely depleted. There is the possibility that with no support of manpower the opportunity to continue the momentum to wage the war, and win it, would have been lost. The Germans, for their part, had the responsibility to prevent those transports from ever reaching the United Kingdom.

It conjures up the notion that the end result would have been very different to how it actually was.

The Battle of the Atlantic was a 'tonnage war'. In actual fact, the cargo transported was reported to be the vast amount of 164 million tons. In the one-to-one battle that continued it was a case of Britain's need, and Germany's determination to stem the flow of war necessities and service personnel accumulation in readiness for some future Allied invasion of occupied Europe.

* * *

A Meeting of the Giants

During the time of the ongoing sea engagement it was decided, in consultation with Mr Churchill and a still professing 'neutral' President Roosevelt of the United States, that the distance across the Atlantic needed 'stop-overs' for refuelling purposes. Iceland was the chosen location and so it came to be. A second site chosen for this enterprise was a point off the coast of Greenland. That plan was known as 'The Mid Atlantic Gap'. The majority of those manning the sites were Canadians.

A further responsibility directed towards the Canadian fleet proved once again its prowess and capability. Following the Fall of France the powers in charge were under no illusion that Hitler's invasion of Britain was imminent. It called upon the Canadian navy to 'police' the English Channel and the route into London. Fortunately the expected assault did not materialize. I guess that off-duty matelots might have discovered that English misses were not dissimilar to those back home. Maybe the accent was a bit different, but then again what has speech got to do with the language of love?

Churchill and Roosevelt had other things to ponder and worry about. With the possibility that the UK was invaded and we failed to defeat the Germans, Hitler might expand his plan to occupy Europe and look for other fields to fulfil his grandiose projections, namely North America. The friends met in August 1940 and preparative concepts were discussed and put on the impending file, 'just in case'. If such a situation should arise and it did appear to be a certainty, key points on that continent would require policing and monitoring, and the responsibility to undertake such an assignment would fall to the armed forces of Canada, taking into consideration that the east coast of that country, for example Newfoundland, is the first port of call across the Atlantic.

Additional localities under British influence were also considered: the West Indies, Bermuda, Jamaica, and the Bahamas. Canada provided and posted troops to these sites as another 'just in case' situation. It appeared that Canadians were policing the world as well as our own British Islands, and of course the Atlantic. Thank goodness that 'wait and see' file was able to be withdrawn. Until that happened I trust that the fellows in those detachments enjoyed their sojourn in those sunny climes and behaved themselves, as all good Canadians do.

* * *

An Ever-busy Navy

In other theatres of the war the Royal Canadian Navy took its place proving again and again its loyalty to its country and to Britain and her Allies. Perhaps the most daunting mission was the assignment which occurred on the 6th June 1944 when in the English Channel it played its part in Operation Overlord, the code name for the landings on the beaches of Normandy. It was redeployed from its duties in the North Atlantic to act as guardians over the invading multitude. It covered the flanks of the invasion fleet, thereby ensuring a defence against enemy submarine activity. Canadians displayed a premier code of practice with a successful outcome. Their naval forces participated in various capacities in South West Asia. A team of navy divers were tasked to spearhead assault sorties across rivers in the campaign fought in Burma. Their warships were assigned to the waters of the Pacific and the oceans of South East Asia. They were visible off the shores of Italy and North Africa when offensive invasions were executed. They were involved in operational duties in north-west and southern Europe. Their ships sailed the freezing seas safeguarding the life-line convoys to Russia. By golly they pulled their weight and more! And the Canadian Merchant Fleet matched that record.

But there is always a balance to consider. Three-and-a-half thousand Merchant vessels were destroyed and 175 warships made a last voyage. Seventy two thousand seamen never again anchored in a home port. It is no exaggeration to express ones deep emotional compassion for those lost, and the ones waiting fruitlessly at the dock gates.

* * *

The Army Takes its Turn

By Christmas 1939 Canadian troops had already arrived on the shores of the United Kingdom. They were the first of our Allies to do so. Some of their divisions joined their British military mates and went with them to France as part of the BEF. I hope with all of my being that the majority were rescued in the Dunkirk evacuation. Some Canadians remained in France, engaged in a rear-guard action; they were deployed at Brest during the dying days of a free France. The collapse of that country to the Germans was imminent and most of the Canadians were taken as prisoners of war. Those who remained here in Britain and were not posted to the BEF were the only fully-equipped regiment in the British army.

* * *

The Tragedy of Hong Kong

Mr Churchill was increasingly perturbed when he studied the mind-set of the Japanese High Command. The mental 'itch' swirling around his cerebral cortex was aggravated by the Japanese cuddling up to Vichy France and to Siam, and to its increasing activity off the coasts of Southern Indo China. Was all of this a prelude to a gathering storm? Did our PM begin to wonder if the old habits of Japan were once again rearing their ugly heads of aggressive rapacity for the acquisition of territory and dominating control? He decided that the British Crown Colony of Hong Kong should be prepared to face a Japanese onslaught and it was imperative to implement the garrison complex in that region.

In November 1941 a contingent of 2,000 Canadian soldiers was dispatched to join other military divisions from Britain and India and local Hong Kong volunteers, as part of a defence force. When the barbarous unprovoked attack on the United States in December 1941 materialized, Churchill knew his visionary qualities had prevailed.

On that self-same day, Japan struck in clear violation of International Law. Japan had not declared war on the then British Empire and the assault on Hong Kong became viable. Shame to the British High Command; those who were responsible for the deployment of those Canadians, raw volunteers, untrained, and untried young men. The 20,000 who faced them were raring to go. Hardened Japanese, fiercely trained troops, greatly outnumbered those ready to fight in defence of that land, by a ratio of four to one.

The garrison courageously fought the overwhelming numbers for 17 days until they were defeated by the superiority of the foe on the 25th December 1941. Of the original Allied defenders, 1,100 were slain in battle and 1,400 wounded. The missing accounted for a further 1,200. Eleven thousand were murdered as prisoners of war during the Japanese occupation of Hong Kong that endured for three-and-a-half years until the end of the war. The cataclysmic episode is aptly remembered as the Fall of Hong Kong and on the anniversary which recalls that infamous day of defeat, it is expressed as 'Black Christmas'. It was a 'wake-up call' of Japanese intentions in the Pacific.

* * *

Their Names Liveth for Evermore

There they lay, the Canadians who died in battle and those who perished in the aftermath of it at the hands of the vicious brutes, their captors. Many were shot or bayoneted to death as they arrived in ambulances at the hospital and in their beds where the wounded were being tended, and they butchered the medical staff at the same time.

There in the Sai Wan War Graves Cemetery in a corner of Hong Kong Island, on a site gradually sloping down to the sea giving a magnificent panorama of the harbour, they are buried. As I stood there, on a stop-over visit on my way home from Australia, I hoped that that view would somehow reach out across the sea to their home in Canada. Enclosed within its wall of flowering shrubs and bushes I stayed and dwelt on the terrible waste of young men taken in the midst of so much horror and carnage. Those who gave their lives in battle and those who bore the subsequent torment and horrific experience of their captivity in Hong Kong, meted out with undiluted barbarism. They suffered starvation, disease, beatings, mutilations and exhaustion. The women were raped.

The Japanese general responsible for such atrocities was tried as a war criminal in 1946 and executed by firing squad. That was all well and good in the circumstances, and it is ethical to carry out justifiable punishment, but that action does not resurrect the men who were murdered at his hands, nor can it give comfort and solace to those families back home that have an empty seat at the table.

A plaque in that quiet place, in the beautifully designed white marble-sculptured memorial building, tells the story of the battle which visitors can appreciate, understanding exactly what happened there and to realize the calamity of it all. A second plaque on The Altar of Remembrance is inscribed thus: "Their Names Liveth for Evermore". I was not acquainted with any of those named and I certainly had no connection with those events at that time, but my memories of that day will stay with me always.

Whilst in sombre mood I stood before the Cenotaph memorial there in Hong Kong, an exact replica to the original in London's Whitehall, my mind dwelling on my memories of my own life at a time when these horrendous actions were in progress. And then I sat awhile in the beautiful Memorial Gardens by Hong Kong's City Hall. The sadness and melancholy remain with me.

* * *

The Blunder of Dieppe

In August 1942 a Division of 5,000 inexperienced Canadian soldiers together with 1,000 British Commandos attempted an incursion on the coast of mainland France near the town of Dieppe. Its purpose was to be a 'dummy run' for a future full-scale invasion on that coast. The Canadians encountered the full blast of a heavily defended fortification, as might have been expected on a vulnerable coastal area, particularly where a town needs to be defended. The invading force was allotted good air cover supplied by a significant number of aircraft. The planners of the raid decided that no naval bombardment would engage. It was thought that an onslaught from the sea would incur too much destruction on the town and too many civilian casualties. That was all very well, and would morally give them the 'high ground' of civilized consideration, but not enough to safeguard the lives of those troops who were participating. The outcome was an ill-fated fiasco: 18% of the 5,000 Canadians did not survive and 2,000 sat out the rest of the war as prisoners.

It was considered by the 'Big Chiefs' sitting in their High Command offices that the raid had been useful, in spite of its shocking loss of life. I pause to reflect that their 'spin mode' musings were the results of an alcoholic lunch. I think that as a result of what I am thinking at this moment, I might indulge in a fluid intake of the same kind.

But it was no laughing matter. I am sorry that I ended the saga of 'The Dieppe Raid' on a humorous note. It more aptly deserves weeping. Overall, of nearly 6,000 who landed, more the 1,000 died and 2,300 were captured. Perhaps after the 'Big Bosses' recovered from their stupor they thought that when the 'big showdown' was planned it might be a good idea to land on beaches and not on blanket-covered machine gun fortifications, safe guarding a heavily populated urban site. Ah me! I think that some of those high hair-brained 'Big Wigs' were ready to be 'put out to grass'!

* * *

Canada in France, Holland and Italy

As I have outlined the activities of the Royal Canadian Army so far, I cannot, with satisfaction, omit their contribution towards a clear-cut victory following the aftermath of the invasion of France on the 6th June 1944.

Although they sustained heavy losses within the first hour, by the end of that day they had penetrated deeper into that country than either of the other Allies who were still struggling to advance further from the beach-heads. In the first month, Canadian, British and Polish Forces faced some of the strongest and best trained of the German Wehrmacht in that theatre of adversity; in addition to divisions of the awe-inspiring Panzers, the German tanks, which far outshone our own. Canadians and the Allies mounted a series of attacks in an effort to take the towns of Caen and Falaise, as part of an Allied plan to liberate Paris.

In spite of a strong opposition, the Allies had made good progress towards their ultimate goal of liberating Europeans from the tyranny of the German occupation, and setting free the population suffering under the yoke of Hitler and his diabolical regimes. The British had liberated Antwerp, a vital port forming an essential supply line from the UK, but the availability of that convenience could not be utilized. The Germans held heavily-fortified gun emplacements at the estuary of the River Scheldt. In the autumn of 1944, during several weeks of arduous combat, the Canadian Army achieved a victory which rendered the port 'up and running'.

Turning their sights eastwards the Canadians played a central role in the redemption of the Netherlands. Their arrival coincided with a crisis in that country. It was a time which bore the inglorious title 'The Hungry Winter', which speaks for itself. The Canadian liberators gave their food rations to the Dutch children, and their blankets to whoever needed them. Bombers were organized to 'food-drop' packets of edibles, relief for the hungry in Rotterdam, Amsterdam and The Hague; with the kind permission of the German occupiers. It was cited 'Operation Manna'. Those unfortunates living under the heel of the jack-booted received succour, as long as the German proviso was adhered to – that the planes delivered from a height not lower than 200 feet. One can wonder if those Teutonics would have acted in similar vein if the position had been reversed. I doubt it!

The well-proven Canadian Army fighting force proceeded to support the Allies on the road to Rome when it was fight-back time in Italy. It was no easy task.

It began a long and hard fought endeavour. Rome was finally taken and Canadians were the first of the Allies to enter that city. It was a job well and truly completed. It is a sad fact, which, whilst one has the privilege to report joyfully on a very successful outcome in the midst of a calamitous time in history, it is one's painful duty to think of those who were never to return to their home and loved ones. In this case it applies to the families and friends of the 25,000 who died there.

* * *

The Boys in Blue Take a Lion's Share

I have expounded on the wonderful input the Allies benefited from the courageous Royal Canadian Navy and the Royal Canadian Army. Let it not be said that the Royal Canadian Air Force was outshone by its brothers in arms. It was there, wherever, whenever or for whatever, the action demanded of it. The men who flew the aircraft earnt their ratings high up on the register of the brave and staunch. They exhibited their ideals of allegiance and duty in their endeavours to safeguard freedom for the nations.

In 1939 Canada, the UK, Australia and New Zealand agreed, together with Southern Rhodesia, to take on the joint responsibility to train air crew for wartime service, to be administered by Canada. It was the initial set up of the British Commonwealth Air Training Plan (BCATP). Training airfields were organized throughout Canada. Training schools were maintained and delivered to the majority of aircrew for overseas operational purposes. Every single aspect of flying operational aircraft was catered for, and every skill needed by those flying them was addressed, and put into practice. The plan delivered 1,500 new airmen every four weeks.

The Royal Canadian Air Force was on duty worldwide as well as at home where two commands were based to protect Canadian coasts and coastal shipping from enemy attack. Close to home they played an integral part in the Battle of the Atlantic providing reconnaissance look-out for U Boat prowlers. Some of their compatriots had come to Britain early in the war and had volunteered for our own RAF, and together with their countrymen, they fought with honour in the Battle of Britain. They flew Spitfire and Hurricane fighters with distinction.

They formed their own Bomber Command within the RAF. They took their share in dislocating industry in German factories by strategically targeting them from the air. Close support to the Allies in Normandy was their remit during the Allied invasion;

and operational duties in North West Europe and North Africa at the time of our spat with Erwin Rommel at El Alamein. The Japanese knew what they were about in South East Asia when they felt the results of Canadian 'ship spotting', giving information to Allies as to where the enemy vessels were located. They flew in the skies over Egypt, Ceylon, India and Malta and gave cover when the Canadian Army was busy in Sicily Italy and Burma: (it writes like my travel itinerary). The United States President Roosevelt sought their assistance when the Aleutian Islands, west of the Alaskan peninisular, were at risk from enemy attack, resulting in the Canadian Air Force giving service in Alaska in conjunction with Americans to cover that eventuality. My! The Royal Canadian Air Force did its share!

With a war record of that quality their reputation of service was recognized by all manner of important people; by other military personnel, by ordinary folk, and everyone else in between, and of course, by me.

* * *

Have They Medals? They Should Have

Military input into the war by Canada and the magnificent aid it offered and gave to Britain rose to an insatiable level. Never in any future history in either of our countries, will Canadians need to be anything else but overwhelming and justifiably proud in the knowledge that they served us right well, and did their duty and displayed their loyalty to King and country in an exceptional manner.

But it was not only in combat, whether on land, sea or in the sky that the Canadians exhibited their qualities. The unsung workers in the factories and in the shipyards are heroes and heroines worthy to be recognized and applauded. They were the fourth arm of that countries contribution. Some say that they were the main spring of the Allied victories. I think this too.

Military production during World War Two included small arms, heavy guns and cannons, aircraft and explosives. The list continues apace. Armoured gun-carriers, anti-tank and field artillery, naval guns, automatic weapons, radar sets, boats and ships. They added to the shopping list synthetic rubber, and as a final item, they dealt with the processing of uranium for the Manhattan Project which led to the Atomic Bomb.

We would have never have been in a position to wage a war, never mind bringing it to a victory, without this tremendous effort of those across the Pond.

Their industry was created from scratch, climbing towards this strong and amazing peak. Their factories were safely out of reach from the bombs which beset those in belligerently active countries. Their output became an arsenal which was the chief supplier of our wartime requirements. They lent us money on an interest-free basis and magnanimously donated their war produce to our Commonwealth Allies unable to take on financial commitments. The cost of the war to Canada was estimated to be in the region of twenty two million dollars. That was old money. Old or new it sets the teeth on edge when one dwells on total cost, and the losses from all sources. Canadian citizens made the greatest of contributions to the survival of decency and justice.

As I stood by that impressive effigy immortalizing the participants of the Canadian Armed Forces I had not an inkling of that fact that one day, a long time hence, I would be telling its story. Recalling the incident of the young boy swinging from the memorial when I first arrived in Canada, encouraged by his laughing parents, I am sorry that I did not have the foresight to ask the family for a forwarding address. They would have received a gratis copy of my endeavours and would perhaps have some feeling of regret for not rebuking their wayward offspring, who I estimate, would be a grown man now in his forties. Perhaps I would have despatched two copies. One for him, and one for his children to read and learn a lesson.

Canadian War Memorial

Tulips, all Colours Especially Orange

Canada and the Dutch Royals have a special relationship which began in a hospital bed in Ottawa. As a result, every year since the end of the war in 1945 the flower beds in and around Canada are ablaze with brilliant colour. Red and yellow, and sometimes mauve, and perhaps blue, but mainly orange. So you might wonder what has all this malarkey got to do with the war, or us.

When Holland fell to Hitler, the Dutch Royal family exiled themselves to Canada. I sometimes think that our Royal counterparts stayed put and remained here to instil what good cheer and encouragement they could to us their subjects. But I am going off the boil so I had better not. The Dutch Queen Juliana was pregnant and she expected to give birth to her youngest child. (It may surprise you, but I can still remember her Mum, Queen Wilhelmina. Wow! Thinking of that family today, that was four queens ago!).

It was obvious that the new baby had to hold Dutch citizenship but how was that to be possible so far away from home? The accommodating Canadians came to the rescue. They declared that hospital suite extraterritorial, and a day after the Princess Margriet's birth the Dutch flag flew from atop the Canadian parliament building. It was the only time in its history that a foreign standard has wafted in the breeze from that place. To double up on the celebrations, it was the Canadian Army who were responsible for the eventual liberation of Queen Juliana's homeland. In 1945 the people of Holland sent a gift to the people of Canada in the shape of 10,000 hand-picked tulip bulbs, their national flower, which were planted out in prominent areas. The following year 20,000 were sent to the hospital in Ottawa. Since then tulips have proliferated and bulbs arrive every year. It is an outward sign of international friendship and an appreciation of help in difficult times. The Canadian Tulip Festival is held annually in May. I understand that it is quite spectacular and I am the sure that it is an amazing affair and a real treat to be there.

Chapter 28
The Price we Paid

It had begun in September 1939 and it ended in August 1945, although related conflicts began much earlier. But the war was over. With just a few exceptions, every nation of the world had been affected. It was the most widespread war in history. Directly involved were more than one hundred million of the population. The 'State of Total War' as it is called, demanded the major participants to gamble their entire economic, industrial and scientific capabilities and military resources into the war effort.

There was no distinguishing between civilians and the military. All were caught up in the bloodshed and they all suffered, marked by mass slaughter and strategic aerial bombing, which culminated in the last air-raid: witnessing the unleashing of atomic energy. That one incident, apart from the effect of the war in its entirety, changed the world forever. Since then, with certain countries governed by unreliable leaders, having the capacity to hold the rest of the world to ransom, we worry that this planet is less secure than it should be.

The war brought into being the Holocaust, and mass murder of those serving in the military of their respective nations, and the wholesale annihilation of those living under occupation. The calamity brought to the fore modern lethal weaponry used on land, sea and skies by the armed forces; we perceived the courage and manifest bravery of the people who fought for freedom, no matter which flag they allied themselves to. We must never forget those stout-hearted fighters of the Resistance movements.

It is not possible to trace the development of a conflict between warring nations without a summing-up of the casualty list. It is my painful obligation to do so. It is estimated that over 80,000,000 people lost their lives, taking into account those who died due to military action, crimes against humanity, war-related disease and famine.

To show more clearly the breakdown of each country's loss I will attempt to record the numbers of each of the major protagonists. Thirty countries were engaged in this cataclysmic era of the world's most devastating history. Approximately 3% of the total global population died. Every nation had its quota, down to the smallest islands and those with the least population.

Military losses of the United Kingdom, including Malta, were 390,000.

Civilian losses 6, 000. Australian casualty numbers registered 40,000 of the Armed Forces and 700 civilians. Canada was deprived of 42,000 of its serving young men and women, and 1,600 of its civic population. British India's militia suffered a depletion of 87,000 souls and 2,000,000 of its stay-at-home people. New Zealand lost 11,700, of its fighting brave and loyal, and South African loved ones mourned the death of 12,000 who did not return home from enlistment. British Burma sacrificed 2,600 of those serving and the shocking multitude of civilian loss accounted for 250,000.

In the United States the families and friends of 407,000 men and women who had served, received the news that they were never going to be reunited with their loved ones, whilst 12,000 who did not leave home shores added to that number. The Soviet Union archives record the numbers of those lost in the defence of their homeland to be 7–10,000,000 in addition to its civilian populace diminution of 10,000,000.

German armed forces losses are estimated to be 5,000,000 or more. With a further estimated number of civilian deaths of 1.5–3,000,000, the Emperor of Japan had 2,000,000 less of his fighting subjects to welcome home, and having to oversee the internment of an estimated 800,000 of his civilian people.

Study those numbers. They roll off the tongue, but how do they affect one's heart and mind? It is beyond comprehension that anyone, anywhere, should seek to engage in an antagonistic confrontation. But they still do. It causes one to wonder, is the human race integrally flawed? Will they ever learn?

World War Two altered the political alignment and social structure of the entire world.

It was the deadliest conflict in human history.

Chapter 29
Conclusion

Is it just my age that has given me the advantage of looking at what I see and having the ability to examine the 'whys and the wherefores'; and the 'rights and wrongs'? Years ago, and not too far back, I could and would have accepted most at face value. Now it is not so easy. I have come to this realisation whilst writing this book.

Overall I think that I have done so in a balanced and fair-minded format. Take for example my comments concerning the bombing of Japan or the aerial warfare on cities on both sides of the spectrum. My thinking now is was it justifiable, to fight evil with evil? Years ago I may have thought differently. Was I right then or am I right now? It is my enigma.

Setting down my thoughts on the Second World War and its issues has given me much to think about and worry over. One thing is clear: war, for whatever the reason, is bad. Surely people can talk, reason, debate and come to a compromise arrangement without resorting to bombing, humiliation, devastation, violence, killing, murder and so many other activities which spell out all that war brings with it.

Religion or cultural differences as reasons for war is a lie. The differences in belief systems and practices are not arguments for war. Countries and people fight over land. Look at all of history and you will see the proof. Not so long ago it was the case in Northern Ireland and today it shows itself in the Middle East. Religion is an excuse. It has been so since time immemorial.

Greed and envy and intolerance are also causes; the curse that gives rise to the mayhem. A person, usually a man, or a group of like-minded people, have dissatisfaction with their entitlement. They seek to appease discontent and assuage their greed. Avarice and jealously combined produces a ferment of hatred and the rearing of an ugly menacing head, and the redress is sought in war. And we all pay the price.

Transcribing my thoughts into the written word has highlighted my abhorrence of war. I think of the waste of life, particularly of the young, who are gone without the chance to fulfil an entitled destiny, and denied others who might have benefited from their presence. Consider the waste of time that conflict consumes. Time that could be better spent producing the concepts that merit mankind.

Examine the waste of resource and the colossal cost of financing a war. Money could be channelled to improving infrastructure, rather than destroying it, and utilized for the education of the young, training them in life-skills instead of instruction in the use of machine guns. This is a terrible indictment of those who practice the policy of bloodshed.

Is it possible to find an answer? What can be done to address such a dilemma? Will it always be war that we bequeath to those who come after us? The tragedy of history is that we never, ever learn. I hope that my story will perhaps be an inspiration to others who share my view and to change the view of others who do not agree with me.

I am finding it difficult to draw this saga to a conclusion. Writing it has not been a problem. I was actually reliving my history. It has been surreal. Incidents were surfacing from my subconscious that I had not thought about for decades. Sometimes more than eight! I felt as if they are happening now, in the present time, it is as if other aspects of my life have faded into obscurity. My own personal story as written in this book would be just one aspect if I were to take up my pen again to chronicle a complete autobiography.

My story is now told – all that I have wanted to say has now been said.

I will now have time to change the focus of my musings, and have time to tend the tomatoes growing in pots on the balcony of my flat. I wonder if the spirit of dear old Mr Smith from the farm in Laleham all those years ago will watch over them.

* * *

One Final Word

Re-reading those last views and statistics I began to think how depressing it was to write "Finis" on such a miserable and sour note; so seeing that I am a bit odd in the way I have presented my stories and an even more unconventional manner of expressing myself, I thought well, I might as well finish my scribblings in a similar vein and so you have yet more to read. And perhaps I can happily close now with a lighter frame of mind. I hope I have achieved that aim.

So I will now sign off, pull down the shutters, and sit with my feet up in the lounge and watch the telly, which I ain't done for yonks. It will make a nice change from writing 'stuff' for you to read.

Quirky to the very last word!